Robin Ince smells of libraries and charity shops. He hopes to eventually bottle and sell this smell as a popular fragrance. He is an award-winning comedian and writer, the sort that appears on Radio 4 shows including presenting science series *Infinite Monkey Cage*. He does not believe the books discussed within are bad books, they are just different.

To Suzanne
Vets get angry
when horses
knees hurt

Robin Ince.

when horses
... love.

ROBIN INCE'S

Bad
Book
Club

**One Man's Quest
to Uncover the Books
that Taste Forgot**

SPHERE

First published in Great Britain in 2010 by Sphere

A CIP catalogue record for this book
is available from the British Library.

ISBN 978-1-84744-269-7

Typeset in Bembo by M Rules
Printed and bound in Great Britain by
Clays Ltd, St Ives plc

Papers used by Sphere are natural, renewable and
recyclable products sourced from well-managed forests and certified
in accordance with the rules of the Forest Stewardship Council.

Mixed Sources
Product group from well-managed
forests and other controlled sources
www.fsc.org Cert no. SGS-COC-004081
© 1996 Forest Stewardship Council
FSC

Sphere
An imprint of
Little, Brown Book Group
100 Victoria Embankment
London EC4Y 0DY

An Hachette UK Company
www.hachette.co.uk

www.littlebrown.co.uk

*This book is dedicated to my father
and mother for bringing me up in a
house filled with books.*

Author's Note

This book is not an authoritative encyclopedic guide to weird literature and second-hand published oddities; after all, it is only one book. To do justice or injustice to the many misguided guides, banal beast books and peripheral poetry pamphlets would require a monastery of monks sworn to dedicated study to cover the historical romance novel alone. This is a personal collection, one that has driven my wife to the edge of insanity as the tattered killer crabs novels were eventually stacked higher than our only child. Sadly, you will not find books for the amateur taxidermist here, or a guide about hobbies that can be undertaken by invalids unable to leave their sickbed, though both exist. I have looked far and wide for *Hobbies for the Bedbound*, but sadly it has never been on any charity shop shelf that has fallen under my gaze. The same can be said for *The Amateur Taxidermist: A Step by Step Illustrated Handbook on How to Stuff and Preserve Birds, Fish and Furred Animals*.

My obsession – and be warned, it never used to be an obsession – has been fuelled by my life as a comedian travelling from Truro to Inverness. This has allowed me the opportunity to visit every Oxfam and local hospice shop I could find, each time hoping to discover something out of the ordinary amongst the numerous Dan Brown novels and Trinny and

Susannah clothing guides. I've had to impose rules along the way, otherwise the exercise would have just been silly. For a book to make it into this scattergun collection, it had to be purchased by me in a second-hand shop for less than £3, or to have been donated by a fellow enthusiast, or to have been found on my travels in a skip or on a train seat. It cannot be purchased at full price, bought from a pulp book internet specialist, or be made up for the hell of it. There are a few exceptions. Sometimes I have paid over the odds; it would be surly not to when the money is going to poorly pets or monocles for the elderly or a new tobacco pouch for the owner of an underperforming junk shop. Other than that, I have been strict.

This is the harvest of five years of touring art centres and old pubs, performing at night and walking the streets by day. There is no end to this book; it is just the beginning of a quest that will dog me until I am in my bath chair. I am not man or beast; I am bibliosexual, and a seedy bibliosexual who haunts the streets, laden with carrier bags held by blistered fingers, stooping under the weight of the rucksack that has brought on sciatica and a Dickensian demeanour.

Contents

Preface

Ever held a book in your hand, only to wonder the next day if it might have been a dream?

Over the last five years, people with hazy memories of something that sounded too peculiar to exist have recommended many books to me: *Cooking for Spitfire Pilots on the Go* or *How I Married a Ghost and Gave Birth to a Poltergeist* or *Learning to Love your Leprosy* or *The Amish Guide to Dentistry*. After investigation, they have usually proved to be the stuff of nightmares or hopes.

There is one book that almost falls into that category, but it is real, it definitely is, and you must take my word for it. Let me tell you a tale of sexy girls.

I held it in my hand, I read from it on stage. Others have held it too. One man even stole it for a while. He was caught at a bus stop in Stirling and forced to return it by a helpful mob, though only after I allowed him to have a page from it. He begged for a page; his eyes almost bled with pleading.

That is how potent this particular book is. I gave him the one page. It had a photo of a naked woman on it lying back and looking enticingly at the reader, telling them to fall into the page; it was the dullest page in the book.

The man stuffed it down his trousers, maybe thinking it

might be safe there from all the grasping hands that would want just a hint of this book, and embarked on his public transport trip.

What book could drive a man to thieve and beg for just one page of it?

The Secrets of Picking Up Sexy Girls, that is what book.

It is a book that I will be writing about shortly, probably in Chapter Two, so I won't spoil it by telling you too much now, but there is something you must know. It is a very peculiar book. I worry you will not believe it exists beyond my imagination. It is a book that cannot be found in the British Library, as it is without an ISBN. This makes it contraband on the shelf. It is also a book with strange ideas, many, many strange ideas. It contains sentences that even someone looking right at them might question their existence, thinking it was a pornographic mirage. Why am I going on about this now? Surely if you want to question me I can just pull it from my rucksack? No, because my copy is gone. One Scottish thief was thwarted, but the second time someone somewhere scarpered with literary fool's gold. I can't pinpoint exactly when it happened. When did I last know that I had it?

I remember reading from it at the Wychwood Festival. This is one of the more civilised music festivals. It is at Cheltenham racecourse and so has plenty of real toilets made from concrete and porcelain. By the paddocks, I briefly showed it to the organiser of a Christian music festival, and from here it gets hazy. I believe it came back with me to my tent.

It is always a book that creates interest. People have to hold it after a reading to ensure I didn't make it up on stage. A curtain designer at the Daphne du Maurier festival in Fowey asked me if I could photocopy the whole thing for her, otherwise she thought her friends would imagine she had gone quite mad when she told them of the contents of the book.

Sometime between reading from it at Wychwood and performing at the Hay philosophy festival the following night, it disappeared from my travelling preacher-like bag of books.

Had it been snatched by the Christian camp organiser while I slept under canvas? Did A.C. Grayling see it in the green room (or rather green yurt) of Hay in between philosophy lectures and suffer an irresistible urge?

Had it merely fallen out on the train, to be found by a bemused and disgusted carriage cleaner?

Whatever events occurred over that forty-eight hours, the book was gone.

I wanted another copy, not because I needed to know the secrets of picking up sexy girls; I knew them off by heart by now, and my wife didn't like me using those secrets anyway. Would anyone believe me as I stood on stage reciting every secret of picking up sexy girls verbatim, like a pervert at the end of *Fahrenheit 451* who, rather than memorising *Crime and Punishment* to save its words from the book-burners, had chosen a short book on the disadvantages of having sex in shop doorways and how to remove tights without looking like an undergarment-removing amateur?

I put the title into a search engine. Fortunately there were a few pages of results, but then I read those results.

The first was one of my own blogs talking about the book; the next ten were descriptions of a show I was touring where I read from the book. Then there was another blog from a man who could barely believe it was a real book but who had seen it close up at my gig in Basingstoke.

Forty-three results and every one involving me.

I went on to auction sites, book sites, any form of internet jumble sale; there was nothing. A few months on and there is still no sign of the book's existence beyond it appearing on stage with me, or in blogs by or about me. There is not even any photographic evidence. It has begun to become a book from an H.P. Lovecraft story, a book conjured up by a pact or found in a witch's grave, now turned to dust, while its possessor is increasingly driven mad and drunk by those who jeer at him for inventing such nonsense. It really does exist. If you don't believe me, I'll find the curtain designer somewhere in Cornwall; she'll say it was real . . . won't she? The existence of every other book mentioned in the ensuing pages can be checked with reasonable ease, but *The Secrets of Picking Up Sexy Girls* . . . I had it in my hand, I really did. If I return to the shop where I bought it, will the shop still be there or will it have burnt to the ground in mysterious circumstances? Or will I be told there never was a bookshop on that street? Sometimes I think I can hear the book, pages turning of their own volition under my floorboards.

The sort of sexy girl that you find in the dunes if you follow to the letter the rules of *The Secrets of Picking Up Sexy Girls*.

Introduction

The Library that Dare Not Speak its Name

Pornographic pamphlets for the pedantic

I'm staring at a wall of books with titles that include *What God Does When Women Pray* (Nelson, 2005), *Memoirs of a Tattooist* (Pan, 1960) and *Temptation in a Private Zoo* (Constable, 1969). Sometimes I daydream that these are the shelves of an acquaintance or an odd doctor's waiting room, but they are not. This is my sitting room, these are my books and I am keeping them despite advice to the contrary.

Sometimes they are at the front of the bookshelf, sometimes hidden in the second tier, depending on the level of dignitary visiting my house. By dignitary I mean friend of my wife who might think that I should be forced to live in the attic in a gender-reversal *Jane Eyre*.

How have I, a middle-aged comedian who sometimes taints Radio 4 with his presence, found myself as self-styled curator of all these published peculiarities and rapidly yellowing tat? I have become the Ralph Richardson librarian of *Rollerball*. My hair has grown thinner, my cardigans dowdier, but my zeal is greater than ever.

As the new century dawned, I thought I was on the threshold of leaving assertive pencil marks in the margins of *A la Recherche du temps perdu*, beginning to comprehend *Finnegans Wake* and about to enjoy a sound working knowledge of Heidegger's influence on the early Beat movement, or at least pretend that was where I was at. But I sacrificed it all in order to be able to precisely quote the opening line of Cliff Richard's autobiography – in which the author ponders the swimming skills of monkeys.

Some critics claim that the greatest opening lines belong to Kafka's Gregor Samsa waking as an insect in *Metamorphosis*, or Meursault pondering his mother's death in Camus's *L'Etranger*, even Hunter S. Thompson's desert acid trip of bat imagery in *Fear and Loathing in Las Vegas*. But how many of those critics actually bothered to read *Which One's Cliff?* (Hodder & Stoughton, 1990).[1] With its lack of Latin and minimal existential angst, most critics probably made their excuses and dipped their noses back into their York Notes pass books. Great works routinely throw up philosophical questions on what it means to be human and clinging on, thanks to gravity, to a spinning orb of rock in an indifferent universe. So Cliff's first line hooked me in: 'To this day I can't be sure whether monkeys swim underwater.'

Do Camus or Thompson or Kafka come near to replicating the image of Cliff Richard bribing a zookeeper to hurl a hapless long-tailed macaque monkey into a pond to check out his monkey–breaststroke theories?[2]

---

1 Cliff Richard has obviously lived a full life as a pop star, celebrity celibate and vintner, but I would say *Which One's Cliff?* is his most psychologically and philosophically rigorous work.
2 Apparently crab-eating macaque monkeys *can* swim underwater.

Despite Cliff's questions of evolutionary advantage in the deep end, *Which One's Cliff?* is a book that fits more neatly in the existential autobiography section than Des Lynam's *I Should Have Been At Work* (more in the logical positivist autobiography section) or Les McKeown's *Shang-a-lang: Life as an International Pop Idol*. Cliff is asking a question – which one is Cliff? Is he who he thinks he is, or is he what others project on to him? Are we ever any more than what is thought of us? What difference between Cliff on roller-skates wired for sound and Cliff on a double-decker bus somewhere near Belgium?

Don't think that I only boast an intimate working knowledge of Cliff's animal quandaries. If I hadn't spotted *Which One's Cliff?* in that Scope charity shop in 2003, I wouldn't have bought *Sex is Not Compulsory* in the Help the Aged next door. This suggested that one charity shop donor spread their goodwill shop by shop, as the two books seemed perfect companions. And if someone hadn't seen me reading from *Sex is Not Compulsory*, in particular the paragraph dealing with lack of sexual desire in Antarctic explorers, they might not have recommended one of the odder rabbit care books on my rabbit care shelf.

I am the proud owner of Denise Cumpsty's magisterial fascist tract *The Book of the Netherland Dwarf* (Spur Publications, 1978) because of an Antarctic sex conversation with a man called Charlie, and so am now familiar with the correct way of killing a particular breed of miniature rabbit. Stretching it sharply appears to be one method, though beating it across the back of the neck with an iron rod is, according to the author, 'probably quickest and kindest'. Cumpsty's defining work is so crammed with methods of dispatching rabbits that one can only presume they're either a sickly breed or so hugely annoying the owner will find any excuse to get the iron bar out.[3] Once the first link is revealed, everyone wants to help weld the chain.

How many out there were aware of the genre known as Christian gynaecologist romance? I have only one novel in that sub-genre and still wonder if I will find more. The one I know exists is *Sign of the Speculum* by Jessica Russell Gaver (Manor Books, 1979), a beautifully crafted concoction of Jesus and genital exploring tools. Next to the 'Faith/Gyno' collection I store my 'Nature Gets Angry' fiction. In this surprisingly substantial genre few animals are deprived the opportunity of wreaking revenge on depraved, beastly mankind (though no one seems to have yet involved the sea monkey).[4] I enjoy a very thorough working knowledge of Guy N. Smith's Crab series.[5] Some eulogise *Crab's Moon* while others rave about *Night of the Crabs*, but for me it's always going to be *Crabs on the Rampage* (New English Library, 1981), mainly for its description of the heady excitement in 'Barmouth' when the Radio One Roadshow comes to town.[6]

Then there are those books that defy genre conventions. *The Day the Gods Came*, which happens to be my favourite book retrieved from a skip, is a collection of non-fiction

---

3 According to a vet I know, the Netherland dwarf is also 'poor tempered'. Who wants a tetchy rabbit?

4 Sea monkeys were advertised in American superhero comics of the seventies. According to the ads, they would grow into fabulous gilled creatures that smoked pipes underwater. This was a lie.

5 There are those who belittle Guy N. Smith's Crab novels. D.B.C. Pierre's Booker prize-winning *Vernon God Little* changes hand on the internet for 1p; Smith's *Crabs: The Human Sacrifice* is currently changing hands for £75. Guy N. Smith also won a pipe-smoking championship in 2003 and D.B.C. Pierre did not.

6 The Radio One Roadshow was the BBC's epic attempt to ensure imbecility was distributed to every corner of the United Kingdom. It involved their most popular disc jockeys going to a seaside resort and 'being bonkers'. This mainly meant throwing buckets of water on people while everyone screamed. Many of these DJs are on very local radio now and quite bitter.

conversations from outer space. While drying some dishes, 'Dr' George King was apparently told to: 'Prepare yourself! You are to become the Voice of Interplanetary Parliament.' This is what King heard: 'Mars Sector 6: Very acceptable. Neem neem two six eight two eight, this pattern – eight seven totally enclosed in this pattern – nim nim.'

So – unlike you – I know when the gods are going to arrive. I'm ready with a tray of flapjacks and a tin foil hat.

My odyssey to collect the world's odder English-language books hasn't all been fun. So great is the addiction that I am now reduced to squirrelling new purchases away under the shed. I'm familiar with the sad, confused looks a man in his late thirties obtains when reading Mills & Boon on public transport. My wife spins out of control when she spots Joan Gardner Loulan's *Lesbian Erotic Dance* (Spinsters Book Co., 1991) lying provocatively on our coffee table (in truth *Dance* is merely a collection of graphs to find out how butch or femme you are. I turn out to be surprisingly femme) and over the years her Christ-Robin-what-have-you-found-this-time?s have multiplied exponentially. The counter-argument that thanks to all my charity shop purchases Third World children will get more porridge and sandals has lost its saving oomph.

For priapic cinephiles only

But I would never have become the hopeless addict I now am if I hadn't come across the following sentence in a Notting Hill second-hand bookshop in 2001: 'A feminine hand is wrapped around an erect penis. As the camera backs off, a man wearing a false beard and glasses is sitting on a bed, nude.'

I had actually been scouting for a book about Crick and

Watson's DNA research; failing that I needed a spare copy of Jacob Bronowksi's *The Ascent of Man* so that I was ready when I felt a friend might need something to explain humanity's move from the nomadic to the agricultural. One thing I had known at the beginning of that day was that I certainly wasn't after a book about an aroused man wearing a false beard. Despite that, and aided by the lack of books on double helices that afternoon, I kept reading. It would take more than one sentence to make me buy a book. There was another sentence, however, that made purchase absolutely essential and accidentally threw me off the straight and narrow of acclaimed books to the more pungent cellars of absurd publishing decisions:

'Her labia are well-defined, not flappy, like many girls of her stature.'

What on earth?

'Her labia are well-defined, not flappy, like many girls of her stature.'

You can't get to this point without re-reading that quote at least three times.

'Her labia are well-defined, not flappy, like many girls of her stature.'

That's what I had to do before being certain those words really existed on a page and it wasn't a manifestation of some weird bibliophile nervous breakdown. But there it was: out of a man's mind, through a sophisticated typesetting, printing and binding process and into book form. This was no amateur photocopied, staple-bound fanzine. It was a real, fully bound trade paperback book with a proper spine, and on that spine – set in a severe, no-nonsense typeface – lay the words *The Stag Movie Review*.

As regular browsers of second-hand bookshops know only too well, you can judge a potboiler by where it falls open, the spine acting as a well-oiled hinge. Obvious examples include the work of Harold Robbins from the sixties and seventies – I had a personal weakness for *The Lonely Lady*[7] – and Shirley Conran's *Lace* (which contains a vivid, Monet-style description of nipples floating in water like 'delicate water lilies'). Twenty-five years ago these authors promised the elixir of soft porn for febrile teenage minds like my own. Nowadays, with the readily available porn of the internet and mid-shelf magazines that hide the nipples on their cover with red stars saying 'Golly!' and 'Gosh?', teenagers would scoff at the youth of yesterday.

The hinge test proved completely redundant for *The Stag Movie Review*. Every page was hinged because it was packed with sex and further enhanced with fantastically pedantic information about the make of nylon slacks briefly covering the men (pornography fans being hugely picky when it comes to the sartorial elegance of performers) or the likely country of manufacture of furniture within the room of csopulation:

'The boys have on white open-collar shirts and sport slacks. The blonde has on a light skirt and sweater. Her attractive friend wears a dark miniskirt, topped with a matching sweater. White knee socks highlight her attire.'

With its bland spine and cheap red print on a pale blue binding, *Stag* looked innocuous – more 1950s industrial manual about why asbestos is essential in primary school construction[8] than genuinely groundbreaking work of

---

7 *The Lonely Lady* was turned into a film in 1983. It is recognised as Pia Zadora's third best film after *Hairspray* and *Santa Claus Conquers the Martians*. It was also Ray Liotta's first film, though he forgets to mention it on his official filmography. He played Joe Heron.

8 The outstanding 1950s promotional film about the joys of asbestos is *According To Plan: The Story of Modern Sidewalls for The Homes of America: A Jam Handy Production*, though *Introduction to Asbestos* comes a close second – 'Asbestos, untouched by time's dark captains rust and decay.'

pornographic scrutiny. Boasting no ISBN (something to startle the more pedantic bibliophile) and with no publisher's imprint, it felt like a maverick outsider. In an act of devotional duty the author, one H.C. Shelby, had taken it upon himself to catalogue hundreds of stag movies. But the man hadn't just catalogued them. Here was a trainspotter of sex films noting every detail, however tenuous. For readers unaware of the genre, stag films were pre-video-era one-reel movies specifically designed for guys to watch with a keg of beer while the women were off attending prayer retreats or knitting circles. All these films follow the same basic plot structure. A man has sex with a woman. Two men have sex with a woman. Three women have sex with two men. A woman has sex with a boxer (I thought *The Beauty and the Boxer* was going to be some lewd union between Sugar Ray Leonard and a go-go girl, but actually it's a boxer *dog*). The myriad sexual techniques there described offered zero eroticism.

'Rape plots are rarely done any more . . .' Even forty years ago, the long arm of political correctness was stymieing the narrative invention of the low-rent pornographer. 'They have had bad connotations due to the number of sexual maniacs running amuck in society. The Peeping Tom theme is still popular as it does not involve force.' This keen insight is from the author's musings on *The Mugger Lover*, but Shelby's critical eye misses nothing; any detail felt to influence the stag party's decision is studied. His examination of *Teenage Orgy* remains my favourite in the fastidious art of the pornography reviewer: 'The couples are attractive and the room where it was made rather well-furnished. The television set is English.' It is all well and good to be certain of the length and breadth of filmed genitalia, but poor feng shui and ugly armchairs can disturb arousal amongst the young bucks.

Despite the manifest social risks involved, I finished reading *The Stag Movie Review* on the train home. The binding was poor and every page loose – at any moment one could have come adrift and fluttered out across the carriage. I glanced at the middle-aged woman opposite and wondered how harshly she would judge me if *Skin Lollipop* with its superb opening line, 'He prods her moderately hairy grotto', landed at her feet.

I wasn't the only one to be mesmerised by *The Stag Movie Review*. Try quoting a few lines from Thomas Hardy's *Jude the Obscure* aloud in a bar and people might nod or smile in a melancholy way (but choose your bar carefully – not every theme pub is filled with Hardy fans; look for a few hand-pulled bitters suggesting a Wessex frame of mind).[9] With Shelby's masterwork I merely had to declaim one line and hordes of people would be clamouring for more. That line was: 'The flamenco dancer walks out of the picture frame and pops a crown on the erect Frenchman's head.' *Stag* was printed heroin and the catalyst in my quest to discover and collect the world's most incongruously dreadful, downright odd and bizarre books.

A lifebelt thrown to love

Any uncertainty about my fate was sealed a week later in a village on the Cornish coast where, incarcerated by rain, I was poking around our tiny holiday cottage for reading matter. The bookshelf sported the usual dreary collection of *Reader's Digests* and Robert Ludlums, but also one single Mills & Boon. Like most men, I had never read a Mills & Boon;

---

9 Hardy didn't really do sex; as far as I remember, it was hinted at with mention of a leaf falling or some roses blooming.

unlike most men, I was about to start reading one, and it would not be my last. This one seemed specifically selected by the cottage owner to fit in with the flinty theme of her sea-view home; it was a story of crashing waves and crushed love.

That landmark book was *Stormy Vigil* by Elizabeth Graham (Mills & Boon, 1982), destined to become my favourite in the substantial 'Lonely Lighthouse Love Story' genre. 'Turning back from the window, Sally went with a nervous stride into the sky-lit kitchen, where her self-made dinner of lasagne in spicy sauce bubbled joyfully in the glass-fronted oven. A meal fit for the gods, only there was no god to share it with her.'

It was my inaugural Mills & Boon experience, and I'd been fortunate in that it was from the house's eighties heyday, offering far more action than their staid earlier publications. I'll go to my grave maintaining that *Vigil* belongs right up there in the very best of Mills & Boon genres – a metropolitan, headstrong woman (and parvenue light-house-keeper) out of her depth in the natural world of storms, waves and big woolly jumpers. For all the sub-merged passion and devil-may-care rescuing of drowning sailors, it wasn't the adventure that really hooked me in but the recipes and crockery descriptions. 'Sighing, she flicked off the heat on the stove and extracted the reddish-gold Italian-style dish from the oven. Not for the first time she regretted the absence of another person to share it with . . . a man who would praise the subtle tastes of garlic, tomato paste, spices that recalled the unique flavour of Southern Italy.'[10] The only thing that slowed down the pace of this

---

10 Not all lasagne recipes use tomato paste; many use tinned tomatoes and simmer them. Spices are also not usually used in the traditional recipe. It might have been lucky that Sally had no one to share her dish with, as the inauthentic use of spices might have driven potential suitors away.

romance was the need to stop and knock up a few of the tasty suppers described within.

It would be injudicious to suggest that *The Stag Movie Review* and *Stormy Vigil* occupy common ground, but Elizabeth Graham and H.C. Shelby share a passion for hyper-detailed descriptions of trousers and knitwear: 'He had shaved, she noticed in one all-encompassing glance, and changed into a heavy flannel shirt of mid-brown and thick twill pants of the type he had worn on the day of arrival.'

Now that is a glance of tremendous dexterity, a glance worthy of Columbo.

Graham underlines another essential element of budget 'shall love ever be mine in this windswept outcrop' novels – a love of extraneous detail to achieve word count without overreliance on plot: 'She groped for the bed lamp switch and peered owlishly at her watch, taking in that the hands pointed to three fifteen.' Nothing is left to chance or the reader's imagination. Sally can't just look at her watch, she must take in the hands.

By the end of my Cornish holiday I'd ransacked all the local second-hand shops, increasing my M&B collection tenfold. And I wasn't collecting willy-nilly either, ruthlessly discarding anything not involving an out-of-her-depth woman in a man's world. Notables in this – yet again – surprisingly substantial sub-genre were *Diamond Stud* (girl forced to leave Swinging London for 'darkest Yorkshire'), *Frozen Heart* (saucy Antarctic adventure with anoraks) and *Where the Wolf Leads* (swarthy Frenchman Dracon Leloupblanc at large).

Cumin revelations of a pier-reviewed celebrity

'The food was curry, which I really like, as does Cliff, I think.'

We know he is uncertain about monkey swims, but we can get closer to Cliff now we know his possible dietary requirements. Who has spied on him to turn over this stone?

These are the immortal words of Syd Little from the popular double act Little and Large.[11] And so – like most things in British culture – everything comes full circle to Cliff Richard. Syd's *Little Goes a Long Way* (HarperCollins, 1999) completes the great triumvirate of books that spurred me into action. It is the only one I ever bought where the postage cost 275 times the purchase price.[12] It was bought on a hunch. Firstly, I was drawn to the pun, 'Little Goes a Long Way'; secondly, I couldn't help but wonder what lay behind the thick-lensed face of the man who kept trying to play his songs before Eddie Large caterwauled in and ruined the mood with a Deputy Dawg impersonation.

Some enjoy showbiz autobiographies for the magnitude of the life experienced, but I prefer the magnitude of the self-delusion. Ever since David Niven's magnificent *The Moon's A Balloon* (Hodder & Stoughton, 1972), any old weather forecaster or beauty queen has felt compelled to tell their story. Is there really a difference between winning an Oscar for *Separate Tables* then leading a thrillingly urbane life in Hollywood, and opening a dry cleaner's in Prestwich?

---

11 Fortunately Little was smaller than Large; the disparity in girth therefore heightened the mirth. Laurel and Hardy were also different sizes and Bobby Ball was shorter than Tommy Cannon. Mike and Bernie Winters were brothers and quite similarly sized, and so less funny.
12 The postage was £2.75.

Syd Little, a man who just wanted to sing his song, but he never knew when Eddie Large would march in and ruin it by pretending to be Deputy Dawg.

I think there is, but I couldn't even name the current line-up of the Sugababes, so what do I know?

Some celebrities use their foray into autobiography to show there is a depth in their thinking that may well have been hidden by their career in variety. They might know how to receive a pie in the face, but that doesn't mean they don't have a corner of their brain reserved for philosophical pronouncements. Little is never afraid of showing off his more philosophical side (though there's still plenty of leg room for anecdotes about curries and panto or the excellence of green-room chicken sandwiches on *This is Your Life*): 'Being childless is a bit like getting a new car, say a Ford Escort. Before you bought one, you never took too much notice of them, but as soon as you buy one you see hundreds.'

Little's publishing history is a stark object lesson in what happens when you employ a ghost-writer. *Little Goes a Long Way* seems to be Syd's own work; it lacks the gloss of the ghost-writer's hand and that only adds charm and authenticity to the words of Syd. But the TV comedian and sometime pantomime Baron Hardup, and Cannon and Ball sidekick in the Christian proselytising game, was far from content with *Long Way*, and five years later, Canterbury Press unleashed *Little by Little*, this time with the helping hand of ghost Chris Gidney, who religiously ironed out every kink that had brought such unalloyed joy in the previous publication. Compare the following two descriptions about encountering Cliff in the Taj Mahal restaurant, Ealing. First, *Little Goes a Long Way*:

> We met him once after he'd recorded 'A Little in Love'. He came over and said hello.
> 'Thanks for dedicating the song to me, Cliff,' I said.
> 'What do you mean?' he asked.
> 'Well,' I replied, 'a "little" in love.' He did laugh.

('He did laugh.' This is one of the most important sentences in the book. It is a sentence of brevity – a mere three words, but a very important three words. Syd makes it emphatically clear that Cliff laughed. People often described Eddie Large as the funny one in the double act, but in this Ealing restaurant we know who is wearing the trousers; it is Syd.

Now, in 2004, *Little by Little* retells the same story. This version does add some historical references to the changing nature of Indian food served in the UK, but it destroys Syd's trademark anecdotal delivery.

> I couldn't resist going over, saying hello and thanking him for the new record he had just released in our honour, 'A Little in Love'. I'm glad he got the joke.

But how does the reader *know* Richard got the joke? Five years before, Syd allowed us those three precious and wholly unequivocal words, 'He did laugh.' Now some of Little's more regular readers are beginning to suspect that the erstwhile Shadows frontman might only have proffered a smile, or a vague nod of recognition. Possibly merely a glassy stare.

With the purchase of *Little Goes a Long Way*, my destiny was set.

When I should have been chatting eruditely about Proust and Joyce in literary salons, my life would now be spent poring over books by psychic women who believe they were John Lennon's lover in sixteenth-century Dorset. But more of that one later.

I have spent a great deal of my life in second-hand bookshops and book fairs in the back rooms of hotels and village halls. I had been mining books on science, philosophy and imaginative fiction, but now, as I returned to those village halls I first encountered when my trousers were short and my voice was higher, I had to retune my eyes for new spines and peer down at shelves that I had never rummaged through. When I was ten I had looked for Edgar Allan Poe; when I was fifteen it was the Beats and other self-involved coffee-bar jazzniks; when I was twenty-five it was anything that would help refine my anxiety, the work of Frenchmen and Colin Wilson. Now, in my mid-thirties, it was stories of irradiated rats and lonely women hopeful to wed one day.

The pilgrimage to discover the truly odd, the sometimes bad and the occasionally baffling has been challenging. It's easy to find a classic – there's no epic journey required to get your hands on one. Simply walk into a bookshop, demand to know where the classics are and choose your

tome. The decision about what is deemed worthy has
already been made. How much trickier it is to track down
exquisite drivel, horribly misguided prose plumbing
unimaginable depths, dreadful hacks who traverse the mundane to make the bland blissful. You can't walk into a
bookshop and say, 'Where are the wrong books, please? Do
you stock any books that should never have been published?' I've tried, but they won't tell you where they keep
them. By the end of this book, your eye will be so keen for
the gloriously pulpy and your senses so sharp that you will
be able to smell a killer-toads-try-to-take-over-the-world
book from two hundred feet.

1

Sex

(or the satisfaction of donkeys
and other bucket-requiring acts)

'Sex! I have to have it, at least twice a week, or
else I'll explode'
'Twice A Week' – The Bigger the God[1]

The dubious world of a fondler's manual

From ancient urns portraying giant penises being carried by
slaves with increasing back problems to continental postcards displaying voluptuous women reclining in velvety
bordellos, there has always been trade in sexual images.
Sometimes they have been fashionable and acceptable,
something to show off in your living room, since they
clearly demonstrate your taste and sophistication; at other

---

1 Technically not a book quotation but a charming line from The Bigger the God, one of
Oxford's most underrated bands. 'Mum Steals Boyfriend' is the only song I know that
includes the phrase 'then he gave her one'.

times they have been the reason for a wooden shed erected by the compost heap or something rolled up in the trunk of a dead tree. When sex has been shameful, there have been ways of getting around the blushes of face-to-face purchase. As sex seems to have always been shameful in Britain, there have been even more ways there.

Book clubs are now groups of people pretending to read Gabriel García Márquez or Thomas Pynchon so they can justify a social gathering with an aura of intellectual credibility. It is the literary replacement for the supposedly popular swingers' parties of the seventies where wives were swapped in Walton-on-Thames and herpes sores were formed.[2]

The reading group sit in a lounge and get drunk and argumentative whilst totally forgetting to talk about magical realism and rapidly moving on to whatever TV series has been successfully spun by the PR people into your weekly must-see.

Before it became a social gathering, before even Oprah Winfrey or Richard and Judy had one, the book club was a glossy lure in the back of the *Sunday Times* colour supplement. They offered hefty tomes of history, classics you wanted on your shelves but probably wouldn't read, and deluxe editions of *The Thorn Birds*. Like a sly smack dealer, the club would offer you three hardback books for a tremendous bargain price; once contractually hooked, all you would have to do was buy six more books at a far less

---

2 Herpes was the dread sexual disease of the late seventies and early eighties. It became such a problem that it was the subject of a TV movie of the week, *Intimate Agony*, in which herpes spreads through a stylish resort bringing painful shame to the rich and tanned. By the time the film was made, the herpes panic had been superseded by AIDS. In *This is Spinal Tap*, the band all share a cold sore after a shared groupie disaster. This is definitely funnier than them all getting AIDS.

reduced rate, then constantly forget to cancel your membership. This meant regularly receiving the editor's choice, normally a book about railway carriages of the 1850s or a glossy volume on Britain's favourite eccentric hedge designs.

So why did people join these clubs when they were walking into a trap?

For many, it allowed them to buy near pornography without the embarrassment of going into their small-town bookshop and asking the old lady with the necklace of rainbow beads and the knitted demeanour, 'Errr, do you have any books on erotic photography? It's not for me, it's for my wife or something. I hate female nudity, it makes me sick. Ask my wife, I vomited on her bra once,' etc. When the old lady is the woman that used to teach you piano, the situation gets even trickier. Bookshop assistants do gossip around the rotating paperback stand.

All of these books were 'tasteful' – books for men who were keen to learn the correct way of photographing naked women, even though they didn't own a camera or know anyone who would take their clothes off for them; or they were books on physically agonising Oriental sexual positions for hairy swingers one step away from entering A&E with a slipped disc. The internet bookstore has removed this necessity.

I understand why these book clubs had to exist; my greatest embarrassment has been collecting books to fill this particular bookshelf – the strange sex compendium section. I am sure the old ladies loudly talking of kidney stone problems at the Cancer Research counter have seen far worse things, like war and death and those they love being lowered into the ground. Surely all worse than a man in a cardigan approaching them with a book of in-depth lesbian photography where pudenda are photographed like woodland, with figurines lurking in the hair,[3] but I still have to buy other books to stack around my guilty purchase. Hopefully a copy of Susan Faludi's *Backlash* and a fiction-alised account of the Pankhursts will make the elderly cashier think, he may be a pervert, but at least he's a feminist pervert.

Over the secret garden wall

It began with *The Stag Movie Review*, but while that appears to be unknown to anyone save a few specific porn cineastes, sex book number two was a best-seller in its time. It was a critically revered book that blew the lid off the chaste 'well if we must I'll drop my drawers but make it quick I'm making Chelsea buns' image of the sexual imagination of women. Did all women want to lie back and think of England, or whatever country they came from, after all?

'I too am a "crotch watcher".'

No, some of them were crotch watchers, others much more than that. Some of them were even crotch watching the crotches of other species.

This book didn't have a single flash-photographed nipple or wet-T-shirted nymph in a wicker chair to sell it, just words.

The 'crotch watcher' is from *My Secret Garden* (Virago, 1975), the book that lifted the lid on the energetic fantasies that sprang from the febrile minds of women trapped in a mundane missionary position of love when their husband returned from a successful sales conference. The book that finally revealed the true desires of women driven half mad by the tedium and sterility of their existence.

---

3 I think that book was called *Stolen Glances*, but it was lost somewhere in a storage box in Peckham Rye many years ago, lost or purloined by a lusty removals man.

The author of this and further revelatory books was Nancy Friday, and her fantasy collection makes me happy to be an uptight English prude whose sexual desires are generally about having sex with someone, not about congress with the dead or a dog's bottom.

Nancy Friday interviewed many women for *My Secret Garden* who revealed their yearnings, some made flesh, others active in the mind. In the seventies, this sort of thing was described as brave and open and honest. To my English eyes much of it seems like mad piffle, suggesting that many women enjoyed winding Nancy up, or that everyone is teetering on the brink of a psychosexual breakdown and even when Freud was most wrong he might have been right.

'I am found guilty and sentenced to be fucked by the donkey'[4] is just one of the sentences that might make a polite gentleman's monocle pop out. This fantasy will be further scrutinised in later pages. You may skip to the next chapter now if you wish.

My Secret Garden is broken up into themes and case studies. Some seem like solitary orgasmic screams for help, whereas others would have had Jean Charcot placing the speaker on a public plinth and declaring she was the archetypal hysteric. Charcot was a pioneering neurologist who particularly enjoyed making displays of women he deemed hysterical. There was fierce competition to be one of his chosen hysterical women, who would rave in front of an audience of physicians and the interested. It was the *Britain's Got Talent* of its day. He believed that it was really only women who could be

---

4 I have looked into obscure sentences and punishments such as seesawing to death, something from Roman times, where two convicts would be at either end of the seesaw,

hysterical, obviously with them having a uterus and so forth, but he did believe that some men could get hysterical if they had flabby testicles. I suspect these men may have become hysterical after Charcot squeezed their testicles and declared them flabby. Both the uterus and the pull of the moon are used far less when diagnosing mental illness in women now.

No woman in *My Secret Garden* fantasises about a man with flabby testicles; perhaps that is another reason why these slack-sacked men are hysterical.

Enough about flabby testicles

My Secret Garden does not have to be read in chronological order; it can be dipped into, though I would not class it as a loo book. I would use any loo that had a copy of Nancy Friday in it with some trepidation.

Who wants to peer at sentences such as 'looking at men, front and back, is a favourite pastime. I like to study the shape of their asses and wonder how they use them when thrusting into a woman, or I wonder what it would be like to penetrate their anuses with a dildo' as you sit on the porcelain? It's like placing *The Orton Diaries* in public toilets.

Chapter headings include 'Black Men', 'The Earth Mother', 'Sounds' and 'Rape'. For my first reading, I decided against 'Black Men' and 'Rape' and scanned down to find 'Zoo'. This sounded reasonably non-threatening. Silly me.

---

going up and down. Then, to spice up the seesawing, vicious animals would enter the arena, thus leading to frantic seesawing to try and remain in the air while your opposite number was devoured. Of course, once your opposite number *was* devoured, you'd sink to the ground and be gored by the lion or leopard, and what's living a few seconds more if it's just sweaty seesawing? Anyway, I have found no historical evidence of punishment by donkey intercourse.

Once you have chosen your topic, you can then choose your fantasist. For 'Zoo' it was Jo, Rosie, Dawn or Wanda. I chose Wanda, as it is a good American name and there are so few Wandas nowadays.[5]

For a zoo story involving a Wanda, the details were more startling than I had imagined. It is here that the donkey fantasy begins in earnest. My issues are both with the detail of the donkey/woman union and also with just how disappointing a zoo would be if a donkey was the featured attraction rather than a lion or rhinoceros. Donkeys for beaches, lions for zoos, but why quibble when something utterly disgusting is about to happen and it is this: 'I wouldn't have believed it, I am being fucked by a donkey!'

Wanda's fantasy begins innocuously enough; well, not that innocuously: she's kidnapped, blindfolded and taken to a farmhouse where three swinging couples are waiting. One couple are involved in the time-honoured profession of donkey studding.

Wanda is tried by these orgy enthusiasts; her crime is the usual made-up rap sheet that judicial donkey sex enthusiasts cobble together. She's been surreptitiously watching a man and a woman manually mate a donkey, a heinous crime in donkey studding: 'I am accused of being a peeping tom, of watching the man and woman mate two donkeys.'

Once sentenced, she is taken to a stable, stripped, then has long black nylons and a suspender belt put on her. I don't know whose benefit this is for: Wanda's, the donkey's or the voyeurs'. Perhaps it's just an extra detail

---

5 Britain's most popular Wanda is probably Wanda Ventham, who appeared in *Carry on Cleo*, *UFO* and *Hetty Wainthrop Investigates*.

she fancied putting in for the geometry of the scene.[6] So you want to watch a woman being mounted by a donkey, but that's still not enough for you, you find it a little coarse. Oh don't just let her be taken naked, that won't be arousing at all; pop some suspenders on her too. That's better, now it's not seedy, it's erotica worthy of Henry Miller. I've never actually read any Henry Miller, but from seeing his book covers in my youth on my father's bedside table, I presume stocking tops are a theme.

If you'll excuse me, I will skip some of the details, because there are a lot of them. This is a fantasy that has been worked on, not some casual musing as a dreamer was distracted by a scene of grazing in a summer meadow. Should you wish to read the entire account, *My Secret Garden* is still available in new or well-thumbed copies. We'll rejoin the scenario here.

'. . . just as I am overcome by excitement and reaching my orgasm, the donkey gives a sound', and once you imagine that donkey sound in your mind, you know it will be echoing in the cave of your mind every time the light goes out.

There is much juice and residue detail added and then a basin is introduced to collect it all.[7] The reader experiences no analysis afterwards to find out why Wanda should desire to be joined to a donkey in front of a large group of spectators. Did something happen when she was in the school

---

6 In Leviticus the Lord states (for it's him who did a lot of the writing, they say), 'And if a man lie with a beast, he shall surely be put to death; and ye shall slay the beast.' This seems pretty unfair on the beast; however sexy a donkey is, I hardly think it could be deemed complicit.

7 It was at this point, when I read this passage aloud, that people started experiencing a cramping in the stomach.

© MEPL

The sort of image that used to spring up when donkeys were mentioned, now erased by the graphic donkey fantasies of *My Secret Garden*.

nativity play? Was she never cast as Mary mother of Jesus and so her revenge would be to take the donkey behind the stable and rut and Eeyore loudly while the Three Kings tried to distribute their gifts? Nancy Friday doesn't judge; she is a chronicler not a moral arbiter. She lifts the stones in the skulls of women and is not scared of what scurries out of any of them. Take Margie.

'Before I was married I went out with a crazy guy, not black, but very far out,' she declares. Margie has discovered that even non-blacks can be far out. She also doesn't want to be peed on in real life, but while masturbating she has quite a specific image to help her through a surreptitious suburban afternoon before her husband gets home in his Chevrolet. 'This idea of a very well-endowed black man peeing for ages on to my clitoris, it's a winner every time.' Another image involving geometry and an arc.

Men with very big bladders and perfect aim rejoice: Margie will be happy to meet you, but in dreams not flesh. For many years the hack comedian has relied on the observation that men just can't find the clitoris; Margie dreams that they cannot merely find it, but aim at it with the precision of an avid child with an air rifle whose pellets are made of wee.

Should a man feel encouraged to spice up his partner's love life after reading of Margie, it would still be best to bring up the idea before going ahead and soaking the sheets.

Nancy Friday's collection was published at just the right time to be a sensation. Now sex is omnipresent and few autobiographies by women (or men) are complete without a blandly candid revelation of their fantasies, or failures by them or their partners (as we now know, Jodie Marsh's garden is not secret; it's open to any horticulturist voyeur). Now that sex is in the open, do fantasies become more bland because they are no longer a revolt against oppression, or are the suburbs still filled with women dreaming of a loving mule, a randy greyhound or a well-endowed nineteenth-century slave called Mogambo?

Nancy Friday's *Men in Love* suggests that men's sexual desires are more banal than women's; this might be because they are idiots who understand so little about women and sex that being able to talk to a girl is already a madcap fantasy. That's what the next book suggests.

How incorrect blouse removal can ruin your sexual encounter in a railway siding

Are you an 'unskilled girl hunter'?

Do you want to hunt girls but you just don't know how to?

Where can you be educated in these ancient skills?

The council seem to have cancelled that evening class since the tutor was arrested while skulking behind the chicken wire of the local convent school. Of course, there is a place you can learn all you need to know about the girl hunt; that place is 1975. This was when a manual was written especially for you, the confused sex hunter. It covers every single base, nook and cranny. No element of mating remains beyond the boundaries of scrutiny. This book will turn your world around and unveil the covert techniques of sexy girl stalking.

Welcome to *The Secrets of Picking Up Sexy Girls – The Complete Guide to Picking Up Sexy Girls*.

Don't know how to talk to girls? Covered.

Don't know where to talk to girls? That's sorted too.

Worried about how to remove their cardigans? Fear no more.

Worried about *where* you should remove their cardigans? That too will be comprehensively dealt with.

I didn't find this book in a charity shop, but on the way to a charity shop. It was retrieved from one of those outlets that from the outside looks like a rundown, grubby second-hand bookshop, predominantly selling yellowed copies of M.M. Kaye's *The Far Pavilions* and Lucy Irvine's *Castaway*, all with broken spines and loose pages. I had found myself in those shops before, innocently believing that I'd find a couple of Hell's Angels novels and a cheap copy of a soap star's memoirs.

'How can they make a living from selling this tat?' I would ponder. Then I would peer towards the counter and beyond and realise that the 'we just sell stinky paperbacks purloined from a widow's house' was a front. I had accidentally walked into a shop of porn and love beads. If you are missing a copy of *Razzle* from August 1978, here is where you shall find it, the heads and feet a little yellowed, but the breasts, belly and genitals still glossy within. The same quandary greets me each time: should I stay in until the sun has gone down and I can retreat from this embarrassment in darkness, or should I rush out now and risk bumping into some nuns who'll tut and imagine me in hell?[8]

The Secrets of Picking Up Sexy Girls was not considered so arousing that it had to be behind the counter of this particular shop. It was mixed in with a couple of *Woman's Owns* and some astrology magazines from the early eighties. I bought one of those too, so I could wallow in the nostalgia of remembering just how wrong some astrologer in a wizard's cape was in his predictions for the hot August of 1981. I never did meet that saturnine man with a folded umbrella and ivory cufflinks. I was twelve years old, so that was for the best (maybe the wizard meant my geography teacher, Mr Letts; he also had a Peugeot). The shopkeeper had played the canny game of placing the book in a sealed bag. By mere dint of sliding tat into a clear plastic bag, the message to the brain is 'Why, this must be the most collectable of items and truly worth the £10 price tag. It has such a sense of antiquity and collectability it has to be sealed for fear that air reaching the manuscript will taint the history and worth within.'

---

8 Certain sex shops in London's Soho fill their shop windows with any old books to build a wall hiding the lust within. The shop windows remain dusty and untouched for years. One day, a friend of mine was wandering by such an emporium and noticed that a book of historical essays by an ex-tutor was in the window. The shopkeeper looked quite perplexed when he was asked how much the book was. Didn't this fool know what glories lay beyond the window dressing? He went into the window, cursing and confounded, and no one on the street knew as my friend left the shop with a broad smile that his guilty secret was not titled *Naughty Nurses Nonstop Naked Nights* but *Napoleon's Russian Retreat and other Emperors' Disappointments*.

The cover was a collage of inviting women, the sort of inanimate women who used to urge men to buy more peanuts from the cardboard rack behind the saloon bar. In the seventies, boozy men were lured into overeating peanuts in pubs via the ingenious tactic of placing the packets on a display stand with an image of a foxy model. The peanuts appeared to cover up her nudity. With each purchase of nuts, there seemed to be an increased likelihood of seeing a nipple, but as the final packet was pulled from its cardboard rack, it would be revealed that she had been covered up all the time in something scanty. This did not stop the vain hope of Watney Red Barrel-drinking men that maybe next time there would be a hint of puckered flesh. *The Secrets of Picking Up Sexy Girls* is definitely a book for men who buy peanuts in the hope of getting a glance of nipple. The cover design and title seemed to scream out 'buy me!'. I believed *The Secrets of Picking Up Sexy Girls* would reward me with untold oddity. I was correct.

If the lure of peanuts coated in thick salt were not enough, wily bar snack manufacturers would lure fools into buying too many peanuts with the false promise of possible nudity under each packet.

The pornographer shopkeeper offered me a brown paper bag to put the find in, but I declined it. I reckoned that anyone seeing me leave with an item in a brown paper bag would presume the article within was not something as innocuous as *The Secrets of Picking Up Sexy Girls*, but some magazine for those with a penchant for octogenarians with eighty-inch busts (*Over 80 and Over 80*, it might be called). I left the shop in daylight; the street was fortunately devoid of nuns (the only nuns in that street were to be found in the videos on the shop shelf, and I have an inkling many of them had not taken orders).

Once I unwrapped the antiquity, it turned out to be even more intriguing than I had imagined. The back blurb promised that I would learn 'how to bend her will to yours'; what is more, the secrets of erotic kissing lay within and 'how to tell how old she is' for the gentleman fearing he will be duped by foundation, eyeliner and lies.

This book was so wrong on so many different levels.[9] Was it secretly a parody, but a parody that the loveless men who bought it couldn't see?

How should *The Secrets of Picking Up Sexy Girls* begin? There are so many conundrums when approaching a sexy girl, so many questions to be answered. The author, however, realised that there was one question that must be answered before anything else could be considered, a question as old as time, gender and fornication: 'Chapter One: What is a Girl?'

---

9 Perhaps the most wrong thing on so many different levels is a song by Peter Wyngarde, formerly coiffured heartthrob Jason King. On his eponymous debut (only) album he sings a song called 'Rape'. Here is a sample lyric . . .

In France of course, where fun is greedy,

The women are a little more seedy.

And rape is hardly ever necessary.

The album was withdrawn quite quickly, but now exists again as *When Sex Leers its Inquisitive Head*.

The I-Spy Book of Females

Like a student cookbook that begins with how to cook baked beans, *The Secrets of Picking Up Sexy Girls* is not scared of starting with the very basics.

If you want to know the secret of picking up sexy girls, you must know what a girl is. This may be where all your difficulties have arisen in the past. Hours of wining and dining and then it turns out to be your cousin Duncan, who is somewhat surprised by the amorous advances in your beige Ford Cortina. You think women always punch you and scream that you are a twisted pervert when you advance, but it's just your male cousins who are rejecting you. You may not know what a girl is, but you will do after reading the opening chapter. Already your expenditure has been worthwhile.

Once you know what a girl is, you then must know what classifies a sexy girl. Evolutionary biologists might say the sexiness of the girl will be defined by the male's level of amorous desire, but you may be unsure what is amorous desire and what is heartburn, so you will be told just which girls are sexy and which are not.

Author Michael Walsh leaves no girl unturned. The reader is taken through all six categories of female – infants, teenagers, girls, women, older women and pensioners: 'This category includes females of 65 or more and girls from groups 1 to 5 who are sexually inert for some reason. Thus frigid girls and lesbians are "PENSIONERS" for our purposes.'

Walsh warns the reader away from the underage, 'for mainly legal reasons', with a warning to the curious that through clever use of wigs and make-up you might end up (as he did) with someone on the cusp of their thirteenth birthday. Why are children so devious? They'll do anything to trap an old man for sex.

The most pertinent girl/woman/pensioner information is summed up in a handy chart that can be cut out and secreted in a pocket in case the girl-hunting man is faced with uncertainty in a pub, club or sheltered accommodation.

Important things to remember, apart from the legal ramifications of infants, are that females between 38 and 50 years of age may have 'more sexual experience than we credit them with', older women 'are not of any particular interest' and pensioners – that's 65-plus and lesbians obviously – are 'of no interest whatsoever'.[10]

So now you know what a girl is, the next question is, where do you find these XX chromosome creatures?

It appears that girls are in many different places.

There's dance halls, obviously, but it is important to remember that there are four types of dance hall: discotheque, ballroom, old-time and parish. All these can be a minefield, packed with musky men and mistaken signals; perhaps somewhere a little quieter would be better to start your foray into sex with the sexy. Michael Walsh suggests you try conservatories and zoos instead. Unfortunately, this might entail some revision. Conservatories here meaning botanical gardens require a basic knowledge of botany, as girls who hang around them will have lapped up Latin and plant knowledge; and zoos obviously require zoological

---

10   For a refutation of this, see the wonderful film *Harold and Maude* (1971), the beautiful story of two funeral-obsessed lovers, one an octogenarian, the other a teenager.

   MAUDE: The earth is my body; my head is in the stars. [Pauses] Who said that, Harold?
   HAROLD: I don't know.
   MAUDE: Well, I suppose I did, then.

knowledge.[11] Orchids are always an exciting topic of conversation, though this can seem racy on a first date.

If you feel that your Latin and zoological knowledge or your old-time dance steps are not up to scratch, there are still many other options: field events, rugby, exhibitions, concerts, swimming galas, public houses, greyhound meetings and most other public sort of things that existed in the mid-seventies with the exception of all-in wrestling. All-in wrestling seems a strange omission; surely many relationships have begun after a young lady has been mistakenly concussed by an old woman's brick-laden handbag?

Again, for the man who doesn't want to get bogged down in all this reading, it is neatly summed up with a grid of locations and percentages.

For those seeking Type 2 girls – that's 16 to 21 – you'll want showjumping or discotheques, because there's nothing spooky about a single man hanging around teenage showjumpers, is there? For those looking for Type 1 – 0 to 18 – you'll do best at concerts (hippy). Remember, concert (hippy) is totally different to concert, where you'll mainly find Type 3. Those interested in pensioners and lesbians will do best down the parish dance.

Michael then tells the reader of his seduction of Helen beside a rotting support stanchion as he pretended he was mainly interested in photographing her and just needed her breasts out to get the lighting right; it was nothing to do with seeing her nipples. Possibly, after experience of peanut

---

11 Zoos don't require zoological knowledge; they just require people to shout at crocodiles believing it will make them move and to tap the glass on snake cages. How I wish that man I saw showing off to his girlfriend at San Francisco zoo by hollering at a lion had fallen into the pit and been torn limb from limb, but by the time I got within shoving distance he had moved on to berating a red panda for being lethargic.

purchase disappointment, he did not even believe such things existed.

Every page of *The Secrets of Picking Up Sexy Girls* has something magical or perplexing on it, so here is the whistle-stop tour for the girl-hunter. There are things to embrace and things to be wary of:

1) Hatted girls are more conceited than bare-headed girls. Headscarves cover something sinister.[12]
2) 'Genuine albinos have very fine white hair and PINK EYES!' Those are Walsh's exclamation marks and capitals, not mine. It is one of the rare uses of capital letters in his book, which contains many more startling ideas, but this is a world where couplings in railway sidings are more normal than PINK EYES. Other words and phrases that Walsh believes deserve Caps Lock status are: 'THE GIVEN ADDRESS SHOULD ALSO BE THE SAME OF COURSE'; 'WOMEN'; and 'ON NO ACCOUNT PURSE YOUR LIPS'.
3) The dyeing of hair is ultimately a sign of deceit.
4) A woman wearing a wig is obviously deceitful, and there are ways to sniff these out. Walsh believes that those who have functional ribbons in the hair are very unlikely to be wearing a wig; however, this does not mean you should tug at the hair of a woman without ribbons. (Any wig-wearing ladies: now you know how to fool that man you have your heart set on. Just place a functional ribbon in your wig and he shall be yours.)

---

12 And yet I find Princess Anne the least sinister of the Royal Family.

Walsh is not dismissive of women with eyewear, a radical proposition in the seventies, when spectacles would carry shame on the bridge of your nose. The movie shortcut to suggest a plain Jane was a pair of heavy-rimmed glasses that would be removed in the final reel, when the leading man would pronounce with astonishment, 'But Julie, you're beautiful without those spectacles that disfigured your face like a Tor Johnson Halloween mask.'[13] As Dorothy Parker once rhymed, 'Men seldom make passes at girls who wear glasses.' Though as comedian Jenny Eclair noted, 'I don't know, most men I know would fuck a tree.'

Walsh shows that the girl-hunting movement has advanced since Dorothy Parker's day. He is less complimentary to contact lens wearers, who he warns might well be vain. Statistics on contact lens wearers who dye their hair versus glasses wearers who go grey are not readily to hand, but I believe the spectacle-wearer has greater honesty and less fear of ageing.

But what about hands?

'Squat, warm and podgy' is how Walsh likes his girls' hands to be. This would explain why he does not give a jot about gloves, which I would have thought could be deceitful too, as sometimes long-finger gloves may merely be padding out stumpy digits.

Walsh is certainly not a body fascist, and is vehemently anti the bra. This has nothing to do with his inability to handle the clasp. In his story of the rotting stanchion and the topless girl, he was adept with her clasp. It's more to do with God, apparently, as 'Girls' breasts are meant to droop and sag all over the place because that's how God made

---

13 A very specific reference to Swedish wrestler and star of *Plan 9 From Outer Space* Tor Johnson.

them; the other higher apes seem to get on quite well without them [bras] so why not girls?' So why do girls wear bras? Because 'they collect badly sagging breasts into manoeuvrable size and texture'.

By Chapter Three, the reader knows what to say to this girl now that he has detected she's not wearing a wig in her beribboned hair, her hands are clammy, her breasts are free, and her zoological knowledge is not so overwhelming that you'll look foolish with a misplaced statement about a pachyderm.

Now that you have your girl, where should you take her for the coupling? In modern Western society it seems there is an embarrassment of riches when it comes to places to canoodle and beyond.

Parks, trains, boarding houses, railway property, ships, public buildings, shop doorways and industrial estates are all acceptable, though Walsh warns there are disadvantages as well as advantages: 'Cats, dogs and even hard-pressed drunks have been known to treat shop doorways with less than respect.' Rampant canoodling in an ironmonger's porch may lose its appeal when the stench of wee assails the nostrils. If a blue-drink-fuelled ne'er-do-well is blurrily oblivious to your rapture, then you may end up sprayed, generally a metaphorical and physical dampener, though if you are with a woman like Margie, this might be the stuff of dreams (you remember Margie? The woman after a man with a big bladder and a good aim).

What if a girl gets nervous? You've done everything right, but then a hand tremor is noticed and you realise the situation is increasingly dubious. 'Calming nervous girls' requires 1 to 4 fluid ounces of cognac. You may also wonder *how* you can sense whether a girl is nervous; you must be as rigorous as a Victorian physiognomist in your facial analysis. Look for this telltale sign: 'The eyes are very round, wide moist or staring. They may have a "faraway" glazed look in extreme cases.'

If the girl is reluctant to part with any of her belongings Walsh reminds us that we shouldn't snatch her brolly or laugh in her face. Also remember: if you have failed in seducing your girl, you may well not have gone wrong, as she 'might have been frigid or a lesbian'. In other words, she was 'a pensioner'.

'They [homosexuals] deserve our pity rather than our acceptance . . . like all other minority groups homosexuals are sensitive about their position in society and can be quarrelsome and even violent when unwittingly provoked.' Annoyingly, Walsh doesn't elaborate on how one might unwittingly provoke these grumpy gays. Who knows what it might be: a casual slur about Judy Garland's performance in *I Could Go On Singing*, an offhand remark about Ted Heath or an ill-thought-out summary of *The Naked Civil Servant*. You can only find out by experience.

On frigidity, the reader is told that Walsh can never work out whether a woman is frigid or a lesbian, as the two are so similar. This is clearly a man who has never been on a Gay Pride march, where frigidity is rarely witnessed, especially after the placards are down and the cognac is flowing freely.

Can you ever manage to overcome the deference of the frigid? With effort and hankies, yes, as 'some frigid girls can eventually be seduced after a lot of sympathy'. A simple 'I am so sorry that I seem to have scared you into rigidity and marble coldness' followed by a long 'ahhhhhhhhh' with concerned eyes might do it.

Should you have managed to sympathise for long enough with your frigid girl, there is still the issue of undressing her.

Do the trials before consummation never end? Hats, head-scarves, gloves, blouses, cardigans, vests and more besides are all dealt with in Walsh's inimitable fashion.[14]

'Blouses – with a willing girl this should be first pulled out of her skirt before the buttons are undone. With a recently calmed girl, the opposite rule applies.' This sums up whatever sort of genius Michael Walsh possesses. It's not the underlying idea that nearly every chapter seems to be on the cusp of rape situation; it's the logic. As if Walsh is a few words short of hitting the publisher's target, but finds himself with nothing to say about blouses. He stares at the topless calendar from his local glazier that hangs from a drawing pin above the oil stain from his lawnmower. He looks at Pamela from Swindon, representing April by stand-ing near a concrete fountain in a damp, untucked blouse. 'Hmmm, she looks happy in her untucked but buttoned blouse; but how would she feel about this situation if she was recently calmed?' He flips to June. Lyndsay looks less happy in her blouse, and yet it too is buttoned and un-tucked, if a little damper to represent the summer month. And thus Michael comes up with a valuable blouse theory and hits his word count at one and the same time.[15]

And so, with your sexy girl undressed, Walsh leaves you to get on with it, but for one final masterstroke. What would be a fitting finale to this vital manual for the lust-laden man? The graph. The last three pages treat us to graphs on sexiness, child-bearing potential, sense of humour, intrinsic intellectualism, and greed, and end with a very cruel graph on the possession of beauty based

---

14 I am using the word 'inimitable' in its usual fashion. It would actually be quite easy to
    imitate it, but it's marginally idiosyncratic.
15 This is conjecture.

around the girls' chances of winning a crown at a beauty pageant.

Now you know it all. Get to the discotheque or zoo or concert (hippy) and start to pick up those sexy girls, but beware wigs and PINK EYES!

'Will I ever spank Boy George?' pondered the confused girl

Members of both sexes who have failed to pick up the secrets of picking up anything can always find solace in their dreams and fantasies, and some people have more vivid imaginations with an exciting menagerie.

Do you still have the gummy Blu-Tack marks on your wall where your Sheena Easton poster used to peer down at you? Did you fall asleep imagining she would walk out from the wall, then wake up confused and embarrassed by your sheets?

Did you look at Boy George and think of spanking him as he lay over your knee?

Did you sometimes wish that Debbie Harry and Chris Stein were seriously ill and you were sexually manipulating them in their agony?

If so, your fantasies are what makes up the magnificent fan fantasy omnibus *Starlust*.

Fred and Judy Vermorel's *Starlust* is a staggering compilation of explicit dream fantasies about pop stars from the seventies and early eighties. Haircut 100, David Bowie, Boy George – all are vigorously defiled, rescued or revered in the imaginations of obsessive fans. Picking this off the Shelter charity shop shelf, I saw one sentence on the back cover that meant *Starlust* would be coming home with me: 'If there was a nuclear war I would be thinking, is Boy George safe?'

Here lie the twin fantasies/nightmares of the hormone-addled teenage brain: the love for Boy George as your parents tutted about what he/she was, and the terror of waiting for a mushroom cloud to rise above Woking. It is a sentence that sums up the eighties (as long as you miss out most of the other historical details of that decade, such as the rabid crushing of the trade unions and the seedlings of rampant consumerism planted by a bleak and venomous administration).

Not all Boy George fantasies are as compassionate or fearful, unfortunately: 'I always imagine popstars in physical pain. At the moment it's Boy George.'

If spanking Boy George seems mild, then Lillian, also a twisted fan of CBGB-spawned pop, imagines Deborah Harry and Chris Stein suffering a terrible and mysterious disease. In Lillian's fecund imagination, a black magic expert informs Chris and Debbie that the only cure is sexual intercourse. They are weak and the intercourse is agony, but Lillian likes this. As you will see, her mind is vivid: 'I often fantasise about hepatitis or migraine. They're two things I've come across in other people and I think: oh, they're very painful.'

And so Lillian imagines Boy George with hepatitis 'from a girl he has slept with'. She also imagines a further cast of celebrities to populate her fantasy, including the finest DJs of their day. Boy George is in agony and so he is picked up by Kid Jensen and John Peel, who drive him home, but not before picking up another former Radio One DJ, Peter Powell, who helps Boy up the steps to his house. It is a fantasy that fuses the banal and the agonising. Where is Lillian now? Did she marry a local radio DJ who she cruises down streets with searching for diseased celebrities, or did she get picked up by the police after attempting to syringe smallpox into Nik Kershaw's porridge? Or is she a nurse who discreetly hides her disease peccadillo as she bed-baths another patient with sores and cracked skin?

Some fantasies are medically intricate, some are mundane, so mundane that there are male masturbatory fantasies that are about the male fan masturbating. Some voyage across stardust galaxies while David Bowie, the Thin White Duke and most potently enigmatic of the seventies pop icons, sheds skin and shoots fire from his orifices. And while Bowie was the pin-up for boys and girls who thought they were a little strange, there was another who provided the lust for the more mature, trapped in marriage and monotony type: 'When I make love to my husband I imagine it is Barry Manilow. All the time.'

This is the simple but heartbreaking fantasy from contributor Joanne. She is one of the many women whose lives are dominated by Barry Manilow. Who is the more piteous, the woman who is envisioning her husband as Barry Manilow while in the midst of intercourse, or the husband who must put up with the orgasm cry of 'Copacabana!' before his wife opens her eyes and looks with disgust at a man who has most definitely never been Bette Midler's piano player.

For Joanne, the fantasy is real until intercourse ends, eyes reopen, 'and when I realise it's not Barry Manilow, I cry myself to sleep'.

Joanne's Manilow fantasies go on for some pages and their intensity is damp with melancholy, but the mood is lightened by the next dream, 'Stephen's fantasy about Bruce Foxton', former bass player with The Jam. There is a certain nonchalance to Stephen's dreamt-up school toilet cottaging scenario: 'Bruce started moving his blazer pocket and brought out a pack of cigs. He handed me one and we both had a smoke and a chat whilst wanking off.' Though he doesn't leave out some of the more lurid details of his imagination: he reveals that Bruce 'smiled at me and showed his mouth full of fresh spunk'. I can only presume that at this point the smoking has reached its conclusion.

The book is littered with letters to David Bowie, who is viewed as everything from the ultimate manifestation of what humanity is, to some sort of sun god and occasionally Satan. Bowie can project the mystical in a way that the Bay City Rollers couldn't. He was not the boy next door; he was the star child from a species the world had never known. A creature whose mismatched eyes and feather boas when tested for DNA would come back from the lab with the result: not of this earth. While his disciples imagined Bowie as the last survivor of an alien species who would ejaculate stardust, the Bay City Roller fan can only dream of Derek wiping the chip fat off his hand and then kissing them with a vinegar-tainted tongue. *Stardust* was compiled in the eighties, so the Bay City Rollers are absent from its pages: pin-up lust dies as chart positions fall.

The letters to David Bowie collected here acknowledge that he receives multitudes of fan scribblings, but each author thinks that theirs will be the one that slips in. After all, Bowie is the only one who could ever know how they feel, because aren't they also the Bowie of their own small town, be it Midhurst or Barrow. Aladdin stripes were on the faces of the acolytes in the suburbs. 'You are the most important thing in my life, the only human being for who I would be capable to do sacrifice,' implores Cosima, another youngster hoping to become best pals with Bowie.

And if a double-decker bus or a Bedford van would do . . .

Just as Nancy Friday's books reveal a gap between male and female fantasies when imagination is required, so *Starlust* also highlights the banality of sexual deviance from a male fan's mind. Most of the men have no time for prosaic interludes or drawn-out fantasies. There are few long conversations or pastures walked through; they are just popping their fingers into Debbie Harry's pants and that's that. Well that's not that: there are some ugly details of things spurting, purple expansions and frequently an undercurrent of angry sweating, but it is usually all contained in the minimum number of sentences possible. In the male dreams there is the suspicion that at the time of writing, these boys do not believe their hands are so far from Ms Harry's undergarments.

In the female fantasies, there is more often a sense of desperation. They are the knowing Billy Liars, the Billy Liars who understand they will never get on the train to London, even though that would bring them closer to Nick Heyward.

> Dear Nick,
>   I think of you all the time, wondering where you are or what you are doing. I get so frustrated, knowing that your life is happy, but mine is miserable without you. Please don't laugh at this letter and throw it away.

For one Nick Heyward fan the solution seems obvious – be involved in a major road accident that results in a coma. Once she's in a coma her parents will get in contact with Nick Heyward's people, then Nick will come to the hospital bedside and sing 'Love Plus One' until she's out of the coma.

Some male Sheena Easton fantasies even bring out the prude in the fantasist. One unnamed young man has dreams of bumping into Sheena in the street and she offers to make him a cup of tea back at her hotel. When she goes out to pop the kettle on, she obviously slips out of her things and into something more comfortable, if a low-cut black bra is more comfortable. Once she gets to the point of commenting, 'Isn't it awfully warm?' our boy fantasiser says, 'I better be going now.'

That is a proper British fantasy, 'I am awfully sorry, but I think this fantasy has gone quite far enough, young lady.'

Then there's the unnamed man who would 'like to stroke Debbie Harry's bum', and Lawrence, who loves Bucks Fizz, particularly Cheryl Baker: 'When I masturbate I imagine her sort of stood there.' Of all the outpourings to pop deities, there is one letter to Bowie that stands out amongst the madness. It is difficult to cherry-pick highlights as the letter has such momentum it would feel like filleting *Finnegans Wake* to edit it, but I must:

> HOW ARE YOU? I'D LOVE FOR YOU TO VISIT ME, MY TRUE IDENTITY IS GOD, I SEE UFOS – QUAZARS OCCASIONALLY . . . DO NOT SPEAK EVIL, YOU ARE THE DEVIL, I AM GOD, WE ARE FRIENDS, LOVERS PERHAPS, YET IT WOULD BE IMPOSSIBLE FOR ME TO BE YOUR WIFE. BUT I STILL PLAY YOUR SONGS ON MY GUITAR . . . I'M DYING FROM THERMONUCLEAR RADIATION . . .

This correspondent has plenty to say in addition to these theories, including words on the Queen, homosexual dissemination, Todd Rundgren, Scientology and artificial eyes. But what makes his letter so charming is the signing off.

After his all-capitals theorising on UFOs and his own satanic nature, does he end with 'yours, Xargor the unquenchable' or 'Beelzebub Soulsucker'? No:

> XENONS HAVE SIX EYES, LIKE SPIDERS FROM MARS
> BUT THEIR GRAIN IS SUPERIOR TO HUMANS . . . I AM A
> RAT IN A CYBERNETIC SEWER.
>   YOURS, SIMON

Where is Simon now? Is Todd Rundgren still mighty? Did the thermonuclear radiation get him in the end?

In the world of *Starlust*, it seems that the only pop creatures worthy of adoration were Nick Heyward, Debbie Harry, David Bowie, Barry Manilow and some members of Kajagoogoo. Some remain adored twenty years on, others are just a painful reminder of the fickle but excessive nature of teenage desire. Does a now grown woman somewhere still worry if Boy George will be safe when the atomic Armageddon comes, or does she just think he should stop painting his neck black and avoid chaining rented paramours to his radiator? Or does she not worry at all any more? The nuclear bomb never came; now the young wait to drown as the icecaps melt. Is anyone saying, 'If global warming does destroy the earth, I'll be thinking, does Joss Stone own an inflatable dinghy'?

Lure of the crocodile, lust of the cockroach

When it comes to animal sex, Nancy Friday is not my favourite author or fantasies compiler (it's the bucket detail; I can't see the window cleaner now without imagining donkey drippings. Every smear on my windows makes me think he hasn't rinsed out the bucket since his weekend shenanigans). For really animal animal sex, I know just where to turn.

Sex Link – 'everything you always wanted to know about the sex lives of animals – and then some' (*Chicago News*) – is a natural history book that specialises in studying the variety of ritual and coitus in the animal world. It is I hope technically accurate (the sex lives of animals is not one of my strong suits), and is packaged with the air of the sordid in the obvious hope that that will shift more units.

The taster sentence for each animal engagement has the ring of a circus sideshow barker luring foolhardy couples into tents full of copulating locusts or a tagline for a grindhouse sex epic that might have graced any 42nd Street fleapit during New York's pornographic heyday. 'The Callicebus monkey – love thy neighbour – and then some' is up there with 'To him, every bed is a battlefield' from *I Feel it Coming*. 'The cockroach – ugly, but oh so sexy' perhaps challenges 'So adult it smarts' from the poster for *Come One, Come All*, while 'The moth mite – to rape, add incest' might lead you to debate whether to go and see *The Spread Eagles*, with its tagline of 'they were flying high and laying low', or go to college and become an entomologist. Other lines are quite unassailable, sounding like a late-night drunken prank by some Hanna Barbera animators secretly spicing up *The Flintstones*: 'The mud snail – group orgy in a chain gang'; 'The crocodile – call the rape squad!'; 'One man's meat is another man's bottom.'

If *Sex Link* has lured just one prospective adult film actor away from the crushing world of pornographic movie-making and towards bonobo studies, then it has done its work.

Calm yourselves you filthy swine

'On television recently Germaine Greer stated that one of the most potent female carcinogens was the unsheathed male penis.'

If the books in this chapter aren't really your sort of thing, then you might enjoy *Sex is Not Compulsory*, described as the book 'that launched a tidal wave of controversy' though no one I've ever met has ever heard of it, so maybe it was more of a tsunami of sod-all. The author, Liz Hodgkinson, sets out to prove that a couple can remain blissfully coupled while celibate. Hodgkinson's book was seen as a brave plea to a sex-soaked world that it was time to dry off and realise that sex wasn't nearly as natural as biological research might suggest. As a man who dislikes seeing tottering youths barely covering their flesh with vague undergarments and the merest semblance of a top, or hearing couplings against my tin bins as I try to sleep, I could have agreed with Liz, but the book reads a little too much like a declaration of 'just because I am celibate does not make me mad, thank you, it is the copulators who are crazy'.

Firstly, as Germaine Greer stated, sex gives you cancer, and that is just the starting point. At times the author seems to believe that we are the only species that has sex for pleasure as well as procreation: 'We, as humans, indulge in sexual activity far beyond the needs of continuing the species.' Sociobiologists have spent much time chronicling the shagging about of sex-happy beasts. The bonobo, still my favourite great ape, seems to have sex whenever possible. Should tension in the camp be brewing, the simple solution is to rub genitals, heterosexually or homosexually. The bonobo ruined many an angry evangelist's argument that it was only sinful man who had same-sex shenanigans; that and the ten-spined stickleback as written about in Desmond Morris's *Patterns of Reproductive Behaviour*, essay number one, 'Homosexuality in the Ten Spined Stickleback' (1952). Even the Bible-chained zealot who escapes the Gomorrah of the city can have his reason and goodness disturbed as he tries to fish quietly on a bank only to be disgusted by some queer fish.

In Chapter One, 'Does Sexual Desire Really Exist?', Liz reveals that the celibate suffers the same shame and cliché as the atheist and the vegetarian, namely the 'oh but Hitler was a bit like that' dullard's comment. He wasn't an atheist, and though he was a vegetarian it was not out of love for animals but due to buying into a health regime, so it was narcissistic vegetarianism, which is different from the 'as a youth I used to weep in butcher's shops' vegetarianism. As for his libido, well, genocidal dictators are rarely given a clean bill of sexual health by biographers; they are either

The Bonobo ape, a keen fan of sex to calm feuds and also one of the few beasts with a fashion sense. Should they find a dead rat or cockroach, they will wear it as a hat. It's a bit like the Grand National, but less revolting.

angry, libidinous rapists or men with mutant genitals and a fear of 'doing it'.

Hodgkinson uses what appears to be a sentence of empiricism when really it is just a made-up but suitable fact: 'If we look at the animal kingdom – and biochemically we are extremely close to certain animals – we will find that none of them have sex except when there is a possibility of reproduction.' Bonobos, genetically one of our closest relatives, have already been discussed. Dog and cat owners are mentioned as another illustration of the non-deviant behaviour of pets. This holds true as long as you have not been an embarrassed boyfriend trying to push a pumping dog off your trouser leg. There have been no reports of any trouser puppies being born, at least in this century.

There is another fact that may be questionable in its veracity: 'Those who are deprived of sex because they are, for example in prison, widowed or on an Antarctic expedition do not usually speak of their sexual frustrations.' Maybe Scott and Amundsen forgot to write in their diaries how difficult they found wanking in mittens was. I believe that when you are undertaking your lifetime's work with huskies, sleds and the possibility of blizzard death, sex drives can be forgotten. Prisons, according to some reports, are places where sheets are rigid and the prettier young pickpockets are wary.

'I do not believe we as humans possess genuine sexual desire.' How have we got this far through evolution, blind luck and sex hatred alone? Liz believes sex is the natural state for humans, but celibacy is a better state overall for day-to-day functions; celibacy in the supermarket, bank and workplace is quite right. If that sentence is taken as 'you shouldn't just rut non-stop everywhere', then I would agree, but maybe that isn't her point.

It is a thought-provoking book. I never knew that Mormon males wore a special all-in-one undergarment to prevent premarital desire, or that nuns were less likely to have blood pressure problems.

Liz's boldest move is to presume that she is all women and all women are her. Having come out of the free love and *Cosmopolitan* 'have better orgasms' generation, it seems that only disappointment was waiting: 'God, we tried. But somehow it didn't work. OK, sex was all right for a bit . . . but never did the bliss last, never did it add to the sum of happiness. Unless they constantly kept it at the forefront of their mind, most women found they were in distinct danger of forgetting all about sex.'

Unless they are donkey lovers or hankerers after historical slave sex, between the women of Hodgkinson and the women of Friday, a happy medium might lie.

The top-shelf journey continues with you

I have barely scratched the surface with a clawed velvet glove when it comes to books and sex. There are hundreds of versions of the *Kama Sutra*, some with line drawings, some with the archetypal sixties bearded man, others with hairless slippery people since we have entered the age where porn has decided to banish hairiness with the exception of an occasional Hitler moustache of hair above the clitoris. The subgroup of erotic massage books alone will fill many shelves. Then there are the erotic novels that attempt to service every penchant dreamt of in a lonely recess. The world of the pretend 'rubbish paperback' bookshop disguising porn awaits you.

What have we learned?

- Wigs and ribbons don't mix
- The inner mind of some women is more disgusting than previously imagined
- One to four fluid ounces of Cognac will relax a nervous girl
- Arctic explorers are snowblind to lust

Oh, and I wonder – do lesbians really read lesbian fiction that is 'especially designed by lesbians for lesbians' or is it as full of old men fantasising as many internet lesbian chat forums?

Further Reading

What are the secrets of The Lust Ranch?
'Carol found her curiosity growing about Rancho Erotica'

Tiffany Twisted
'Slowly he let the toy slip between his nether lips and enter him'

Sex and War: How Biology explains Warfare and Terrorism and Offers a Path to a Safer World
by Malcolm Potts

2

Poetry

(or the rhyming dictionary for kings and rockets)

I didn't realise you wrote poetry, I didn't realise
you wrote such bloody awful poetry.
'Frankly Mr Shankly' – The Smiths

Should I compare thee to some marmalade?

I like poetry best when it is used to create lesbian detective
crime thrillers set in Sydney, Australia. Unfortunately it is
not as frequently used for that purpose as it should be.[1] So
far the only book I have found that has satiated this need is
The Monkey's Mask by Dorothy Porter. So if you are currently debating whether to start that lesbian detective
thriller poem, then go for it, the market is currently wide
open for more; it's one of those sub-genres that just does-
n't have enough authors. I don't mind which geographical
location you use.

---

1 My favourite book about a family of Jewish intellectuals individually searching for notions
of God with a spelling competition backdrop is *Bee Season* by Myla Goldberg.

For many people, their only brush with poetry beyond school is when they open a greetings card. They may be the lucky ones.

Actually they are not the lucky ones.

The lucky ones receive a card where the blank space within has been filled by their friend's words rather than mass-produced sentiment from a sweat shop of rhymes. Can Purple Ronnie or Snoopy say as much about how you feel about your birthday / fiancée / poorly cousin / bereaved mother as telling them how you feel by using your thought and imagination?

Confronting poetry has its problems.

Firstly, many men fear poetry. Despite Byron, Shelley and Ted Hughes demonstrating that you can be virile, manly and write poetry, it is seen as the occupation of the effete read by the peculiar and occasionally the faux punkish.

For many years, the best way to keep reasonable space between you and the halitosis-heavy masses on public transport was always considered to be by reading a book of poetry. A slim volume was meant to suggest some sort of cottaging code or that you would turn to anyone near you with wide eyes and spitty lips and declare that you were the Duchess of Gloucester. Sadly this technique to create personal space has faded since the London Underground used advertising space for poetry and the BBC allowed Griff Rhys Jones to wander over hills demanding that the British public tell him what their hundred favourite poems are. They lie. They pretend it's John Donne when it is more likely a limerick.

I recently tried gaining personal space with a copy of some fey nineteenth-century poetry and still found myself being swallowed into the surly, panting human who was dripping next to me on the Bank branch of the Northern Line. If you really want space on public transport you should carry some pornography from the 1970s and a pair of children's safety scissors, then delicately cut out all the eyes of the glamour models whilst whistling. Every now and again mutter, 'Why are women more beautiful when they are eyeless?' You will be able to stretch out, though this can have ramifications such as ending up on a police list or being run out of town.

My taste in poetry is blandly English, which means the misanthropic and melancholy. If a poet obsesses about faded billboards and flies in jam, I can generally be persuaded to read a few verses. I mainly read Philip Larkin with a hint of John Betjeman and a little John Cooper Clarke if I want to imagine I had legs like wispy calcium tendrils and hair to envy.

I have attempted tackling the greats. I read T.S. Eliot's *The Waste Land* when I was eighteen, but I read it on the Metropolitan line between Chorleywood and Finchley Road as if it was a pulp book. So I haven't really read T.S. Eliot's *The Waste Land*, I've just seen the words that make it up.

Like jazz, I want to love poetry, I am sure it will give me more depth and a more interesting taste in hats, but it doesn't seem to happen. I know enough about poetry to make the more brutish slap me around the head with a bin lid, but I also know so little about it that the suave, well-read poem lover would consider me a halfwit Neanderthal and laugh at my bin lid scars. It may be the only time that the brutes and the effete enjoy themselves together, laughing at me concussed.

The King will never die in ABAB rhyme

My return to poetry occurred around London's Berwick Street market, home to noisy satsuma merchants and location for one of the blandest album covers ever conceived – Oasis's *(What's The Story) Morning Glory*. As I was meant to be doing something with a deadline, I ducked down into a second-hand record shop hoping the deadline wouldn't notice me and would savage someone else instead. Just next to the Akira Kurosawa boxed sets, and above the contemporary country and western, was a bookshelf with a few biographies on. Something about Metallica, a volume on the Osmonds, and a glam rock word-search magazine.[2] I didn't need to know any more about Mormon harmony singing, and the glam rock word search had been defaced with lewd images of Gary Glitter, but just below them was something I instinctively knew would soon be mine even before my brain had really registered what it was.

> Did you ever see a star shoot over the earth
> And wonder if it landed what it would be worth?
> Well, now you know, for Elvis was here for a while,
> And he was priceless as a man and a child.

This is the poetry of Joan Buchanan West. Joan Buchanan West has a very specific area to focus on. She only writes poetry about one thing, and that thing is the King. Not a king, THE KING.

---

2 That's how I remember it, but as research has shown, the memory can play tricks, especially with word-search magazine covers: Dalton and Fenchurch, *Gender, Subordination and the Post Modern Idyll – the dream of masculine heels in Wordsearch Magazines* (East Anglia Further Education Press).

Elvis: His Life and Times in Poetry and Lines, published by Exposition Press, Hicksville, New York, is in my top seven second-hand book impulse buys.

I knew I could trust it because:

a) The cover was not the work of some average Joe graphic designer; it was clearly the work of the author herself or one of her Elvis disciple friends.

b) Well, it's poetry about Elvis Presley, isn't it?

The illustration of the King's face might not betray professional artistic ability, but it is obvious that there is love in every brushstroke. I would rather have spent an afternoon surveying Joan's artistic output than those hours wasted at the Tate Modern Pop Life exhibition of dead calves and stapled porn mags that were meant to make me think about . . . well, dead calves and stapled porn. There is no irony or cynicism in Joan's work, no hankering to sell to a Saatchi, just honest love and the desire to tell the tale of a man very special to her. Every artist needs their muse, and what greater muse than a man who has, in his life and death, been worthy of black velvet paintings?

A black-and-white photo of Joan Buchanan West herself covers the back. She has the face of a kindly Baptist who wants to make sure the world is overflowing with love. Her eyes suggest she knows how to pour more love in. The recipe for further jugs of love to fill the world? Poetry – poetry that celebrates the almighty Lord and the Abrahamic God too. The only quandary in Joan's life is deciding who is her one true king, God or Elvis Presley. She finds equilibrium by loving Elvis but knowing that it was God who made him. As her poetry proclaims, it would be sacrilegious not to worship Elvis; after all, the existence of something so perfect is proof of God's omnipotence and imagination.

Nevertheless, should Joan's church declare Presley adoration a sin, it is certain she would face excommunication rather than destruction of her copy of *Viva Las Vegas*. I'm not sure why the church would decide Elvis praise was a sin, but organised religion does have its quirky moments, such as burning Giordano Bruno for considering that there might be life on other planets, forgetfulness when it comes to paedophile priests, or the banning of the film *Grease* by the Legion of Decency.

Published just two years after Elvis Presley's unfortunate death, much of the work is Joan trying to smile through the agony of the King's demise, and hopefully help other fans cope with the pain. It does not use its rhyme scheme to cover sandwiches made from a whole loaf of bread, bacon and jam, even though that culprit may have figured in his demise.

Joan is very clear from the outset when she explains what ELVIS is. ELVIS and GOD are firstly worthy of full capitals wherever possible in this book. According to Joan, no one Before ELVIS (BE) and no one After ELVIS (AE) will ever bring as much joy to the earth as he did; he was a gift from GOD. This will not be an Albert Goldman smear campaign of the dead in ABAB rhyme scheme.

It is unseemly to deride Joan Buchanan West's ELVIS poetry, because it is so well-intentioned. Like Don Estelle, through amateurishness beauty can arise. As the Lake District was to Wordsworth, and cold chips and the immorality of the *Daily Express* are to John Cooper Clarke, so Presley is to Joan. It may be clunky, but its heart is so perfectly placed that derision says more about the critic's cold granite innards than Joan's poems. To tackle the legend of Elvis in poetry or prose can trip up many writers.

Aloha inadequacy

If you have ever picked up a copy of *Elvis: The King on Film* (you may well have missed it as it had quite a limited print run), you will find two abysmal essays within. To call them essays is already elevating them. They are just lots of words that stop once the word count is reached. One looks at the Elvis concert documentary *Elvis in '72*; the other word jumble attempts to put karate funfair motorbike film *Roustabout* into some context. It is the worst critique of a karate funfair movie I have read; it is also the worst critique of a karate funfair movie that I have written.[3]

Truman Capote's acid comment, 'that's not writing, that's typing'[4] would almost summarise my work, and it wasn't even very good typing. If you place just one monkey in a room with a typewriter, eventually he writes an essay on *Roustabout*.

There is an aura around the worshipful church of Elvis that turns us into gibbering wrecks. For the disciple, their love blinds them to the ineptitude of their praise, like a hymn written by a man in a cave who is clothed in moss and hand-pierced tattoos of Jesus. To the writer merely commissioned to write of Elvis, there is the fear of terrifying reprisal from the psychotic whose every tea towel has the words of 'Love Me Tender' printed on it.

As with the majority of deities, Joan does not believe ELVIS can die. Though he has left his mortal body, his dates remain '1935–Never'.

---

3 Both pieces were written by me and my stomach still knots when I think of their clumsiness. They appear to have been proofread by Don Estelle.
4 This was Capote's assassination of the work of Jack Kerouac.

What would be scorned as prose can be revered as poetry. The mere use of rhymes means that even the most artless words gain some kudos because the author has rhymed 'leather' with 'weather'. If they fail to rhyme, points may also be scored for making the poem a pretty shape. Joan predominantly sticks to the former, keeping her rhyming dictionary warmly by her side.

Elvis: His Life and Times in Poetry and Lines opens with a work simply entitled 'Elvis'. It is biography in rhyme chronicling the major events of Presley's early years, such as the death of his twin in childbirth.

> Little Jess Garon, who was named for his granddad,
> Was to meet his fate quickly, how very, very sad.
> Elvis Aaron, named for his dad, was the second one
>   born,
> And would grow up loved and respected, never scorned.

Should it lose marks for poetic style, it makes them back again for historical accuracy, except for the 'never scorned' element.

Elvis Presley was frequently scorned, particularly by his venal manager Colonel Tom Parker. It was Parker who ensured that Presley was trapped in trite films for most of the sixties, churning out some of his worst songs and wearing too many Hawaiian garlands in helicopters. In his later years, Elvis was offered the leads in *Midnight Cowboy* and *A Star is Born*, but by then it was too late, and the money probably wasn't enough to keep Colonel Tom at the craps table.[5]

---

5 Eddie Murphy was a huge Elvis fan and once met Colonel Tom Parker. He was surprised when Colonel Tom rubbed his head. Apparently amongst gamblers of a certain generation it was considered good luck to rub a negro's head. Hmmmmm.

Joan notably decides not to use her rhyming dictionary to praise Elvis's movies, which is a pity, as *Jailhouse Rock* would have almost rhymed with 'swivelling hip shock'. *Viva Las Vegas* could have had 'the pleasure he gave us', but *Kissin' Cousins* would have been trickier.

Here is my own *Roustabout* haiku.

Poison Ivy League
Karate chopped
Not Barbara Stanwyck's best

This is infinitely superior to the thousands of words I used in *Elvis: The King on Film*. I made £100, not enough to buy all the copies and burn them, or pulp them and use the papier mâché to make great big Elvis balloon heads, a far more fitting tribute than my sentences.

Joan's tributes knock mine into a cocked quiff. To her, Elvis is mystical. The question of his existence is not scientific but metaphysical.

There was an aura about him which cannot be explained
It was like the mystery of air, after it has rained.

What is the mystery of air after it has rained? I am sure if you asked a meteorologist or ecologist they would give you a reasoned answer with the use of evidence and charts. Is Joan suggesting that the aura of Elvis could be easily explained if you were prepared to put the effort in and check with an aura expert?

If he could not have sung a note at all
We would have loved him, this man who stood so tall.

It cannot be denied that Elvis Presley was a very good-looking man and a dab hand with the hair dye, but Joan is going too far here. Had Elvis been the most handsome squirrel shooter near Memphis he might have had some adulation in local bars, but it is certain that his singing, and that singing being placed on records that were distributed across the states, was a major part of his being loved by so many. To put it all down to the cut of his trousers, whether leather or silk, suggests that he would have had the same swooning fans had he been an underwear model.

Joan then goes on to blame herself and the other fans for Elvis's tragic death, but still looks forward to joining him in heaven. And all of this is dealt with in the first poem of the book – where can Joan go from there? Into realms of Presley poetry undreamt of by most minds, that's where.

> Dear Elvis, we promise your memory will be kept alive,
> And no matter what happens it will survive;
> So happy now and sing your songs
> For the glory of God and we'll join you before long.

Ian McShane and iambic pentameter

Books of fan poetry are not found so frequently now. The internet is the natural home for odes to *Blake's* 7 characters and boy band heroes; you don't need to sneak in and use the office photocopier and staple gun any more.

Just before the internet became another limb of our life, Arrival Press of Peterborough published *As Seen on TV: Your Favourites* in conjunction with *What's on TV*. It is the best collection of TV fan poetry about Bruce Forsyth and selected weathermen I have ever found behind a splintered radiogram in a covered market in north Devon.

The amateur poets within may have dreamt that one day their work would be read aloud by Cyril Fletcher on *That's Life*. Amateur poetry with a sledgehammer satirical edge seems very much the domain of the English in the shires. One of the most interesting poems dwells on Esther Rantzen and her charity work. The poem starts off in a jolly manner, expressing joy at the larks of the *That's Life* team, but then goes to another place.

Young people may be traumatised,
If beaten, raped, abused.
They need someone to help them
When frightened and confused.

Four verses in and memories of funny foreign place names that sound like toilet are long gone. And it's difficult to mix fun rhymes with child abuse.

As Seen on TV was published in 1993, so the poetry creates a jigsaw picture of the public's taste in the early nineties. It is a world of Ian McShane, Pop Larkin and Fred the Weatherman from *This Morning* with Richard and Judy, immortalised in 'Ode to Fred' by Mary Hazeldine.

Mary declares her respect and love for the TV weatherman who leapt across a floating image of the British Isles in the Albert Dock, but still there is that hint of the psychotic. The weatherman is celebrated, but Mary can't help but imagine his death by drowning due to the absorbent nature of his knitwear.

The majority of the poems offer love in stanza form to these TV celebrities, whether it's Russell Grant, Magnus Magnusson or Gordon Honeycombe, the TV newsreader who was also the narrator of Arthur C. Clarke's *Mysterious World*, bringing authority to footage of men in gorilla

This is not Fred Talbot, but it is a weatherman in an exuberant jumper.

costumes being mistaken for Bigfoot. However, there are some exceptions. Sean Vincent uses his moment of rhyme to lambast not merely Paul Daniels, but also his son Martin, and ends it all sticking the boot into Debbie McGee.

His son's as bad, another trick
And as for Debbie she makes me sick . . .

And there lies the danger of excessive TV exposure. When Paul Daniels first appeared on television, he was feted as the new king of magic with his sleight of hand and Yorkshire wit. Then, via omnipresence initially caused by public demand, the public decided they had had enough of him. What once was delight in his cheeky showmanship was transformed into loathing for his smug, almost arrogant way with a magic teapot.

While Daniels is derided by Sean Vincent, others who would face public ire later in the decade were still loved in 1993. *The Big Breakfast* had captured the hearts of the *What's On TV* readers, and while this Zoo TV style, with its caterwauling presenters and energetic floor managers, would wear thin as the decade moved on, at this point in time it was an anarchic early-morning delight shaking up the placid mainstream breakfast telly that was home to the demure. Chris Evans, Paula Yates and Zig and Zag are all revered in *As Seen on TV*. 'Sir Bob's Wife' is a eulogy to Paula Yates' interview technique, which involved her cheekily flirting with celebrities on a bed.

> Paula's bedroom ways and manners put rich and famous
>   at their ease,
> As she drapes herself beside them, showing, ankles,
>   boobs and knees.
> Eddie Shah prostrate beside her, one could hear the
>   mattress groan,
> Other heavyweights included dear old Bruno, Frank
>   Stallone.

Though an avid watcher of *The Big Breakfast* in my youth, I have no memory of Frank Stallone's appearance on the bed. I imagine it was to promote *The Rollerblade Seven*, the fabulous remake of *Seven Samurai* ON ROLLER-BLADES. As well as starring Sylvester Stallone's brother, it also stars Martin Sheen's brother and Karen Black from *Airport '75*.

Some of the poems are mere adjectives away from being the words of a stalker written in the condensation on their celebrity's bathroom mirror. Moira Stewart, who is definitely in my top three newsreaders of all time, is the idol/victim in two poems. Joy Iyengar's 'Moira Stewart' depicts her as a woman hiding her moral outrage behind a professional newsreading face, but ready to spring into actions of justice one day soon.

We are sure you'd really like to say
'May all those bombers be blown away
Why have wars that kill in vain
And cause such heart and body pain?
And why should children starve today
When so much food is thrown away?'
Oh Moira if you had your chance
You'd make the politicians dance.

What the world needs now is for Moira Stewart to stand up and shout, 'I'm mad as hell and I'm not going to take it any more.' Unfortunately, the majority of journalists who shout that they are as mad as hell appear to be clinically mad and on Fox News (Ann Coulter will be discussed in a later chapter).

While Joy Iyengar gets her moral outrage and sense of injustice from Moira Stewart's broadcasts, Desmond A. Masters' 'Miss Moira Stewart – News Presenter' insinuates that his reason for tuning into the news has little to do with his interest in current affairs.

'Good evening' said in a husky voice
Enslaves my heart, I have no choice
Meticulously groomed and dressed
Our news presenter looks her best.
That special face, I'm being absurd
I watch her lips speak every word.

And all this before he calls her his 'Moira Lisa or Temptress of the Nile'.

The line between adoration and psychosis can be thin; sometimes the fan does not know they have overstepped the mark until they look down and see the lock of hair torn from their idol's scalp dripping blood in their hand. *As Seen on TV* is a rhyming discourse on where that line can be drawn, a middle-age, supermarket version of *Starlust* (see Chapter 1).

There was an old prophet from Gaza

Do you enjoy bible stories? Do you especially enjoy the stories with lots of damnation, pustule plagues and God being moody? Are you annoyed that time constraints are limiting your enjoyment of the full text? Do you wonder if time could be saved if only a simple rhyme scheme could be used to sum up Exodus? Then *The Old Testament and Apocrypha in Limerick Verse* by Christopher Goodwins will be the answer to your overly specific prayer.

Here's Proverbs 31: 10–31:

A virtuous woman is rare.
To find one where would you look – where?
But find one whose word
Shows that she loves the lord
And no one will with her compare.

I prefer the one about the old woman from Ealing (I really don't know how she makes it reach the ceiling; muscle control, I suppose). Neither Revelation nor Leviticus gets a going-over, which is a pity as they would be a challenge, though a rewarding one, to any limerick writer seeing how far they could push this art form. Leviticus mixes instructions for stoning a variety of sinners – the usual assortment of animal fondlers and sex deviants – with top tips on how to remove mildew from a stained tent. One moment you're stoning two gay men to death; the next you're rubbing salt on your canvas – that's what it was all about when you were tramping through the desert with occasional visits from God and locusts.

Sodom and Gomorrah also gain a jaunty rhythm during the purging of the sinful, making the whole affair quite jolly.

> There's one thing you must do – Not!
> In Sodom the men want you, Lot!
> But quit there for Zoar
> Don't look back! But go . . . er
> Bad news, your wife's now become salt.

The limerick also gives a little suspense: what the heck is the author going to find to rhyme with Zoar? Ingenious, he adopts a conversational style, 'go . . . er', which also increases the comedic vision of a man now wedded to a pillar of salt.

Christopher Goodwins, a vicar, has taken on a mammoth task with this collection, and to his credit he even manages to include Mephibosheth (though smartly, he didn't place him at the end of a line).

Other authors take the challenge of a rhyme and create something quite intriguing and confusing. There are some things we all talk about when we talk about love, and some things you might be surprised to find out that some people talk about when they talk about love.

True love wails

What is a hectopus? Why does an octopus represent the failure of love? Or is it the arms of love?

There is only one person who would know. The author of 'Octopus Hectopus'. It is not a New York Lower East

Side contemporary beatnik dance poet. It is the multi-millionaire romance author Danielle Steel. Not content with splintering the bookshelves with her heavy, gold-embossed romantic tear-inducers, she produced a less weighty book entitled simply *Love Poems*. By my calculations, *Love Poems* weighs approximately 73 per cent less than the average Danielle Steel such as Danielle Steel's *Season of Passion* or Danielle Steel's *To Love Again*.

I have never read any of Danielle Steel's novels of romance, though I have watched some adaptations on late-night TV. Danielle Steel's *Jewels* is about the English aristocracy, American visitors, war and jewellery stores. Danielle Steel's *Secrets* is the story of a glamorous TV soap, blackmail, and male models who may not be as straight as a die. Danielle Steel's *Message from Nam* is about a message from Nam. The films are brief; the books will get you from London, England, to Auckland, New Zealand.

I prefer my romantic fiction to have brevity, which is why I have remained true to the considerably briefer (and lighter) Mills & Boon. The gap in my Danielle Steel knowledge means I have no idea if either octopi or hectopi make appearances in her novels. I hope they do. There are not enough romance novels combining love and giant monsters of the deep with varying limb numbers.

Love Poems is a poetic Rolodex of memories of love and defeat that have become 'woven into the fiber' of Danielle's being. The first thing to notice about the poetry is the beautiful symmetry. All poems are immaculately shaped; it is a topiary expert's expert cutting of words.

Sometimes geometry in poems can convey what words fail to. Then again, sometimes geometry is just geometry and tells us nothing whatsoever.

Danielle uses frogs, peacocks, champagne-filled shoes and jam to convey love won and love lost or still waiting. The fears, the victories, the joys and the pain can all be conveyed through sandwich spreads and amphibians. But what of the worries of love? Danielle bares her internal organs with her rhyming honesty, wondering if her nipples are too small, and what would happen if she got lost in an anthill.

Further insights into her psyche are revealed when she buys eighteen nails to forget that an ex-lover is getting married. The reader is not told how these nails are utilised. Is the lover crucified, Kray style, to the floorboards of a decrepit warehouse? Or is Danielle one of the many people nowadays who use angry DIY to block out the pain of an ex's new-found happiness?

While Danielle's novels are renowned for their value for money in terms of word count, her poetry is sparser. Her poem 'Peeling Away' is just thirty words on one page. Maybe that's the trick of poetry: it's an art form for the lazy or for people who don't like proper sentences. Even her titles are short and specific. 'First Meeting', 'No Choice', 'Bereft', 'Friend', 'Comfortable', 'Bill', 'Silence', 'Free' and of course 'Jam'.

Jam.
    There must be jam
        You told me
            Firmly

And Danielle sticks to her promise: when jam is demanded by a lover, then jam there will be, whatever the breakfast.

Toast.
   Eggs perhaps
      Double coffee
      Some milk
Maybe juice
  But always
    Always
      Jam.

When does poetry become a list; when does a list become poetry: these are the sort of questions that niggled at C.S. Lewis every day. I'll try not to give away too much about the ending; suffice to say that it involves scrambled eggs and ham. Oh yes, and jam.

Verse in zero gravity and a spacesuit

How does jam float in zero gravity? Who knows how toast is spread in space?

Perhaps the modernist poet can help.

The tedium of the Cold War was warmed by the space race, the battle between the USA and the USSR to see who would conquer space first. In the sixties, space was a grand distraction. Worried about the Vietnam War disaster swallowing up all news coverage? Quick, send another rocket into space packed full of chisel-jawed military men who embody the American dream. By 'conquer space', what was really meant was dipping your toe in a bird bath and pretending you had dived into the Atlantic Ocean. Incidentally, do not dip your toe in a bird bath; due to its height you may fall over and be trapped under it, and end up as a re-enactment on a TV accident show.

Technically the size of space is very, very, very big.[6] Even the numbers of verys needed to convey how very big it is is more than the number of verys that were said in the whole of the twentieth century.[7] The dream of reaching the stars infiltrated every child's mind, displacing previous dream jobs. Who'd want to be a zookeeper, mucking out giraffes, when you could be eating mush out of a tube as you floated through the Van Allen belt. Few media were unaffected by the dream, from TV to novels, and even poetry. *The Frontier of Going*, compiled by John Fairfax, is a collection of poems inspired by the possibility of adventures in space.

The Frontier of Going includes work by D.M. Thomas, George Barker and James Kirkup. Kirkup, despite a very lengthy career in poetry, is best remembered for the 'rude dead Jesus cocksucking' poem, also titled 'The Love that Dares to Speak its Name', which was the last piece of work successfully prosecuted under the blasphemy libel laws. I saw 'The Love that Dares to Speak its Name' performed by Ian McKellen at some blasphemy do a few years ago. I thought it was rude and funny, like an X-rated biblical seaside postcard. I am told that at the time of publishing it was seen as a very serious look at centurion sex through a spear-made gash. Maybe I am childish.

The Frontier of Going doesn't include any messianic mauling, but does include 'Love in a Spacesuit' and 'Tea in a Spaceship', both of which are tricky propositions in a NASA vessel. James Kirkup's mind is again concerned with

---

6 It's not even that. If we were the size of a grain of sand and took a paddle in the Atlantic Ocean it might be a little like conquering a corner of the Milky Way, but still leaving out quite a few billion other galaxies and all the empty bits in between.

7 Stanford and Tucket, *Accurate Accounted for Uses of Very and the sub-male myth* (East Anglia Further Education Press).

sexual union later on in the book, when he attempts to cure the astronautical problems of congress in space.

> Nay! Before I will renounce
> My lust for earth and love of you
> I shall have us both, dear, fitted
> With a spacesuit made for two.

It is a rather charming 'Daisy, Daisy' for an astronautical endeavour.

George Barker contributes 'From: Nine Beatitudes to Denver (iii)'.

> It strikes me as, well, the height of erotic presumption
> Suppose she prefers the attention of Mars or the
>   respectable ring of Saturn.

Barker worries that by sending up a spaceship we are having sex with space, or more particularly Selene, the goddess of the moon. These are wonderings made by many scientists with a Freudian perspective: 'Will Selene appreciate the impregnation by that germless ball?'

Peter Redgrove's 'The Haunted Armchair' concerns us all ending up dead, leaving nothing more than greasy stains on an antimacassar as far as I can comprehend. I am not sure why this is in a book of space poetry. I have either missed the point of his eulogy to undiseased bodies becoming diseased, and being no more than an armchair imprint somehow actually referring to Yuri Gagarin, or John Fairfax had to occasionally be liberal in his choices when attempting to fill a whole book with poems pondering on space. I accept that lives being no more than a stain could certainly be happy in a compendium of existential limericks.

Whatever the ultimate judgement on *The Frontier of Going*, it shows that there was a time when excitement about space, discovery and rocket ships was such that it even deserved its own book of poetry. Now the only space poems you are likely to find are just for under-tens, and frequently they are not even specially composed on a space theme. They are a case of 'take nursery rhyme and replace "plum pudding" with "stellar nursery"'.

Little Miss Muffet sat on her SPACE ROCKET
Eating her ASTRONAUT FOOD
When down came a ROBOT
And frightened poor Muffet INTO A WORMHOLE.

Composers of CD baby space compilations are wily.

What have we learned?

- Observe your lover's toast accompaniment well; it may be your fondest memory after love turns to tears
- Armchairs are not just the past, they are the future in space too
- Leviticus is more palatable when rigorously edited and given the addition of a jaunty rhyme
- The true holy trinity is Father, Son and Elvis Presley

Further reading

Poetic Gems by William McGonagall

Such a legendary bad poet that I spent my youth believing his existence was a fabulous con trick by Spike Milligan.

A Lifetime of Love by Leonard Nimoy

Does for poetry what William Shatner did for Beatles cover versions.

And I've never read the collected poetry of Charlie Sheen or Ally Sheedy, due to their expensive and collectable nature, but the snippets available on the internet suggest they might be worth seeking out if you are a wealthy aficionado.

3

Autobiography

> We are easily breakable, by illness or falling, or
> a million other ways of leaving this earthly life.
> We are just so much mashed potato.
>
> *Sing Lofty: Thoughts of a Gemini*, Don Estelle

The narcissism of the cracked panto dame

Philip Glass's soundtrack for *Koyaanisqatsi* boomed out of a
damp but prepossessing amp in an Edinburgh basement as I
bombastically read that anecdote about Cliff Richard,
Syd Little and a curry to a drunk but strangely receptive
audience. It was on this stage that my love for the 'self-
aggrandising without self-awareness' life story was reawak-
ened. That year, Syd Little's words were my solace and the
straws I clutched as my new show for the Edinburgh Fringe
festival sank in a quagmire of ill-thought-out ideas and lack of
preparation.

The Award-Winning Robin Ince, Star of *The Office*,

Series One Episode Five (First Bit) was meant to be a satire on celebrity self-delusion and the trite nature of television. I played myself, but a lunatic version of myself, struggling with failure. To make the show more pertinent, it was a failure itself. And so ideas eat themselves.

Unfortunately, despite being surrounded by Warholesque images of *Hi-De-Hi!*'s Su Pollard and Brian Conley and ending the show punching a melon that represented Vernon Kay's face until it exploded, most people thought it was real. To the audience, I was a man genuinely having a nervous breakdown because he believed that he had created everything that was good on television and radio.

Even as I sang 'Mustang Sally', weeping and covered in melon bits, the audience looked on in scared bemusement – blackout. This proves one of three possibilities:

a) I am a brilliant actor.
b) People are idiots.
c) Shows dreamt up with Danny Wallace at 2 a.m. in a London cellar bar may ultimately be misconceived.

The author celebrating the work of Stevie Smith.

The saving grace was my delving into passages of Syd
Little, an iconic figure in my fictional self's mind. So after
I had finished failing in my own show, and still stinking of
tropical fruit, which was rotting on my lapels in the heat,
I would find strange late-night clubs where I would read
from Syd. Soon Syd wasn't enough, and I spent my days up
and down Edinburgh's charity-shop-festooned Nicholson
Street seeking out other celebrity self-servings. *Rags to
Richie* by Shane Richie offered up a fabulous story of dis-
appointment: Shane hoped to strike up a rich conversation
with Robin Williams as they had much in common. Not
merely were they both comedians, they had both been in
Peter Pan. Robin Williams played Peter in the Steven
Spielberg multi-million-dollar film *Hook*, and Shane Richie
was Captain Hook at the Cliffs Pavilion, Southend. In
addition to this there was *Acts of Faith* by Adam Faith in the
Shelter shop, *Behind Closed Dors* by Diana Dors in the
PDSA store, and Ed Stewart's *Out of the Stewpot* in the
British Heart Foundation. Only Michael Flatley's autobiography disappointed by avoiding even the slightest sense
of pun with the self-fellating title *Lord of the Dance*. That
was its only failure; in the self-aggrandising stakes, it was
Lord and King and, perhaps, God.

Nearly every chapter of Flatley's triumphalism begins
with a quote to remind us just how astounding, loved and
adored he is. Bono, J-Lo, Hugh Hefner, Catherine
Deneuve and Plato are all quoted to remind us that Flatley
is better than you. Plato doesn't actually speak of Flatley;
rather his words are used to remind us that Flatley's great-
ness of mind means that he does not fear death, unlike you,
you woolly-thinking, lead-footed sloth. I never got round
to reading *Lord of the Dance* live on stage; I just couldn't find
the right music. I tried 'Turning Japanese' by the Vapors

and the Buzzcocks' 'Orgasm Addict', but sadly they just didn't fit.

Apart from a brief period of childhood where I read any biography or autobiography of anyone who had so much as cleaned out their tobacco pipe next to Boris Karloff or Vincent Price, the autobiography corner of the bookshop hadn't much bothered me; now piles of them teetered around me. It didn't matter if I hadn't even heard of the subject; if a publisher had decided this personality deserved a book of their own (and it was under £3 in the charity shop) I was making black holes in my mind reading their words.

My struggle . . . to glue sequins

With the domination of television banalities, the 'business' side is increasingly bold as the 'show' side timidly cowers behind the marketing importance of sexual confession, drug lust and booze shame. Neither are these final confessions as final as they used to be; for some celebrities, the new volume of autobiography is an annual event, like amnesiacs returning to their preacher's confession booth.

The profitability of those who have lived a little in the tabloids requires publishers to swoop in, snatch up and rapidly manufacture a life story with glossy pics before the public have moved on to the next one. One wardrobe malfunction on a red carpet, and a couple of blow jobs to a premier-league footballer or a boy-band background dancer can be highly profitable as long as you are not shy in describing a misshapen foreskin or how you threw up afterwards.

How debased the word 'star' has become. Once it was Bette Davis and Clark Gable selling Lucky Strikes and lighting up the Hollywood canteen; now it's shamed news-paper editors selling burgers and arrogance, and pneumatic women who are married to quick-tempered soccer play-ers.[1] It's as if an astronomer mistook sputnik debris for Alpha Centauri.

Silicone-inflated flesh texts

'Some people may be famous for inventing a pencil sharp-ener, I'm famous for my tits.' Jordan/Katie Price is being very generous here as, sadly, the inventor of the pencil sharpener is barely known at all. The handheld pencil sharpener was patented by the Eureka company in 1865. After that there was a boom time in pencil sharpener design, which, according to officemuseum.com, petered out in 1910. The breast craze has still not petered out though and looks to continue as long as the male human brain finds evolutionary advantage in leering.

While the population's knowledge of office equipment is limited, this tittle-tattle-submerged island has never been so ravenous for every detail of lewd antic or melancholy agony that has befallen those who have been on the telly or a supermarket magazine cover in some capacity. An auto-biography entitled *Dogging, Drugs and a Big Cup of My Tears Spilt over my Tits* is what the people want.

When the public spent more time living in the literal rather than the literary gutter, they wanted stars to have been sent down from Olympus, but not any more. They want anyone who seems to have a better life than them to be tor-mented by their past, present and future. They want to cheer on prospective pop stars on TV shows, then, when they've

---

1 Fill in your choice of stars here. I might have meant Piers Morgan.

spent £374 phone-voting for them and they become winners, they want to throw vodka-soaked glacé cherries in their faces in some nightclub in Kingston upon Thames.

If one sentence sums it all up, it is this from Jodie Marsh: 'All I remember from then are two things: Dane was really impressed with my plasma screen television, and we had sex.'

Jodie Marsh is typical of the celebrity who has attained notoriety by mooning on red carpets and showing her enhancements like a flamboyant John Merrick in a medical theatre. She is celebrated like Quasimodo on fool's day, a crown placed on her head, then swiftly knocked off when people feel they have seen enough of her tattoos and nipples in media cocktail bars. So what kind of voyeur am I to have her book by my bed? Well, if I hadn't purchased it, the British Red Cross would have been £1.75 worse off when it came to bandage-buying.

Jodie opens with a good pull-back reveal gag: 'So there I was: naked, screaming and covered in a thick, gooey substance.' The reader presumes she is sharing a tale of splattery sex; actually she is recalling her birth. My disappointment came a few weeks after reading this. In Brighton, I met the author of this line, and it was not Jodie Marsh (beware: there are more ghastly revelations like this ahead). The author was the editor of a women's sex magazine; nothing sordid, more authoritative: you can even get it in W.H. Smith. I had met her before when I interviewed her for some failed digital TV documentary and she opened proceedings by pulling open her drawer of vibrators; it was a very big drawer, and colourful too. It was she who dreamt up Jodie's first salvo.

Jodie Marsh's *Keeping It Real* sums up the death of civilisation for anyone who fears Armageddon is around the corner or under the mat. Whether it's rank consumerism in the world of lust and white goods or Z-list parties, Marsh gives every detail for the reader who thinks you can only buy books next to the chicken dinosaur shapes in the supermarket. It's all lap-dancing and Dean Gaffney. It is Marsh who goes so far as to describe the disappointing foreskin of a celebrity. I would reveal who had the misshapen and annoying foreskin, but after trying to read the book again, my brain started being sick and some of it leaked out of my ears.

Mumbling with ghosts

The revelation that Jodie Marsh may not have been the brains behind all the words on the page is the first warning to the uninitiated. The truth is that many celebrities do not sweat over their PCs crafting sentences of honesty and beauty for their public.

When you are buying the autobiography of your latest favourite celebrity, you may not know that the auto element is something of a lie. So suppress your surprise when you think, 'I would never have thought Mungo Bongo from TV's *I've Nailed My Head to a Plank* could have written a coherent sentence, especially after winning the show by using the longest and thickest nail.'

You were correct: they can't write. Instead, some bedraggled writer with a skin condition and poor-quality knitwear[2] has to make do with a couple of sit-down chats and then ghost-write the life of these hectic flibbertigibbets. Just be satisfied that they took time out to turn up to the photo

---

2 This is not an attack on writers, just my own confession to a life in cardigans and itching eczema, but I know I am not the only one. Writers frequently suffer from scurvy as they spend their lives locked in rooms.

studio for seventeen minutes to create the cover image. In a few years' time, even the cover will be a lookalike, or digital reconstruction of what the celebrity might look like if they gave a toss.

The problem is that lazy lazy, greedy greedy celebrities have to cram in so many adverts for king prawn garlands, straight-to-DVD movie premieres and nervous breakdowns to ensure their existence is a satisfactory whirl that they can no longer make time to come up with their own life story.

I wondered if ghost writers ever took revenge on celebrities they particularly loathed with a snuck-in made-up passage to shame them. Sadly, I couldn't find a single covert sentence about a lust for pickled eggs, bed-wetting at thirty-five, or a peculiar attraction to chimpanzees dressed in bikinis, probably because there is more financial security in ghost-writing than in creating something original.

After all, many celebrities are no more than walking ghosts, pepped up by their vampire-like management until they crumble like chaff and blow under the carpets of the public's memory, so it may be best that their lives are ghost-written.

At this point, a line must be drawn. I want to focus on celebrities I believe could be bothered to write their own life with honesty, candour and an Olivetti. I may have been caught out by a wily and adept journalist who has slipped into the skin of their celebrity with the ease of a marsupial sliding into a black mamba, but I want to believe that these are truly the words of the author. Occasional disbelief has been suspended.

Over the next few pages, we will take a journey into the not necessarily great lives of the twentieth century. There

may be no generals, film stars or Nobel prize-winning
physicists, but we will discover what it is to be the brother
of one of the twentieth century's more disappointing prime
ministers; the zoological interests of the Peter Pan of pop;
and the philosophies of the seventies face of Rowntree's
fruit pastilles.

Plato of the sitcom

I was lucky to find *Sing Lofty: Thoughts of a Gemini* on the
broken bookshelf of a charity shop in Barrow-in-Furness
(I forgot to note down which charity; tardy). Barrow-in-
Furness is home to BAE Systems, a popular manufacturer
of metal things that kill people. Travelling to it by train
you see beautiful scenery that would inspire an amateur
Lake District poet; when you arrive it is not quite the rural
idyll you might expect. There is a vague overhanging cloud
of depression; this I am told is a common meteorological
occurrence when the main industry of a town is death.
In keeping with Barrow's theme, most of the books in
the charity shop were about battles, regiments and trench
warfare. *Sing Lofty*, telling the tale of a man who played
a sitcom bombardier, fitted right in. At £2 it was
considerably cheaper than the prices I have found on
internet sites, where the book can fetch anything from
£17 to £60. Actually, it might be a lie to use the word
'fetch'; 'be priced at' would be better, as none of the
copies have sold since I began my monitoring. I believe
all will be gone after you have had a taste of the mind of
Don Estelle.

The first thing that struck me as I read *Sing Lofty:
Thoughts of a Gemini* was that this celebrity definitely did
not use a ghost writer. On every page the essence of Don

appears in broad and fleshy strokes, whether in the guise of actor, singer, wronged neighbour or philosopher. One moment he is mentioning the Futurist Theatre, Scarborough; the next he is pondering upon the metaphysical: 'One thing I seem to be aware of more than anything now is the passage of time. The years seem to be flying by . . . it's as if you're on an express train, which of course you are – a Time Train!'[3]

The joy of the autobiography is that it allows the author to show you who they truly are away from the public persona they have had to adopt. You might just have thought of them as the funny fat one in that thing, or the one with the guitar and hat from that other thing, but there is more to them than the things they do on those things while wearing their trademark things. Though they may be best remembered for falling in a big vat of custard, they finally have the chance to reveal the Wittgenstein within, the trap-like mind of the philosopher they had to keep hidden in their variety heyday.

That which we cannot speak of we must pass over in silence, with maybe just the hint of swanee whistle.

Cliff's sodden monkeys again

Cliff Richard's *Which One's Cliff?* has been updated many times in his long career, but the conundrum that plagues him most remains the same decade after decade. Whichever edition you pick up, Cliff returns to his quandary over monkeys swimming underwater.

---

3 Time Train sounds like a great idea for a TV series: a train that can go backwards and forwards in time would surely be an enormous hit. Sadly not: it was made as a series with Vincent Price called *Time Express* and it only managed four episodes despite appearances from *Wonder Woman*'s Lyle Waggoner and Catwoman Lee Meriwether.

And so the issue of monkey breaststroke I mentioned earlier sends the mind reeling into Harry Webb's life. One sentence in to Cliff and already you are putting down the book and staring out of the window, searching for vague memories of monkey splashing in a David Attenborough documentary about Lake Superior.

Cliff Richard has been accused of lacking honesty in the past, and his private life, if it exists beyond tennis and wine gargling, is guarded. He has always been canny enough to know that a true star doesn't dredge around the gutter. Joan Crawford never went on about beating her daughter's head with a hairbrush or posing nude and staining casting couches to help boost her embryonic career. Dirk Bogarde, during an interrogation by Russell Harty where sexuality was vaguely skated over, authoritatively stated, 'You won't crack me, ducky.' Perhaps 'ducky' wasn't the best choice of words when attempting to extinguish discussion about your possible homosexuality; nevertheless, he slammed the lid shut. Somehow Bogarde managed to write numerous volumes of autobiography without the public demanding a few paragraphs of rutting. But enough of Dirk Bogarde, who writes annoyingly well and therefore will not figure in this chapter again.

It is encouraging to know that Cliff is prepared to have moments of total candidness, even if it is monkey-related.

I would have liked Cliff to have resolved this issue by the end of *Which One's Cliff?*, but the question of the sub-aquatic monkey is never answered. Does this mean Cliff is lazy? It took me almost no time whatsoever and just a simple opening of my *Wonderful World of Animals* book to discover that some monkeys do swim under-water.

© Oliver Grove

As well as swimming, the macaque monkey will apparently forfeit food in exchange for pornography in experimentation. This is why they are frequently placed in editorial roles for the mid shelf men's magazine market.

That is a macaque monkey swimming. Now that I have revealed this, is *Which One's Cliff?* ruined? Does the book hinge on the suspense of monkey swimming uncertainty as *The Usual Suspects* hinges on Keyser Soyze's identity? No.

Had Cliff instead mused on the Sub-Aquatic Ape Theory espoused by Elaine Morgan in *The Descent of Woman and the Aquatic Ape Hypothesis*, he might have been on safer ground, as there still seems to be no definite answer on whether we differ from other primates due to a semi-aquatic period in our evolution. Though it is not generally considered very likely by many evolutionary biologists.

Sadly, not every autobiography can commence with such an arresting and revealing thought as Cliff's.

'Life began for me on January 28th 1944 in the Boundary Park hospital, Oldham,' begins *My Life* by Bobby Ball. Come on, Bobby, couldn't you have at least started with 'To this very day I still argue with Tommy Cannon about whether camels can walk up stairs'?

'I love the flute because it's the one instrument in the world where you can feel your own breath. When I play, I can feel my breath with my fingers. It's as if I'm speaking from my soul,' types Michael Flatley in *Lord of the Dance*. Flatley quite rightly declares his soul is wind, but doesn't ponder whether kangaroos can count.

'"Don't call us, we'll call you" is the famous showbiz brushoff. I claim to be the youngest recipient of this award, at the age of two, and from the Big Agent Himself, the Good Lord!' says Jimmy Savile in the opening of *Love is an Uphill Struggle*. Jimmy reveals in his first line that God refused to take his immortal soul when he was small and ill as he knew there was much work to be done on Earth – from presenting *Top of the Pops* to creating some very bizarre rumours just because he keeps all his late mum's dresses pristine in a closet; but he doesn't get unsettled pondering whether rooks know how to sew.

Lemmy of Motorhead provides far safer hands if you want a Satanic birth sequence, even if he doesn't bother with natural history either. 'I was born Ian Fraser Kilminster on Christmas Eve 1945, some five weeks premature, with beautiful golden hair which, to the delight of my quirky mother, fell out five days later. No fingernails, no eyebrows and I was bright red.'

The task of the original *Which One's Cliff?* was to answer one major question: what is Cliff Richard? Like the three-in-one nature of Father, Son and Holy Ghost, there are three Cliffs – a celebrity, a pop icon and a Christian. Can he really be all three in one? Having spent fifty years at the top, Cliff has written numerous volumes, but it is to the first edition of *Which One's Cliff?* that I most often return.

Cliff's words can both dazzle and, sometimes, shock. Reading them now, it's a fascinating example of how language and its impact change over a few decades. This is Cliff mulling over the dance moves at a charity disco night. In the early seventies it would be innocuous, a mere description of amateur choreography; in 2009, it is very different:

'There was the time, for instance, at the PHAB disco. I had the shock of my life to discover that modern music is tailor-made for spastics. Suddenly the jerky movements and lack of co-ordination all absolutely fitted and, as I pranced around the floor with my spastic partner, anyone watching would have been hard pressed to tell which one of us was disabled.'

Obviously Cliff is critiquing the inelegant nature of modern disco dancing while at the same time celebrating its ability to bring equality to the dance floor by making it impossible to define who has a muscular disorder and who doesn't. He is declaring that 'we are all spastics when dancing to modern music'. When I share this passage with people it creates an enormous amount of discomfort. Frankly, I have no idea why I keep reading it out aloud.

By the fiftieth birthday reissue of *Which One's Cliff?* in 1990, Cliff is no longer pondering on his triumvirate nature; this may be because he is no longer three in one, he is in four in one. Whereas once he was celebrity or popstar or Christian, now he is vintner too. Once an icon is multitasking that much, debate about what or who you are ends and you are just Cliff Richard, a singing Christian celebrity tennis winemaker who has earned the right to talk about themselves in the third person.

'I honestly don't relate to the title *Which One's Cliff?* any more. To my mind it's a redundant, old-fashioned question and should be consigned to history.' After the struggles of youth, the agonising internal monologue that tears us apart as we question 'Who am I and what am I?', Cliff knows which one is Cliff. He's the one with the green piping on his jacket.

Despite Cliff's enormous success, he seems to have been mocked for almost as long as he's been an icon of pop music. His vinyl jackets, suggesting costumes of the future as imagined by a 1960s BBC costume designer, his roller-skating, his piety and his celebrity tennis tournaments with Mike Yarwood and Ronnie Corbett have all led to snipes and a thinning of Cliff's smooth skin.

Cliff has robustly defended himself; as he points out, he has had more chart hits than Elvis Presley.[4] He is not shy in reminding his loyal readership that he is definitely best. Cliff knows how to balance the humility with the final boast: start your anecdote with a 'poor little old me, could I really manage such a feat' and end it with 'yes, it was much easier than I imagined, being brilliant'. Dignity intact, stunning proof of great success underlined.

'It's amusing now to remember my reaction when the idea of performing at Wembley Stadium was first mooted. "Can we really fill it?" I wondered. The largest venue I'd ever played in Britain was Birmingham's National Exhibition Centre, and that seats around 11,000. Sure, I'd filled that six nights on the trot . . .'

Deftly done, Cliff Richard. In case you were wondering, Wembley Stadium was an enormous success, selling out two dates. Cliff was also considered to be the nicest rocker they'd had play there and left the stadium very tidy, with

---

4 OK, so Cliff has had an extra 32 years to record songs, but this is just nit-picking. In terms of cinematic contribution, *Summer Holiday* is *The Night of the Hunter* to *Viva Las Vegas*'s *Citizen Kane*.

the only police complaint being that his fans overfed their horses.

Cliff's gospel passnotes

Cliff has also written numerous books about his faith in Jesus. My personal favourite is *You, Me and Jesus*, which combines biblical quotes with Cliff's musings on them. Then, as a bible study carrot to propel you through the book, halfway through there is a colourful splash of photos of Cliff in action.

The subtext is clear: 'Well done, you've read Hebrews 1:1–6 AND Revelation 3:15–19; take a break. Here's me leaning against a jukebox in a vinyl jerkin, oh, and here's me in tight denim feeding a mule.' It might have been this image of mule feeding that inspired Cliff's fans, so eager to ape their icon, to overfeed those horses.

Then it's back to the texts and commentaries: you've had your sexy break from the Bible; it's back to hard study for you. I have not yet found a selection of excerpts from the Koran brightened up with occasional glossy photos of Cat Stevens skateboarding or reclining on a sunlounger. I search in vain.

Cliff can rest easy now he knows which one he is, but will someone please tell him: yes, monkeys can swim underwater.

The whispering of meat paste

What really marks out a truly self-penned celebrity auto-biography of the highest calibre? Is it a broad selection of previously unseen photographs? Is it revelations of youth-ful heartbreak? Is it a loose tongue when it comes to revealing scandal about co-stars? These may be considered to be the makings of a best-seller, but what marks out the truly great autobiography for me is the inability of an author to realise that his reader may be more interested in knowing about his appearance in a Hollywood film with Dudley Moore than his argument with a neighbour who refused to chip in when it came to regravelling the communal drive.

And so we return to the sitcom philosopher, to Don Estelle's autobiography, *Sing Lofty: Thoughts of a Gemini*. It is a mighty book. Let us start with the regravelling anecdote, which reveals the common touch, showing that even those at the top of the show-business game have problems when it comes to resurfacing drives:

'To digress for a moment, sometime in 1976 I had asked all tenants/owners on the part of Warren Road where we all lived if they would like to contribute towards a scheme to improve the "road" . . . all the residents paid their share except our problem resident . . . the whole of my summer season was soured.'

Don Estelle is remembered most fondly for his performance as the short in stature, big in aria, pith-helmeted Lofty in the TV sitcom *It Ain't Half Hot, Mum*. After the sitcom ended, he found himself on the slow slide from the public eye and finally resorted to selling cassettes of his singing in shopping centres wearing his trademark pith helmet. A commonly heard sentence in shopping centres around the United Kingdom is, 'I remember when Don Estelle was standing there, just where the panini stall is now. He was singing "Whispering Grass".'

There are many paragraphs in *Sing Lofty* that betray Don's pomposity and self-delusion, but you can't laugh at him because the melancholy lingers after nearly every chapter.

As he points out, when you're on a roll you don't think it's going to stop, and then one day you look around and find that no one wants your autograph any more and confectioners and crisp-makers don't need your face to sell their wares.

A DJ acquaintance of mine went to interview Don in the mid-nineties. Don invited him into his Rochdale flat, where he had laid on some meat paste sandwiches and a bottle of Marks and Spencer's best wine. Once they were sat in his flat, Don insisted on telling him every detail of his life, every graze suffered while working in a factory, every detail of a disappointing tram ride. With the paste in the sandwiches hardening and the wine almost finished, he had only just got into the fifties; his career highs were still two decades away. Often it is this utter lack of understanding that anyone might be interested in his TV, film or opera work when they can hear his opinions on war or famine that gives the book its plain beauty. Raymond Carver stories are successful not because they are laden with sex and violence; they are successful because somehow the mundane becomes the pointer to what being human really is or can be.

There is a frequent angry edge to the book, as well as some confusion, with facts repeated and chronology uncertain. If it was proofread, it was proofread in a bus shelter or while waiting for the meat raffle. Had Don known about this, he might well have been furious with his publisher, except that his publisher was the Don Estelle Music Publishing Company (CEO Don Estelle).

If tragedy is the fall of a great man, then *Sing Lofty* may not be tragic, but who says that you have to be a general, lord or emperor to feel the harshness of a fall; a sitcom bombardier can experience it as painfully as a man with epaulettes and lickspittles. Don is also insistent on making his identity clear in case the reader becomes confused.

'I know what you're thinking, I sound like Frankie Howerd, but I am NOT.'

Don is quick to summarise his professional work and move on to more about gardens, mortgages and unpleasant neighbours. In the mid-seventies, he appeared in *Not Now Comrade*, which, as he explains, 'starred Leslie Phillips, June Whitfield, Roy Kinnear, Windsor and I. The movie was made at Elstree and was a Bernard Delfont/EMI production.'

That is quite a cast of British comedy alumni, so now that Don has given us the basic facts we might need, particularly the production company, the reader might expect a few anecdotes about what working with these revered individuals was like, but there is no time for that. It seems nothing of any interest happened, certainly not as interesting as the subject that Don leaps straight into with his next

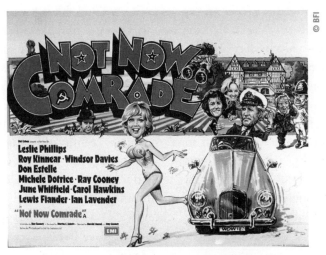

Not Now Comrade — when asylum-seeking was just a saucy romp. What would the *Daily Express* think of it now?

sentence about cottage upkeep. 'Back to the Old Granary. The house was a sixteenth-century property and needed to be refurbished, as I said. The fencing was suspect, and as I had to keep the dogs in . . .'

Many readers may have friends who have told them about problems they've had with fencing or who have suffered a splinter from a gatepost; few of us know anyone who has been in a film with Roy Kinnear, June Whitfield and Leslie Phillips. Don's editorial decision is that what is most burnt into his mind is the memory of problems with that bloody fence, and if that is what was preying on his mind most, then it's probably the issue that will most intrigue his fans. In many ways, he was right. Many auto-biographies namedrop excessively and then tell bland anecdotes about the time they accidentally flicked a pitted olive in Roger Moore's eye; few are obsessed with land rights and disputes over outdoor carpentry. Though Don may not comment about his work much beyond its geo-graphical location and the names involved, he is thorough in chronicling it, making sure that no job remains unmen-tioned, whether Jonathan Miller-directed theatre or snack sales work: 'We also had two major network adverts in April 1977, for Smiths Quavers and Rowntree fruit pastilles.'

The wonder of reading Don is the sense you have that you are actually with him, sharing a couple of bottles of Marks and Spencer's wine and some paste sandwiches.[5] The problem is that as the wine goes down, Don goes through the arc of the man imbibing in the corner table of the saloon bar. He gets tetchier, then repetitive, then ends

---

5 I am told by two friends who interviewed him at his flat in Rochdale that this was the traditional spread. They were non-specific about which paste.

the chapter with a shrug of 'Hey, what do I know, they're all bastards.' In his way, he creates a book not dissimilar to Ice T's *The Ice Opinion*, in which Ice ended each chapter with 'Who gives a fuck.'

There are many facets to Don's character, and he is eager to show what he has mastered. He is keen to demonstrate where his life stands in the context of world history: 'I was born in Manchester on 22nd May, 1933, the day Herr Hitler became chancellor of Germany. He was to give many evil fruits to the world a few years later.' How would you describe the genocidal despot Adolf Hitler? I suppose I would say he was like a malevolent greengrocer delivering evil fruits to the world.

The whole book is a constant reminder of the horror of fame, because more often than not it eventually vanishes and you become yesterday's man. You can't just look back with joy at the time you were the network TV face of crisps and confectionery. Instead, you glare with hate-filled eyes at the new man who is selling snacks and appearing in panto with his name as big as Cilla Black's on the poster, and think, that used to be me, isn't it meant to be for ever, the bastards. Twenty-six years to the day after Don Estelle was born in Manchester, Steven Patrick Morrissey was born there. Though I am no believer in astrology,[6] it seems that this is a good day for birth if you are hoping for a northern misanthrope. Sadly, Morrissey has not yet covered 'Whispering Grass'.

As well as dealing with history and philosophy, Don can also be Rochdale's Marshall McLuhan, with his sociolog-

---

6 The great astronomer and science populariser Carl Sagan noted that there was a minuscule pull by the stars on the baby, but the pull of the midwife was far greater, suggesting a new astrology based on midwifery technique.

ical views on the medium as message: 'TV somehow absorbs all human effort like a sponge, although it reflects public responses; it's like a public toilet, no one is there long enough to make it their own.' Is he really saying, 'I urinated all over television, but no one remembers what my wee smells like now'? Probably not, but only the media studies group at Brunel University can analyse this fully.

However far into his career and mind you venture, Don always seems to return to fences, boundaries and footpaths. His dramatic centrepieces remain his feud over rights of way. He wants to move the right of way that goes through his land from the centre of his land to the edge; as we all know, there's always some busybody or grump who'll obstruct you when you're trying to move your footpath from centre to left.

After two pages of road improvements and solicitors' involvement in right-of-way conundrums, it's back to the world of showbiz. 'Well we got over the summer, hit the clubs and made a new series of *It Ain't Half Hot, Mum* in the autumn.' Again, it appears that absolutely nothing of any interest happened during the filming of this series, certainly nothing that could beat a rusty gate or fence-building.

Later in the year, Don finds himself in pantomime with Jim Davidson. Davidson, a hard-drinking jack-the-lad at the time, does generate some anecdotes from Don. Once a woman in the front row fell asleep with her arms between her legs. Jim distracted Don from offstage by doing a gorilla impersonation and Don could hardly get through his lines. This is the insanity of showbusiness.

Though panto might be fun, as the lyrics of 'Fame' attest, performing and fame come at a painful cost. Don reveals, 'I've found pantomimes heavy going, and when that one finished, I got a cold.' Working with Jim Davidson was such a joy, however, that Don gets a little repetitive. The subject of their first panto together is broached on page 85: 'It was *Babes in the Wood*, with Jim Davidson, which was his first pantomime.' Meanwhile, on page 88, 'Working with Jim Davidson was good; it was his first panto.' These errors do not jar; they add to the joy of the book, a further chance to take a break and tuck into yet another paste sandwich.

For more information on Jim's pantomime work, you could read his own autobiography, which sadly is not called *My Fucking Greedy Ex-Wives and Why I Would Like to Shit on Liberals and Communists*, but *The Full Monty* instead. It is a celebration of drinking, being furious with your wives for being annoyed at your boozing, and getting speeding tickets.

Don Estelle's book really has to be read in full to appreciate the man and what made him. To cut it into bits feels like précising *Ulysses*; somehow it takes away the meaning. Don wears many hats in *Sing Lofty*, and, at this point in his career, he doesn't mind whose feathers he ruffles. The villains of the piece, though, are chat shows, which Don sees as no more than 'self-ego debates' that are 'a grand display of psychic peacock feathers'.

I have found that imagining psychic peacock feathers whenever I am watching a chat show has really brightened up listening to some *Hollyoaks* actor droning on about their modelling career. This book was written before TV really went downhill into the world of reality and freak-show documentaries about dog-headed girls. Could Don have controlled his wrath when confronted by *Touch the Truck*?

As a singer, Don cannot hold back when it comes to the state of modern pop: 'Much of the stuff marketed today, in my view, is aimed at the bestial, basic, sex-mad, drunken louts with an IQ of morons.' Thank heavens he didn't live long enough to see the Pussycat Dolls or the video for Eric Prydz's 'Call On Me'. Although in fairness, when you were once signed to EMI and now you sing in Medway shopping centres, it's hard not to feel a little betrayed.

On the plus side, Don does some cheery home and garden design. 'At our Rochdale house I had put up a chain-link fence and gates to keep Fred the Afghan in the garden.'

Geography can be more enthralling than events. Here is the final *It Ain't Half Hot, Mum* tour: 'This was going to be the final tour of the show, starting in June until October. Some of the other theatres we played at on the tour were: Bradford, Plymouth, Bristol, Ayr, Birmingham, Manchester, Cardiff, Nottingham and Sunderland . . .' Sadly, we will never know if anything of interest happened in those towns and cities, as Don needs to get back to the real story, which involves an impulse purchase in Buckingham and a bridging loan.

So how shall the world remember Don Estelle, if only via his own words? Will they remember a man blessed with a golden voice who graced adverts for pastilles and cheese crisps; or will they remember a man who suffered boundary difficulties and grumpy neighbours? If John Osborne's Archie Rice had a brother who had a little TV success and then watched it slowly drip away, he might have been Don Estelle. More than most autobiographies, *Sing Lofty* gives you a sense of the real man: sometimes pompous, sometimes confused, and sometimes self-effacing, but real nevertheless.

Unhappy in Hitler's shorts

The seventies was a fruitful time to create laughter from World War Two. Perry and Croft wrote *Dad's Army* and *It*

Ain't Half Hot, Mum, and one former singer from Liverpool with an Elvis fixation was laughed at across Britain as he put on a Hitler moustache and paraded around the stage in humorous shorts. But behind the funny slapstick Nazi lay fury: 'He began touching my arse three or four times a day, it got on my nerves.'

Freddie Starr's autobiography, *Freddie Starr: Unwrapped,* is about settling scores. Whether it's the gay producer he punched for goosing him, who then decided to ruin his career, the gay gardener who made up lies about him in the press, or just everyone who hasn't given Freddie what he deserves in accolades and jewels, one thing is certain: few of Freddie's mistakes are of his own making. He concludes his book with a series of pitches for TV shows that he should be starring in. These include a show where 'he meets the most evil people in the world and gets inside their minds'.[7]

'I've got a degree in the art of intimidation. But no one can intimidate Freddie Starr.' Reader, you have been warned.

The actor and comedian Mike Reid is co-author of one of the brightest autobiographies, *T'rific.* He's not bitter, but he's happy to tell you who needs a slap. This might be because his co-author is Peter Gerrard – the co-author of a number of books about villainous heavies including Lenny McLean, the Guv'nor, and Ronnie Knight, former husband of Barbara Windsor.

---

7 One of my favourite elements of the comedian's autobiography is the declarations that everything now is rubbish compared to them. It doesn't matter how many years you had a prime TV show, accolades and gold-card membership to a club run by Peter Stringfellow; once your show is cancelled it's bloody unfair. Starr is openly derisive of Harry Hill, while Mike Reid in his autobiography *T'rific* initially hides his derision with what appears to be a compliment about how brave modern stand-ups are to write all their own material, especially as it is all rubbish. The general philosophy is 'Well, we had our time, there's a new lot out there now, it's their time. Mind you, they're all crap. I'd like to see them play the Circus Tavern, Purfleet, on a Friday; they'd eat them alive.'

Rather than a backslapping-we're-all-having-a-smashing-time-in-showbiz memoir, Mike writes (or dictates) that he's a bit of a loner and lots of those he's rubbed shoulders with are rude sods. He is presenting TV show *Seaside Special*, and the guests include Cannon and Ball. This could be their break, so 'they were shitting themselves'. Mike offers kind words and some gentle support, but it doesn't help. 'Two hours I've spent with them before they went on, and to be honest when they did, they died on their arses. Terrible.'

What a sharp, shiny nail that final one-word sentence is. Why wasn't Mike just happy declaring that they died; why include the punchline 'terrible'? The reader finds out soon enough. A few years later, Cannon and Ball have made it, and it seems that it's rather gone to their heads. This is Mike's story of compering a memorial gig. 'Bobby Ball was over the other side wearing his coat like a Batman cape and clicking his fingers at me. "Oi you. Yes you – over here." I didn't want a row so I pretended not to hear him.' The next time Bobby Ball plays the big I am with Mike Reid, he gets called an ignorant prick 'and a lot more'. Bobby has since turned from alcoholism and the high life to born-again Christianity. It's a popular arc.[8]

Morning!

The seventies was a good time for 'the entertainer', whether singing opera, goosestepping, or playing records by Brotherhood of Man. Even the ability to place a stylus on a record, create a jingle and froth with badinage was a

---

8 Bobby Ball's autobiography reveals that he did indeed behave like a little sod, but it wasn't really his fault. Satan did it all and now he's found God and he's better (and bitter).

way to access the finest things in life. Though as Radio One's Ed 'Stewpot' Stewart discovered, you may not hide from the critic's eye.

'My most memorable critique of the show was written by Milton Shulman . . . if Martians landed on earth and tried to find some sort of intelligent life, they would only have to watch Ed Stewart and his contestants on *Exit – The Way Out Show* to realise there was none at all!'

Ed Stewart was one of the Radio One DJs of the Golden Age; obviously it was a golden age made of fool's gold, but who would have known at the time? The DJs cavorted at the Radio One Roadshow in Barmouth or Rhyl, displaying their credentials as family entertainers before the microphones went off; after that who knows what went on. The seventies was also a time for imagination and big ideas, and Stewpot was renowned for his catchphrase, a catchphrase that was to sum up the Radio One Breakfast Show: 'Morning!'

Not 'morning', but 'Morning!'

In the seventies, it was so big that half the population were saying 'Morning!' especially when they met people before midday; indeed, it's still common parlance now. Ed Stewart is author of *Out of the Stewpot – My Autobiography*. The 'My Autobiography' element seems extraneous. I suppose some shoppers might see *Out of the Stewpot* and believe the DJ might have written a book about fourteenth-century cooking utensils; best to play safe with a title.

If you are hoping for a book about a DJ receiving fellatio under a blanket on a night flight, this book will make you very happy. 'We returned, giggling, to our seats, and continued to watch the film. Its title really made me laugh – *What's Up Doc?*. The only thing up on that flight was me.'

And the plane, obviously.

I am very old-fashioned and find myself feeling vaguely sullied when forced into thinking about the engorged penises of people who presented *Top of the Pops* while gurning with shiny hats on.

Like most of the Radio One DJs from the early days, Ed Stewart watched the changes that were brought in in the nineties and saw the end of a glorious era. An era of cheery banality mixed with pomposity. Change is always hard to take, and each generation believes they are the last of the decent before something corrupt and vacuous takes over. Stewpot knew what it was like to be put out to pasture; he had suffered this when he was removed from *Crackerjack*:

> '"And who is the new blood?" I shouted down the line.
> '"The Krankies."
> 'So that was it.'

Few of the old-guard DJs seem to understand why Radio One became less popular; they can only see the decline in popularity in terms of the British public's fury that they couldn't hear Dave Lee Travis, the Hairy Cornflake, say 'whack whack oops' on a Sunday. In their eyes, the death of the old Radio One is the Tiananmen Square of radio broadcasting: the people stood up, but the government's tanks rolled in and took Simon Bates from us.

'It all started with DLT's infamous resignation during his Sunday morning programme . . . "changes are being made which go against my principles . . . and I cannot continue to work for the station under current circumstances . . . the only option is to leave".'

A noble speech: changes are being made, they must be

about to sack me, so I'm leaving. I would like to think that the decline of Radio One was the public realising that they should elevate their expectations of what entertainment should be, if not for themselves, at least so they didn't disappoint the Martians when they arrived at Milton Shulman's late behest.

Perhaps one reason there are fewer listeners now is the enormous number of alternatives to Radio One; rather than one station playing pop, there are many. They all play the same pop, but that's the great thing about the free market, the illusion of choice. Shall I listen to Razorlight on Absolute, Radio One, Heart, Capital or Three Counties? Stewpot observes that Chris Moyles is attempting to return Radio One to what it once was, and he has done it with considerable success. It reminds me of Steve Martin's old joke: 'I believe Ronald Reagan can make this country what it once was . . . a large Arctic region covered with ice.'

However much you try, you just can't keep the banal down. The alcopop-drinking, blue-afro-wig-wearing, it's-my-fucking-stag-night, vomiting-in-bins British public have won again. But there is another England . . .

A very English Englishman – bless Bognor

After the sordid sex and acidic recriminations of so many confessions, there is an autobiography I turn to that acts as a balm. It is the autobiography of a very English Englishman. He is Terry Major-Ball, and he was real.

Terry Major-Ball was the surprise celebrity to arise from John Major's administration. For anyone who might wake in the middle of the night with the nagging question, 'I wonder what the brother of one of Britain's less renowned twentieth-century prime ministers thinks about the world, DIY and breakfast,'[9] *Major Major* was the answer to those sleepless nights. The book combines the understated Englishness of an almost forgotten Britain with an accidental humour that could sit neatly next to George and Weedon Grossmith's *Diary of a Nobody*. To sneer at this work would betray a cruelty in your own nature. If it wasn't for the historical record of Terry Major-Ball's birth and death, you would think he was an invention to distract from a crumbling administration.

The cover reveals Terry, in heavy glasses, his lip genetically designed like that of his brother, holding on to a garden ornament. There is no hint of glamour or a man changed by his proximity to a prime minister. As the Majors' garden ornament business had closed many years earlier, the ornament displays the usual wear and tear that occurs after a few years in an English garden. The book's anecdotes create a warmth about the past that almost makes you want to embrace malnutrition and powdered eggs.

'One day Shirley came home from work at Philips with an idea for a holiday. "Terry, how about going to Butlins at Bognor?" she said . . . I wasn't at all keen.' For Terry, Butlins suggests something newfangled and confusing, a journey away from British tradition into modernity. Once at the Butlins in Bognor, however, he sees that he was quite wrong. He is impressed by the outdoor and indoor swimming pools, the putting green, the sheltered garden for reading 'and the woods nearby where you could pho-

---

9 Since writing this I have read a few books on British prime ministers and realise this is a little harsh on John Major; most of them have been more useless than history seems to remember.

tograph squirrels'. He admits that he has never been that
adventurous in his holiday choices; he likes his home com-
forts and obviously his squirrels. The final chapter
demonstrates how his life changed once he became the
brother of a prime minister. Simply titled 'New York', it
sums up that peculiar lack of ambition that seeps through
the English: 'As a young man I often wanted to go to
Heathrow. My friend Ted, who was a bit of a wanderer,
used to suggest going there in his car, but somehow we
never made it.'

To hold such a simple ambition in life – not to fly on a
plane, but merely to visit the place where they depart
from – and never achieve it makes Terry strangely and
pointlessly admirable. In later life he finds himself on board
a Virgin Atlantic plane to New York and enjoying the
attention of an air stewardess who looks like his mother,
something he does not hesitate in telling her. In the Virgin
Atlantic departure lounge he enjoys a cup of tea and a man-
icure. Once on the plane, he notices how first class looks
like the intercity trains he has seen at Victoria station, 'not
that I have ever been on an intercity train – yet'.[10] He
writes of the plane and take-off like a Victorian time traveller marvelling at what this leap into the future allows him
to behold. He jokes with the crew that it's all made of
rubber bands and talks of the 'colossal machine' as if he

---

10 The more I read this autobiography, the more I find it almost impossible to believe Terry
  Major-Ball was real. I fear I am like one of those New York hipster critics who got drawn
  into the saga of J.T. Leroy, author of *The Heart is Deceitful Above All Things*. Leroy was
  a pathologically shy young man who had supposedly spent his youth being pimped out
  by his mother at truck stops as a cross-dressing prostitute and now had the look of
  Truman Capote's shaggy nephew. It turned out the book was the work of thirty-something
  author Laura Albert, while for public appearances J.T. was played by Laura's half-sister-
  in-law, Savannah Koop. As literary hoaxes go, it's a pretty darn good one. But the
  question now stands: are the books as good if they are not written by a sexually abused,
  cross-dressing, hand-relief-giving rent boy with an evil mother? Only you can decide.

were in the belly of a metal beast from Ray Harryhausen's imagination.

Terry charts his meetings at Downing Street with a candour not even seen in the 'very nearly' political auto-biography, such as the snack revelation when invited to stay for lunch at Number Ten. 'I had to confess that I couldn't manage lunch because I had just bought a pie at Victoria station, sharing it with the ducks in St James's Park. I had a good chat with them, however, and a very nice cup of tea.'

Sadly, Terry Major-Ball died in 2007. If there was ever an award for the least egotistical autobiography of all time, I think this prize should posthumously be awarded to Terry, a man who typified understatement and an unlikely Englishness. His was a world of 'bading' people farewell and 'lovely ladies': 'The truth is, I was really rather frightened of girls, but fascinated by them.'

It seems only right that this chapter should end with Terry's views on the British breakfast. 'I'm like John, I'll eat anything. I'm very flexible about breakfast. It depends what I'm doing. I must admit, although it's not politically correct, that I do like bacon and eggs.' I'm not entirely sure that bacon and eggs has quite risen to the status of Roy Chubby Brown and Winterval[11] when it comes to PC, but Terry seems such a gentle soul that I am sure pig slaugh-ter would occasionally prey on his mind as he popped a yolky rasher into his mouth. Rather than the politically correct brigade, it is the biblically correct brigade that might

---

11 Winterval is the favourite myth of the lunatic right who base most of their weekly columns on angry Brie-based dreams rather than looking out of their window. Christmas hasn't been banned for a while, though Oliver Cromwell gave it a go, making holly dec-orations illegal and having a goose-sniffing patrol going around rooting out errant Christmas goose cooks.

look with accusatory eyes at Terry's favourite breakfast:[12] 'And the swine, because it divideth the hoof, yet cheweth not the cud, it is unclean unto you: ye shall not eat of their flesh, nor touch their dead carcass' (Deuteronomy 14:8).

But this is no time to get bogged down in the correctness of bacon.[13]

'To be quick with a cooked breakfast I put the bacon in the microwave, which is healthier than frying it. Sometimes I cook the egg in the microwave as well, usually cracking it into a saucer rather than a plate because it makes the egg smaller but thicker. The egg comes out of the microwave looking like a fried egg, but tasting like a poached egg. Then you add a handsome dab of Lea and Perrins or Heinz, and you have a breakfast fit for a king.'

I think it is highly doubtful that Terry ever ate hummus, or any other chickpea-based dish.[14] It is a great pity that he never wrote a recipe book. If he had, I believe it would have been not dissimilar to Delia Smith's *How to Cheat at Cooking*, which I think was mainly about how to avoid cutting

---

12 According to dietary folklore, eating pork contributes to lack of morality, dirtiness and greed. I can only judge this by the occupants of the greasy spoon café I was in this morning, but I definitely got a sense that the ones who ordered sausages were a bit smellier and spent slightly longer before turning over from page 3 in *The Sun*. The Muslim, Jewish and Leviticus-observing Christian faiths all eschew eating pork, suggesting a lot of prophets suffered from diarrhoea in the desert after some off ham.

13 Angry supercilious meat-eaters will often think they have cocked a snook at a vegetarian should they see them eating bacon-flavoured crisps. 'Oh, you say you're a vegetarian, but I see you're eating bacon crisps.' 'There's no meat in them.' 'Yes, but where do you draw the line?' 'I don't know, slaughter?'

14 The best poem about cooked breakfasts can be found in Hovis Presley's *Poetic Off Licence*. The greatest comedian to come from Bolton and the only one to find the notion of fame ridiculous, his other poems included 'Then I Saw Her Face, Now I'm an Amoeba', 'Not So Much a Leading Light, More a Faulty Rear Indicator' and 'Take me Drunk, I'm Home'. He died in 2005 aged 45. Few comedians have happily shrugged away fame with such casual aplomb. He once had a TV executive drunkenly begging him, down on both knees, to appear on a stand-up show. The knees in his trousers were worn out without success.

yourself when opening a tin of macaroni cheese. This is not a criticism; I have had far more cuts from opening tins of macaroni than I have had meals with raspberry coulis drizzled on them. Perhaps Terry Major-Ball once faced something drizzled on his plate, but I imagine he asked for a piece of white bread and mopped it up like gravy.

Like the man-child in *Bad Boy Bubby*, Terry was released into the world and he saw only wonder. After a month of reading books where poisonous ego informs nearly every page, mixed with boastful anecdotes of ruttings, *Major Major* can set you back on an even suburban keel.

Footnote

I cannot suspend my disbelief any longer; the truth is out: nearly every celebrity book is ghost-written. My hopes of honesty were finally smashed to splinters on the rocks when I discovered even Terry Major-Ball had a ghost writer, James Hughes Onslow. This might explain this sentence: 'Next morning, still fuming, I rang my friend James Hughes Onslow at the *Evening Standard*. I know I should be careful about calling a journalist a friend, but James is a friend, though he can be quite mischievous with stories he thinks are funny.'

So was Terry Major-Ball really the man conveyed to the reader, or an exaggeration by James Hughes Onslow? According to the *Daily Telegraph* obituary, after retiring to Somerset, Terry would sometimes look up at passing air-craft while paving the garden and declare, 'I used to be up there once.' On one occasion his brother was interviewed for two hours and then the interview was never used. Terry considered this a disgrace: 'I could have painted a door in that time.'

I cling to my belief that James Hughes Onslow was Boswell to Major-Ball's Johnson.

What have we learned?

- We are mashed potato on a time train
- Monkeys swim under water
- There may have been a homosexual conspiracy against Freddie Starr
- Ed Stewpot Stewart has been priapic on a plane
- There is greater dignity in the garden ornament business than in politics

---

Further reading

Yes, Mr Bronson – Memoirs of a Bum Actor and **Yes, Admiral** both by Michael Sheard.

He has played Hitler on screen at least four times, was Goering's double in *'Allo 'Allo!* and he knew Peggy Ashcroft.

Larger than Life by Eddie Large

Once you've tackled *Little by Little*, see the other side of the double act.

An Interlude with a Small Rabbit

For much of my life I was one of those men who knew surprisingly little about any small-stature rabbit breeds. If I'm honest, I couldn't really tell one rabbit from another, except by colouring. I am the same with cars. If a cab company calls me up and says, it'll be a 1973 two-litre Ford Mustang in the car park for you at eleven, I have to say, 'Errr, could you just tell me what colour it is? That would be more helpful.' Obviously if the car is a model that has been in a film it becomes easier, but I'm not very likely to be picked up in a Lotus Esprit with submarine capabilities or a 1981 DeLorean DMC 12.[1] My ability to distinguish between rabbits, or more precisely one particular breed of rabbit, took a great leap forward a little over a year ago when I was handed *The Book of the Netherland Dwarf*.

If you have any pressing questions about the Netherland Dwarf, Denise Cumpsty may well have the answer for you.

---

1 Just in case, that's the car that doubles as a time machine in *Back to the Future*, deemed in a recent poll to be the second most famous car of all time. Number 20 was a 1986 Mercedes Benz 560 from the Patrick Swayze movie *Road House*. I do not believe the poll was scientific.

If your question is how to kill the Netherland Dwarf, she may even have several answers for you. *The Book of the Netherland Dwarf* is just one in a series of practical pet guides brought to you by Spur Publications. Other books in the series include *Exhibition and Flying Pigeons* and *Exhibition and Practical Goatkeeping*.[2]

Denise begins her book with a little bit of showing off disguised as proof of her Netherland Dwarf credentials. She has won every major award of consequence, and has been breeding Dwarfs for twenty-two years. If there is anyone who knows more about the Netherland Dwarf I would be very surprised.

The first question that may pop into your head is why the Netherland Dwarf? Why the fascination? This is ably covered in Chapter One – 'Why The Netherland Dwarf? The Fascination': 'First, it has all the undeniable attraction of the miniature. Like a small child it is appealing and vulnerable. Unlike a dwarf in real life, it is not deformed.'

Within the first page of Chapter One, Denise starts to hint at the love/hate relationship between her and her award-winning rabbits. Yes, the Netherland Dwarf is a natural showman, 'like the Polish',[3] but it is also an obstreperous creature: 'One of the worst bites I ever received was from a Netherland, and I carry a scar to this day.' Hang around the bar at a rabbit show late enough and you'll see it turn into a scene from *Jaws*, as the Brody, Quint

---

2 I know less about exhibiting goats than I do about smaller rabbits, but I do know if you are a young person exhibiting goats at the Hamilton County Fair you must wear white trousers.

3 This does not refer to the Polish people as I initially thought, but another breed of rabbit that I haven't bothered reading about. That's not to say the Polish people aren't good showmen. Klaus Kinski was Polish and he loved showing off; he once pulled a paddle steamer across South America so he could turn it into an opera house. It sent him quite mad.

and Hooper of the pet world show the various ugly livid scars they've received from a mynah bird's beak or a gerbil's claw.

Len Askew's drawings are the splendid icing on top of this Netherland Dwarf epic.

These are the sort of magic hands that Netherland Dwarf owners possess. Take a look at that thumb again.

4

Bad Science

If it is not true that a divine being fell, then we can only say that one of the animals went entirely off its head.

G.K. Chesterton

Was God an astronaut?

Erich von Däniken

What planet are you on and which planet are you from?

Hold your hands up to the light. Part your fingers. Dare you look?

Does anything look not quite as it should? Are you as averagely human as you should be?

Have you ever been haunted by a dream of living in an underwater palace?

Do you have a vague memory of lifting a space visor and viewing a savannah full of hairy apemen?

Are you plagued by images locked into hidden segments of your being that tell of man's evolution? The question is, man's evolution from what?

These dreams are quite normal; you've proudly come to realise your true heritage. Be relieved you're not just another standard beast of earth like a gazelle or slime mould; your journey is so much more exciting than the bog-standard one of evolution from gloop to ape.

You are a descendant of Atlantis, and if you are not from the deep (check vague scars where your gill slits once opened), then you have probably fallen from a height. You are from outer space, you are an Aztec spacegirl.

Remember, whatever they say, we are all made of star stuff.

As yet the human genome project has not seen fit to work out which of us can claim gilled ancestors on our mother's side and which of us can claim ancestry with those from a distant nebula on our father's. While scientists shilly-shally around, authors have grasped the nettle and forged ahead, providing their readership with all the facts, or almost facts, or conjecture that could be a fact if you really wanted it to be. I have been to specialist book and crystal fairs and found myself lost across time and across the universe. I have overheard conversations in West Country mystical shops that have made me fearful to walk near any standing stones just in case they return to living form, though that may also be the fault of terrifying children's TV series *Children of the Stones*. In daylight I am a logical empiricist, or the nearest amateur equivalent; once the sun has gone down I can believe in cannibal zombies breaking through my garden gate and haggard bleeding men suddenly being reflected in my bathroom mirror as I look up while brushing my teeth. I am gullible and superstitious in the dark of the night; for the regular readers of many of these books, the sun is rarely up.

Do you like antiquated word search to go with your superstition? Then we'll continue.

Has the Bible got a code?

Will the Koran reveal secret messages if you rub lemon over it and pop it on the radiator?

Could your eyes once have been lasers?

Do angels live in a secret hole in Jupiter?

Are your dowsing sticks sentient?[1]

The pseudoscientist author is dealing with brains that are almost blank slates; as long as they write in a manner that suggests truth and academic rigour, the reader will swallow it. This is also how the crazed conspiracy theory manages to remain in such a vibrant, healthy state. It is another boom that caters to those who think the collapse of the twin towers was a mirage involving elephants and some magician's doves. After all, it's easier to read a book of smoke and mirrors than one issue of *Popular Mechanics*. If only we had all paid more attention when that physics teacher was making us burn peanuts under a test tube, or if only science classes were allowed to be more exciting, none of this might have happened. There is hope for the next generation, due to the popularity of nut allergies; a teacher told me that the energy-of-the-peanut experiment has been replaced with the energy-within-a-marshmallow experiment. Much tastier.

One of the world's leading, and richest, pseudohistorians/scientists is Erich von Däniken, who captured and bottled the public's imagination in the seventies with *Chariots of the Gods*. I purchased it initially for nostalgia; now I am

---

1 In tribute to Gary LeStrange's *Is My Toaster Sentient?*.

middle-aged I am increasingly drawn to things that I held when my hair was thick and my potential seemed to have no limits. That's why I have recently watched Bill Bixby turn into Lou Ferrigno and Edward Woodward equalise eighties New York. The same time that I was watching *The Incredible Hulk* for the first time, I was buying books by Erich von Däniken. Having only recently mastered reading, I was already using it for ill. Did I know what I was wasting my brain for at an age when it was most receptive to ideas? Yet when I opened this edition some thirty years after I had last seen these words, I had almost no memory of them. Had my own brain saved me by making a decision to jettison treatises on alien visitations to Aztecs?

Von Däniken had unearthed the possibility that human civilisation had had more than passing help from an extra-terrestrial hand. What makes this corner of the market so comfortable is that it seems bulletproof to debunking. This is not due to the academic excellence, but the will to believe. Von Däniken's astronautical work has been examined, dissected and discredited, but it is still in print. The pseudohistorian always has recourse to the question 'But why are the establishment trying to discredit my theories, what are they scared of?' As Carl Sagan said, 'They laughed at Galileo, but don't forget they also laughed at Bobo the clown.' Von Däniken's books appeared at just the right time, when the mystical was engaging with a young generation on pot, politics and a general euphoric view that 'the world is not as you thought it was, Grandad'. He opened the Venusian gates to a horde of confused academics and scribblers who had gathered together enough conjecture to sell it as a whole new way of thinking about existence.

Von Däniken begins his bank-breaking first book by

sowing the seeds for his Herculean leap with the question 'Are there intelligent beings in the cosmos?': '. . . the forest of question marks grows and grows as soon as we make a careful study of the facts . . .'

Von Däniken speculates on the likelihood of other life in our galaxy; many scientists have also spent their lives looking into this. There is an organisation called the SETI Institute (Search for Extraterrestrial Intelligence) whose work is to unearth any inklings that we are not alone in the universe. It is one thing for there to be life on other planets, and another to then leap straight to the conclusion that this life will be much more intelligent than us, and able to travel at close to the speed of light and pop down to help our civilisations develop fancy stuff. Luckily for us, von Däniken has made that leap by Chapter 2.

He points out that many generations deemed the earth to be flat and the centre of the universe with a benevolent sun revolving around us. These things were discovered to be untrue due to the broadening of scientific knowledge. Sadly for von Däniken, it is that same rigorous system of proper scientific research that means his theory flounders. Fortunately, book buyers are generally less interested in scientific rigour. That said, Chapter 2, 'When Our Spaceship Landed on Earth . . .', is scientific enough to include equations. Equations are a fabulous tool to sway the doubters.

The attentive reader will have noticed that by this chapter the 'let's presume's and 'it's not impossible's have started to appear. Von Däniken imagines how spear-throwing primitives would react to a spaceship landing; on this occasion the primitives are on another planet, and the ship is from Earth. Early on they would mainly be burying their heads in the ground, as they will presume these visitors are almighty gods. The space travellers, meanwhile, decide they will methodically learn of these primitives' ways as they receive presents and offerings from them. 'It is conceivable that our spacemen will rapidly learn the language of the inhabitants with a computer . . .'

Von Däniken agrees that it is impossible to imagine everything that might happen in such a situation, but he makes a good fist of it. His conjectures include winning over the natives, who will help search for fissionable material so the visitors can return to Earth. Silly travellers for not packing enough fuel. Before the visitors depart, one native will be chosen to be king and given a radio so he can stay in contact with the 'gods'. Meanwhile, 'a few specially selected women would be fertilised by the astronauts. Thus a new race would arise that skipped a stage in natural evolution.'

Von Däniken's vision supposes that, against previous laws of nature presumed by biologists, interspecies sex can lead to pregnancy. It also neatly avoids the evidence from earthlings' exploration of their own planet, in which the discovery of primitive people usually resulted in the explorers decimating and torturing them, turning them into slaves and leaving the survivors in squalid homelands going blind from their addiction to shoe-polish wine. I am afraid that I am with the comic-book artists of the fifties with their *Sinister Tales* and *Weird War* magazines. If a civilisation is so much more sophisticated that it can visit us, it's probable they want to do some snacking on our bones.[2]

By Chapter 3, 'The Improbable World of the Unexplained', von Däniken offers evidence. Ancient maps

---

2 Might I also recommend Alan Moore's invasion of the humanitarians strip from 'Tharg's Future Shocks' in *2000 AD*.

of the world so accurate they could surely have only been made by extraterrestrials looking down from a space rocket in the sky. These maps were once the property of a Turkish navy admiral and were discovered in Topkapi Palace. This remarkable feat was the impetus behind von Däniken's incredible proposition that the only logical solution to the question of how mankind has advanced, created new technologies and done well in the cartography stakes is because something came from another world and gave us a helping hand. Unfortunately, though the maps were pretty precise for the time, they were not so stunningly accurate that only aerial photography from a spaceship was the answer. Six years after *Chariot of the Gods*, under the duress of experts, von Däniken retracted what he had written, saying, 'but this just isn't so'. Since that time, many other commentators have picked holes in the book that would have made it more chasm than book, so they have been ignored.

Throughout the book, the writing screams out, 'Surely this is ludicrous?' unless you are desperate to believe, and it turns out many people are.

'Enormous drawings that were undoubtedly meant as signals for a being floating in the air are found on mountainsides in many parts of Peru.' Undoubtedly meant? There is no room for debate here; there can be no other explanation and there will be no other explanation, because if there is, the whole premise of this profitable book collapses. Every statue that shows a figure wearing even the slightest hat is evidence of a space helmet; every Sumerian straight line a clear illustration of a UFO landing strip.

'The word "impossible" should have become literally impossible for the modern scientist.' Modern science has moved at a rapid pace and has certainly unearthed some incredible new theories, but just as the word 'impossible' is not as useful, the word 'evidence' is still of reasonable importance in scientific discovery.

So 'Was God an Astronaut?' What about Sodom and Gomorrah? Was this actually deliberate destruction of fissionable material; did Lot's wife die because she looked back at the nuclear explosion?

Maybe von Däniken asks more questions than he answers, but fortunately they are questions that aren't burning, so you can mull over them in your own time in a festival field while your thoughts are muddied by hot cider. Meanwhile von Däniken keeps on writing. His latest book,

From *The Goodies Book of Criminal Records* one of my favourite childhood books as it was full of stupid jokes, ridiculous drawings and had a picture of a topless lady (I think it also had a nude Bill Oddie just to keep the balance).

unpublished at the time of writing, is *History is Wrong*. That should be another hugely entertaining slice of nonsense based on more conjecture, myth and avarice.[3]

Tinnitus, or conversations from the gods

'As an Occultist who has practiced Yoga for eighteen years, I am able to bring about a Mental Contact with a Being now resident upon the Planet Venus,' opined Dr George King in *The Flying Saucers*: a report on flying saucers, their crews and their mission to Earth.

Von Däniken spoke of the aliens of the past, but before him was a man who went one better: rather than collate evidence of the aliens that had once been, he went direct to the aliens themselves and chatted about magnetic flux, if not face to face, then mind to mind.

The Day the Gods Came (The Aetherius Society, 1965) is by George King DD. As I mentioned in the introduction, this is my favourite book retrieved from a skip. I was not rummaging around in a skip looking for roof tiles and spokes; it was right at the top of the objects scraped out of the stripped terraced house I wandered past in Herne Hill. I just wish to make it clear that I am not a regular rummager in bins and skips; it's only if the bin has something really good at the top that I might take a peek but will stop once I get to the point where old meat and pastry appear. George was born in Shropshire, and after studying all branches of metaphysics and then practising yoga, he put all his efforts into 'an exact science': 'He learned how to bring the mystic fire of Kundalini under conscious control until he attained

---

3 *Gold of the Gods* revealed that von Däniken had been in a cave filled with the gold of the gods. German magazine *Der Spiegel* found the explorer who apparently led him to the caves and he revealed it was utter nonsense.

the elevated state of cosmic consciousness.' From that point onwards he became dedicated to bringing enlightenment to the world and building a temple to demonstrate a new science, 'the science of shape power'. It was through yoga that he won a battle that meant he could never be deceived.

After reading *The Day the Gods Came*, the reader is left with the big question: is George King DD deceiving us or does he really believe what he's writing? This is one of the toughest questions when dealing with this gaggle of books – has the author consciously set out to profit, either financially or via celebrity, by making up strange extraterrestrial facts, or are they convinced of the truth of their visitation conversations? Perhaps the answer lies somewhere in between, and they started off gleefully making up their new worlds like stereotypical bamboozlers, but later came to believe in the truth of their fictions. Now, as critics question them, they plead like Kevin McCarthy warning oblivious motorists of the danger of pods at the end of *Invasion of the Body Snatchers*.[4] If you borrowed one of daytime television's lie detectors, the ones normally used to discover if a lumbering male simpleton has deceived a lumbering female simpleton by having sex with her best mate in a nightclub toilet, would the alien amour appear to be telling the truth?[5] I suspect George believed right from the start.

After finishing *The Day the Gods Came*, the reader can't help but have a smidgen of desire to be George themselves, even if only for a day. Imagine if you had, or believed you

---

4 If you can't find *The Day the Gods Came*, you could start on Whitley Strieber's *Communion*, the story of how an average writer makes a fortune after his non-fiction personal alien abduction.

5 Though lie detectors are the judge and jury on Jeremy Kyle and other nasty daytime diseases, they are far from 100% accurate and have been debunked themselves. Ask the inventor of the lie detector if the lie detector is 100% accurate while they are attached to a lie detector and you will be none the wiser.

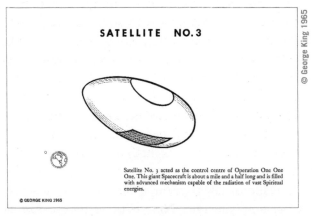

SATELLITE NO.3

Satellite No. 3 acted as the control centre of Operation One One One. This giant Spacecraft is about a mile and a half long and is filled with advanced mechanism capable of the radiation of vast Spiritual energies.

© GEORGE KING 1965

The Kinder Surprise Egg of space goodness – the surprise is being bathed in delicious spiritual energy.

had, received a message from cosmic intelligence instructing you to become the voice of the interplanetary parliament. It must be good for the self-esteem at the very least. Furthermore, in what can only be described as a highly persuasive argument for the enlightening power of yoga, George has been selected as the 'primary terrestrial mental channel' by some higher life form who trusted him to spread the message via the antiquated medium of book. The cynical reader may question whether the yoga of Raja, Gnani and Kundalini are sciences, but that's just our closed Western minds, blighted by consumerism and forgetting to get in the lotus position and tilt our heads to the correct position to receive our stellar messages. Dr King has made metaphysical history, but I think metaphysical history is a little different to the more fact-based history of schooldays involving the Industrial Revolution and the Battle of Naseby. G.R. Elton's *England Under the Tudors* never once bothers to mention spaceships, despite some evidence of Martian involvement in the building of the *Mary Rose*.

The transcripts of George's conversations take the form of an impenetrable radio play or some lost dialogue from *2001: A Space Odyssey* written while Arthur C. Clarke was suffering extreme sunstroke after a day unicycling on a Sri Lankan beach.[6]

MARS SECTOR 6: Acceptable. Magnetic flux?
ZERO ZERO FIVE: The magnetic flux in this area is . . .
    nim nim eight seven eight two eight . . .

The reader is taken through Operation One One One and Operation Nine Nine Nine. Chapter Two, 'Commentary on the Mighty Cosmic Event', then deciphers what we have read so far. Apparently, nim nim eight seven eight two eight and all that surrounds it is about ensuring natural magnetic stabilisation of the solar system. If the potency of the magnetic flux is too great, then the whole darn solar system either falls over or civilisation comes to a similarly slapstick end. The universe will end not with a bang, but with a swanee whistle. George highlights 'July 8th in the Christian year of 1964' as a day of great importance. I have checked my desk diary, but sadly have found not so much as a bank holiday or remembered saint. All I have discovered so far for this date is the release of an Olivia de Havilland film, *Lady in a Cage*, which doesn't seem to have shaken the earth with magnetic flux, or shaken box office records either. The film is about a wealthy poetess trapped in a cage-like elevator and terrorised by a derelict, some hoodlums and a prostitute. It is notable for being James Caan's first featured role in a movie. According to George, 8 July 1964 was due to be the great day when he WILL

---

6 There is no evidence to suggest Arthur C. Clarke ever unicycled on a Sri Lankan beach.

COME (his capitals). Was he waiting for James Caan? Is James Caan the master of the universe? He was very good as Sonny in *The Godfather*.

The cash cow of the spacemen

Erich von Däniken came after George, and has placed a greater footprint in the moondust of this genre. Once he had had his hit with *Chariot of the Gods*, the sequels poured forth and other scientists started to gather up the evidence that proved creatures from beyond the stars had popped down to give *Homo sapiens* a helping hand. After all, who wants to buy another boring book on evolutionary theory over one that promises spaceships and maybe interplanetary sexual liaisons?

After all, 'research into many very old and authoritative records of Earth's chequered history indicates an overwhelming probability that our world has, on countless occasions, been host to extraterrestrial spaceship visitations,' informs Robin Collyns, author of *Did Spacemen Colonise the Earth?*.

From the outset he seems pretty convinced, as I hoped I would be. I was under the influence of an immense sugar rush after some home-made fudge purchased at a school fete, where I was propelled to the bookstall of Jilly Coopers and microwave cookery books. So I bought *Did Spacemen Colonise the Earth?* under the influence of sweetened condensed milk in solid form, something akin to eating magic mushrooms and buying Carlos Castaneda.

How would Collyns prove his theory? What more evidence could you ask for than an occasional image from ancient Egypt that has an apparent orb in the sky. If it is an orb in the sky, then there can be only one answer to the question 'What is it?' It must be a sphere containing aliens, probably popping down to help build a sphinx. A key rule in the collating of evidence of the spacemen coming and building our pyramids for us is that any pictorial image of something round must surely be a spaceship. It might look like two children kicking an inflated pig's bladder, but that is just to the untrained eye. To someone with a knowledge of archaeology, carving and semiotics, it is another alien craft.

Collyns cherry-picks his good science and his bad science. That which can help build up a body of evidence to suggest the spacemen have come is near irrefutable, but the theory of evolution 'is really an unproven faith'. 'It has been increasingly evident to thinking people that neither theological doctrine of "divine creation" nor the theory of evolution can explain the origin of man, flora and fauna, on this or any other planet.'

Who are these 'thinking people'? They obviously don't include most biologists, Crick and Watson, the pioneers of DNA, Craig Venter, Steve Jones, Richard Dawkins or any other silly scientists who have put their trust in facts. In Collyns' world of spaceships he takes the John Merrick angle and declares he is not an animal. 'Man was/is not an animal. Soviet researchers have shown that man's aggressive tendencies are not biologically inherent in his genes.'

Even more interestingly, it seems that because man likes painting and making things, he is not of this earth. It is the return of human arrogance and stroppy-child attitude: I want to be the centre of the universe and I do want to be a dirty ape, so why don't you shut your faces Copernicus and Darwin and let me be superior?

'Indications are that life form bodies for plant, animal and human disease bacteria – microbes, viruses – may have been artificially created in outer space laboratories by possibly evil spacemen.' And it is here that I start to question

Collyns' book, in which the number of what ifs, perhaps, maybes and who knows outdoes even von Däniken's. Who doesn't want to believe that evil spacemen are the cause of all our pain? If you approach *Did Spacemen Colonise the Earth?* with an open mind, and by that I mean a mind that is open air and screaming 'I want to believe in UFOs even if they are Chinese lanterns', then you will leave this book both contented and fearful that the evil ones shall come again. If, on the other hand, you are the type of person who might say, 'Hold on, how come every single sphere in a painting is meant to represent an alien spaceship?' then your nasty, slighting cynicism will leave you unconvinced. But before you dismiss it completely, ask yourself (as Collyns does), are Jewish people the chosen people because they are from outer space? Does the Bible contain computer estimates from spacemen? Why does the Catholic church have a 30,000-word schema covering the possibility of other life in the universe? Then again, you could also ask yourself why they still believe that Cabernet Sauvignon from the hands of a priest and into your mouth turns into Messiah blood.

'Was the star of Bethlehem a spaceship?'

Right, I'm out of here.

There may well be life in the universe; there are so many possibilities it would seem arrogant to believe we were the chosen, stupid, warring few. Why intelligent life would want to travel light years to visit us is another question. Do intelligent human travellers holiday in Crawley? There's a thin line between scientific investigation and smoking too much skunk and believing that *The Twilight Zone* is a documentary. Actually, it's quite a thick line. If you'd rather not skip through *Did Spacemen Colonise the Earth?* but would like to theorise on being on other planets, enjoy a proper scientist's equation.

This is Frank Drake's equation for the likelihood of life on other planets. It is one of my favourite equations which I stumbled upon while reading the delightful *Murmurs of Earth: The Voyager Interstellar Record* (Random House, 1978):

$$N = N^\star \ \text{fp ne fl fi fc fL}^7$$

---

7 N* represents the number of stars in the Milky Way galaxy.
Question: How many stars are in the Milky Way galaxy?
Answer: Current estimate is 100 billion.
fp is the fraction of stars that have planets around them
Question: What percentage of stars have planetary systems?
Answer: Current estimates range from 20% to 50%.
ne is the number of planets per star that are capable of sustaining life
Question: For each star that does have a planetary system, how many planets are capable of sustaining life?
Answer: Current estimates range from 1 to 5.
fl is the fraction of planets in ne where life evolves
Question: On what percentage of the planets that are capable of sustaining life does life actually evolve?
Answer: Current estimates range from 100% (where life can evolve it will) down to close to 0%.
fi is the fraction of fl where intelligent life evolves
Question: On the planets where life does evolve, what percentage evolves intelligent life?
Answer: Estimates range from 100% (intelligence is such a survival advantage that it will certainly evolve) down to near 0%.
fc is the fraction of fi that communicate
Question: What percentage of intelligent races have the means and the desire to communicate?
Answer: 10% to 20%.
fL is the fraction of the planet's life during which the communicating civilisations live
Question: For each civilisation that does communicate, for what fraction of the planet's life does the civilisation survive?
Answer: This is the toughest of the questions. If we take Earth as an example, the expected lifetime of our sun and the Earth is roughly 10 billion years. So far we've been communicating with radio waves for less than 100 years. How long will our civilisation survive? Will we destroy ourselves in a few years as some predict or will we overcome our problems and survive for millennia? If we were destroyed tomorrow the answer to this question would be 1/100,000,000th. If we survive for 10,000 years the answer will be 1/1,000,000th.
When all of these variables are multiplied together we come up with: N, the number of communicating civilisations in the galaxy.
(Taken from activemind.com; originally from SETI project.)

It would be crude to merely dismiss Collyns, as he does ask questions such as:

Does a Milky Way transgalactic spaceship beacon network exist?

Have Atlantean mammoth and mastodon bones been discovered?

Did early New Zealand Maoris learn astronomy from spacemen?

All these books are a bit of a fun, except that they pretend to offer evidence for nonsense, nonsense that a conspiracy-theory-hungry population finds tasty and provocative. Carl Sagan, one of the great modern popularisers of science, wrote of this frustration in *The Demon Haunted World: Science as a Candle in the Dark*. Sagan is picked up by a driver at an airport. Upon finding out who he is, the driver asks him many questions about science, except he sees science as being UFO investigations and the lost city of Atlantis. As Sagan debunks each of the myths, he sees the driver grow glummer and glummer, and realises that 'I was dismissing not some errant doctrine, but a precious facet of his inner life. And yet there is so much in real science that's equally exciting . . . did he know about the molecular building blocks of life sitting out there in the cold tenuous gas between the stars?'

All the nonsense of the spacemen and the ghosts and the mermaids can be an entertaining read, but I still make sure I find time to sit bamboozled as I try to comprehend how something of infinite density and no mass went bang, and I'm pretty sure it wasn't because a spaceman fired a laser beam at it.

What we have learned

- Many of these books of alien visitation are best summarised by the quantum physicist Wolfgang Pauli's statement when facing a physics paper he disagreed with – 'that's not right, it's not even wrong'
- When learning about scientific possibilities it is often best to read books by scientists such as Carl Sagan
- We are the spawn of aliens

Further reading

Signs of the Gods by Erich von Däniken
Return of the Gods by Erich von Däniken
Arrival of the Gods by Erich von Däniken
The Gods and Their Grand Design by Erich von Däniken
Gold of the Gods by Erich von Däniken
The Gods Were Astronauts by Erich von Däniken
History is Wrong by Erich von Däniken

5

Romance

(or a tea cosy for the heart, or how to thaw the heart of the hardiest unreconstructed bull male whilst being involved in an important scientific investigation in a lonely wasteland without taking up more than 187 pages)

Remember the first time you fell in love?

Awful, wasn't it?

You discovered that the object of your affections really liked you, but she really liked you as a confidant. So she told you all about how much she wanted to sleep with your friend, and how nice it was she could talk to you about what a great guy he was and maybe you could help get them together. So you did. And then they noisily had sex next to where you were sleeping and you punched a wall after drinking too many miniature bottles of liqueur you found in a cupboard where holiday memories were put.

And from that point on you believed that infatuation was a mental illness.

The cure for this belief is available in a simple 180-page format and it is called Mills & Boon. It's either a cure, or an alternative to venturing into the battle for love in the first place.

Presumptions are made about Mills & Boon, many of them unfair and made by people who have barely read even one novel involving a shy woman and an Arctic explorer or a city girl relocated to the Outback.

'. . . and the night of that damned storm was nearly my undoing. My God, I went in to comfort you, but if I had stayed any longer I would have ended up raping you.'

'Not rape, my love,' she replied softly, shyly.

I doubt any novice Mills & Boon reader would expect that kind of dialogue. As the avid reader knows, contemporary Mills & Boon has branched out from gentle doctor/nurse stories to tales of hot and bothered sensuality, but this isn't even from one of the modern, racier Mills & Boons; it's from the early eighties.

These musings on storm-tossed rape possibilities are taken from *The Challenge*, a Mills & Boon novel set on the scorched plains of Australia. The hero, Saxon McAllister, may be a lonely cattle rancher who doesn't care for the fancy ways of the urban, but that was hardly an excuse to startle me as I browsed a library sale in Chippenham. It was my first time in Chippenham library; actually, it was my first time in Chippenham, but it felt right that I should find one of the more extreme romantic conversations in this town. I had come there to gig for my friend Wil, a man who combines pink hair, eyeliner and Care Bears hanging from his belt with a former career as a wrestler and anarchist. He is a man of impeccable integrity and we are bonded by our love of crazed religious cartoon books that tell you you'll go to hell if you dabble in witchcraft. Dabbling in witchcraft includes watching *Bewitched*. The gig was fine, even though every man in the audience seemed to have the face I had imagined for Saxon McAllister, except for Wil. Saxon was not a man who would dye his hair or his sheep pink.

Just as I had expected less of Chippenham than I should have done, so I had just started erasing my preconceptions of Mills & Boon. In my small-minded and uneducated way, like most others I had always presumed that Mills & Boon was as genteel and prim as an Anglican chutney sale. I believed that every female in their novels was part of the 'true love waits' sect,[1] and every man as honourable as a Quaker. As I was to find out, the world of mass-produced romantic fiction, much like the Women's Institute, is feistier than you might imagine.[2]

So what is this thing called love?

Everyone wants love in their life, with everything from adverts to movies to helium balloons in the shape of hearts constantly reminding you of the fact. So you search for it in clubs and bars and zoos and concerts (hippy) and you find it. It's never what you thought it would be. A moment's bliss and an error of judgement can all too easily lead to a life of bitter

---

1 'Believing that true love waits, I make a commitment to God, myself, my family, my friends, my future mate, and my future children to a lifetime of purity including sexual abstinence from this day until the day I enter a biblical marriage relationship.' This is the promise of the true love waits gang.

2 Despite the image of the Women's Institute being a prim collection of pastry and pottery enthusiasts, they have fought campaigns on equal pay, domestic violence, and AIDS, and that was before they increased their infamy with the celebrated naked calendar. In 2008, they produced an online video guide for spicing up your love life. If they have any involvement with jam now, it is most likely being smeared on naked flesh.

regret, angry argument and erratic vase-throwing. Thanks to love's failure, comedy clubs have air laden with male comedians' whining about their wives'/girlfriends' lack of understanding of football, drinking and farting, and female comedians declaring that the men they've found have failed to comprehend the complexity of sex due to all their farting, football and drinking. Others declare love to be a state of insanity or just another of the brain's chemical imbalances. But for all its potential pitfalls, without it manufactured pop bands would have nothing to sing about, sales of wilted carnations from garage forecourts would vaporise, and coastal charity shops would find their bookshelves nearly empty.

When love is a fictional concept, roses don't cut fingers, romantic sea cruises don't lead to vomiting and diarrhoea, strong and silent types don't turn out to be dullards who have nothing to say. Keep love out of real life, the best place for it is on the pages of a slim novel held in the palms of your hands as you sit by the fire, alone, in your studio apartment.

So why is love in Mills & Boon better than love found in almost any other publisher's output? Love at low budget, and Mills & Boon offers love at a far more reasonable price than most, just seems to be happier; the less you pay for it, the better the outcome will be.

For example, a first edition of *Tess: A Pure Woman* by Thomas Hardy is currently retailing at £1,243.11. For that you will get rape, unwanted pregnancy, betrayal (partially due to not checking under the doormat for post – a foolish error in the days of loose doormats), loveless marriage and cold death. No one ends up happy and some people end up murdered or hanged. Isn't life miserable enough without retreating into more written moroseness, and hefty debt?

ups and downs of finding love

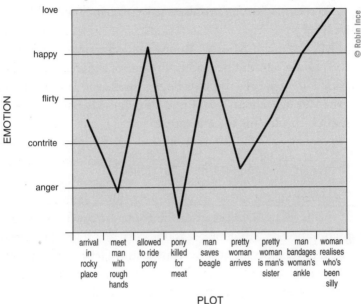

© Robin Ince

EMOTION

love — happy — flirty — contrite — anger

arrival in rocky place | meet man with rough hands | allowed to ride pony | pony killed for meat | man saves beagle | pretty woman arrives | pretty woman is man's sister | man bandages woman's ankle | woman realises who's been silly

PLOT

This is a graph.

A first edition of *Vets at Cross Purposes*, on the other hand, retails at 68 pence. For that money you will get some disagreement over the treatment of colic in horses, some ill puppies that get better, and finally, love in a Land Rover on a muddy lane.

Expensive love fiction is far more likely to end in suicide or, at the very least, a hopeless sense of regret. While the hardback and highbrow is meant to tell us what love really is, the cheap paperback is the story of what it's meant to be. Just as models and actresses in magazines are airbrushed to within an inch of becoming Wilma Flintstone, so the details of love in these novels have many of the hard edges chiselled off and filed away.

So what is the secret of low-price romance with a happy ending?

My favourite Mills & Boons predominantly deal with the build-up to the bedroom, the eve of the marriage. The final page is where the bliss begins, and so it can go on for ever. We leave our lovers in a clinch.[3] There will be no sequel, this love is for eternity.

Is love permitted in darkest Yorkshire?

Diamond Stud is a fine example of Mills & Boon's genius. It is one of my favourites in the romantic artificial insemination horse farm genre. It is the story of a man. That man is called Diamond, and he runs a stud farm in Yorkshire. Hence *Diamond Stud*, you see.

'If there was a more overbearing, unreasonable and thoroughly disagreeable man than Nick Diamond, Sherril had never met him – and he lived in darkest Yorkshire!'

As you might imagine, Sherril and Nick do not get on. She is a southern sophisticate; he is a northerner who believes in tradition, not women's lib. They feud, they brood, they steam and yet the novel ends as Sherril smiles, nods and buries her head 'into the comfortable warmth of his shoulder'.

How could this have happened? After all, barely one hundred pages ago Nick Diamond was not a man whose

---

3 Before typing this I saw the saddest form of clinch, the one-sided love hug. This is predominantly seen at railway stations. A couple hug; one of them is holding tighter than the other and whispering love in their partner's ear, but passers-by can see the expression on her face that says, 'oh god, I really must tell him sometime'. The tragedy of the one-sided love hug.

flesh or shoulder bones exuded warmth or comfort. They were slabs of northern granite, northern granite that wanted to crush anything from fancy London with its effete ways and ignorance about how to stick a syringe into a pony's vagina.

Nick Diamond is a man with a great many characteristics designed to repel any woman with ideas that belong in the twentieth century (save for those who are sexually attracted to Death Row occupants). So how could he inveigle his way into the heart of Sherril? Is the symmetry of horse insemination so alluring?

However, we may be moving too quickly into the specifics of horse stud Yorkshire lust dramas, before we have understood the generic basics. So let's first take time to study the journey that takes two cold and furious people from frigidity to consummation (or nearest available equivalent).

Where is love? From jungle to roller disco

Before beginning the dissection of the narrative arc of bliss, it is important to divide our plots into sub-categories.

Romantic fiction is like music. It would be ridiculous to just declare, 'I love all music.' You might love modern jazz, but hate hip-hop. You might adore Captain Beefheart, but wish to assassinate Snow Patrol. Perhaps Elgar cures you of all ills, but Donna Summer makes you perfect strangulation knots with old rope. Romance publishers know that love fetishists have specific needs. Whereas one printed-love junkie may want to experience passion with a rural earl, another may be disgusted by aristocratic clinches and instead experience burgeoning desire with a pianist on a Mediterranean cruise liner, while another still may want to read about a nineteenth-century gypsy feuding over land rights with a ballet impresario.

In the early days, Mills & Boon was very simple: you picked your profession, generally nurse or jungle explorer, and picked up your book from the railway station newsagent's to read on the way to Woking (or Welwyn Garden City). The most complex the genre got was in combining the two, in novels such as *Jungle Doctor* by Vivian Stuart: 'Anton Kramer, a man of fierce devotion where his work as a surgeon was concerned, could never surrender to an uncompromising love like Deborah's.' All ends when 'His lips found hers and the little silver plane went winging on, towards a distant horizon.' But whose lips met whose? Did Debs' lips meet Anton's or the lips of young flyer Hank Curtis? Even in 1961, things could get complicated.

As the decades went by, the demands of the reader became ever more specific – modern, historical, thriller, hospital, vet, astrological, rude novels, even novels that were 'a bit longer' became part of the publishing house of love.

By the nineties, Mills & Boon's extensive ranges included high-octane, feral stories such as those found in the Silhouette series, where protagonists could tell the difference between an amateur wolf and a trained wolf. You need to know the quality of your wolves if you are running with Paranormal Allied experts such as Kieran Holt. He's a genetically enhanced superagent who has had to leave his wife, Paige, because 'a lab explosion has turned him from scientist to experiment', and finds himself battling with the Beast Within. He's not the only genetically enhanced character in Mills & Boon, though.

'When it comes to matters of the heart, you'll find he

hasn't got one.' Why would he need a heart? He's Nathan Whitmore, embroiled in 'Australia's cut-throat, glamorous world of gem dealing' as portrayed in the six-part Hearts of Fire series.

'"I don't know how I've kept my hands off you," he murmured, as his lips found the tender skin below her ear.' Is Luke Hunter an Aries? Let's hope he's astrologically compatible, as *Hunter's Harem* is in the Starsign Romance series. If you can't decide on what profession attracts you to a romantic hero, instead use the lead of which stars were gravitationally affecting him as he was pulled from the womb.

And so the many faces of Mills & Boon keep on revealing themselves:

- Black Star Crime, home to Margaret Moore's *Tuscan Termination*, where a hilltop village in Tuscany has its secrets uncovered after a corpse is discovered by Hilary.
- The Special Moments series, which offers double bills such as *The Man Behind the Cop/The Single Dad's Virgin Wife*, formerly found separately in the Super Cop and the Wives for Hire series.
- Blaze, which presents another double bill of *Dead Sexy/Heated Rush*. I have no idea what lies within, but the exterior offers a topless buff cowboy, leaning on a fence as lightning strikes. I think this one might be too potent for me to open.

If there is a romance you have imagined, then Mills & Boon will have thought of it, commissioned a writer and printed it.

Those innocent days of the early eighties

For all the exciting modernity in the new, multi-layered world of romance, the Mills & Boons I favour are from the late seventies and the early eighties. This was the age of Jane Seymour, one of the twentieth century's icons of romance. On our televisions she would walk through her Jardin de Romance of perfume adverts promising alluring odour and chocolate-box kisses. Of course there was another side to Jane too, which makes me wonder how she found the time for love. When not in her jardin, she spent much of her time in the old West dodging spitting tobacco and curing Johnny Cash's tuberculosis in *Dr Quinn, Medicine Woman*.

Jane is the perfect Mills & Boon heroine. She may appear beautiful and serene, but she is no shrinking violet; she treats gunfight wounds but she wants a cottage with roses around the door and a great big bottle of perfume hidden in the shrubs.[4] This is women's lib as it should be: mainly tough, sometimes yielding, and smelling nice.

Dr Quinn was a woman fighting prejudice in the old West. It is this metropolitan feminist fish-out-of-water plot that is also the staple of my favourite Mills & Boon sub-genre, which, like Jane Seymour, seemed dominant in the early eighties.

Both the previously mentioned titles *The Challenge* and *Diamond Stud* belong in this period, and in the Venn diagram of heart-shifting writing they have a broad shaded area. One woman leaves London for 'darkest Yorkshire', the other finds herself in the Outback, but both have to

---

4 I would not like to live in a cottage with roses around the door. When I was three I was playing kiss chase with the local Baptist minister's daughter and I fell and grasped a rose bush as I went down, tearing out a tendon. For me, roses are the blight of love, the reason I never kissed the Baptist minister's daughter. They also attract bugs.

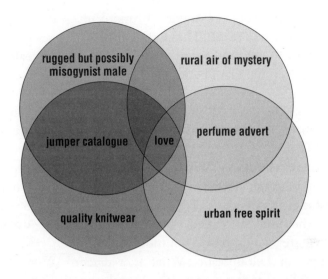

Is this too many shaded areas for an effective Venn diagram on perfection in romantic fiction.

fit in in an alien world and cure brusque men of their preconceptions. Perhaps unsurprisingly, neither woman name-checks Andrea Dworkin, author of *Intercourse*, a book that has been summarised as 'all heterosexual sex is rape'.[5]

The testosterone christening

At the outset, the reader must know that the men their heroines are facing up to are real men. Men who, initially

---

5 I read enough feminism in my late teens to make me permanently ashamed. I realise now that a young man should balance his feminism carefully. Read Susan Faludi's *Backlash* and discover how you are complicit in the patriarchal society, then read some Ernest Hemingway and imagine you are a bullfighter for a little counterbalance.

it may seem, would fit Andrea Dworkin's image of the male as a sexual miscreant. The author firstly achieves this by adorning their protagonist with a name that reveals all before even the first physical description of their musculature.

Nick Diamond. What is a diamond? A sharp, solid, impenetrable object, and so is Nick Diamond, northern stud farmer.

Saxon McAllister. What is a Saxon? A man of the past, a man in rough clothes, a man who is unaware of the feminist movement, and so is Saxon McAllister. Though with the mention of stifled, stormy rape, maybe Viking McAllister would have been more appropriate.

Dracon Leloupblanc. What is a dracon? What is a leloupblanc for that matter? It's a Frenchman, that's for sure, and a Frenchman whose surname literally translates into 'the white wolf'. The reader knows this man is no pussycat (though there is a possibility he has rabies). But it is still too early for me to launch into the virile, exotic world of *Where the Wolf Leads*.

The average reader wouldn't take a risk with a protagonist called Anthony Pudding, though it might be acceptable for the name of the secondary male lead who is a good listener and friend to women due to his wobbly frame. He will never marry the slim, pretty girl, but he may find solace with a plump, lonely girl in specs.[6] The rules are clear: plump for the plump, beautiful for the beautiful, feisty for the feisty.

Before the book is even opened, a brief perusal of its back cover will offer the reader a stern warning. Both they and the heroine within are about to set foot in a world

---

6 I admit it, I've been reading Philip Larkin again.

drenched with testosterone and masculine aggression. Dare they read on?

The lure of cold geography

I will buy a Mills & Boon on the strength of character name alone. But I frequently buy them at two for a pound; the purchaser of full-price Mills & Boons may be less impulsive.

Cover blurb is vitally important. The reader may have been drawn in as far as the second paragraph by names alone, but now they need a plot to make sure they are intrigued enough to make their purchase. There is no time for excessive intricacy; the author only has between 150 and 200 pages to take you from emptiness, loathing, self-loathing and occasional lifeboat saving, via hidden feelings (at times brought forth by lifeboat saving), to the clinch in thick knitwear.

It's a crowded market. The author and publisher must grasp the beating heart of their reader with an iron fist, occasionally clad in velvet.

This is the back cover trailer for *Midnight Sun's Magic* by Betty Neels: 'Spitzbergen, not so very far from the North Pole, would not seem the most likely place to find romance . . .' Betty, or rather the marketing person who has penned this, is luring us into a world of intrigue via geography.

What is the enigma of Spitzbergen?

When I think of romance, I never think of Spitzbergen. Due to a hole in my education, the word 'romance' could be replaced with pretty much any other noun.

Spitzbergen would not seem the most likely place to find spaghetti vongole.

Spitzbergen would not seem the most likely place to find pedicurists.

Spitzbergen would not seem the most likely place to find a china figure of a mournful dog.[7]

I don't think of Spitzbergen as being the most likely place to find dachshunds, dinner sets, devil fish, discotheques, dandies, dim sum or leather-bound copies of *Daniel Deronda*. Until very recently, I thought nothing when I saw the name Spitzbergen. The mentioning of it in a Mills & Boon blurb made me educate myself, and that is what reading is about: learning.

Now I know that Spitzbergen means 'jagged peaks', a name given to it by Dutch explorer Willem Barentsz. This fact will become very important later on when we discover how the Dutch have influenced Betty Neels and her imagination.

Though I may have known nothing of Spitzbergen, I was drawn further in. A question is begged: why is love made less likely by location? I am sure that lust is decreased by thickness of overgarments in Arctic regions, as *Sex is not Compulsory* posited, but whether in the dry heat of the desert, the freezing air of the North Pole or the humidity of a decaying sixties shopping centre, surely love can find a way to blossom?

'. . . but when Annis went to work there for a short time, she managed to fall in love with a handsome Norwegian. The affair was brief and disappointing, though.' Suddenly, the claws of blurb salesmanship are released from my

---

7 This is a popular parlour game, most often played during religious holidays: Could you in Spitzbergen? Each person declares something you could do in Spitzbergen, and the loser is the person who says something you could actually do there: e.g. find the stored seed of a plant long destroyed by global warming, as it is home to a dry seed store especially curated in the event of Armageddon or nearest equivalent.

Barentsz the Dutch Arctic explorer and Fridtjof Nansen the Norwegian Arctic explorer. So who looks sexiest? Only Betty Neels truly knows.

second-hand cardigan. This has none of the pounding fear of an affair in deepest, darkest Yorkshire or a woman meeting a man of mystery in the loneliness of a lighthouse. Annis then meets a Dutchman, Jake Van Germent, and apparently spends the rest of the book explaining that she's not just on the rebound, despite his not being very handsome compared with her polar Norwegian.

Should I have opened the book, what would I have been in for? Apparently, I'd find a quest to discover who is best at loving – the Norwegian or the Dutch – and that just doesn't seem enough to me. Even now, I have never bothered to read *Midnight Sun's Magic* although it sits firmly on my shelves. But it is thanks to *Midnight Sun's Magic* that I was perusing Arctic adventure on the PDSA shelf and found something far more potent. I discovered the Arctic adventurer love story that would define all further Arctic adventurer love stories for me. Betty Neels would return, in Dorset and Amsterdam, but not in the Midnight Sun.

No tears for an eaten dog

'It was Dain Ransome's skill as a lecturer on a riveting subject that had fired Kerin with the idea of joining an expedition to the Antarctic, not the man himself – he had struck her as a particularly unpleasant mixture of arrogance and icy coldness.'

There is no 'brief' or 'disappointing' here; this is a novel that offers definites right from the start. Here is Dain Ransome, an ice sculpture of manliness as if hewn from a glacier. And here is Kerin, a woman attracted to the Arctic by the words of a man she finds repugnant. This should be a sleigh ride of romantic imagination.

If you were a young man having trouble finding a paramour in the eighties, then Mills & Boon's output would suggest that you might do best by walking along some tundra in goggles and anorak. I presume Ranulph Fiennes has an immense amount of female attention; he can barely have enough time to hacksaw off his latest set of frostbitten fingertips before another woman throws herself in the path of his snowmobile.[8]

The reader knows that an Arctic explorer is a man with a wanderlust, but can he exchange his lust for wandering with a lust for stroppy women? They also know that an Arctic explorer is attracted to the cold because like is attracted to like, so how do you thaw the heart of a man whose blood flows like a glacier? What a challenge to a

---

8 Ranulph Fiennes really did cut off the blackened dead tips of his fingers after getting impatient with the elongated medical process around such things.

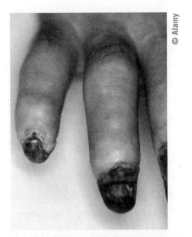

© Alamy

You're only a true Arctic explorer if you keep your fingertips in a jam jar.

woman to reach her hand into this chest freezer of innards and warm it up.

Frozen Heart by Daphne Clair plays hardball with the frozen wasteland love genre. Can Kerin, a young journalist, thaw the frozen heart of Dain Ransome? Will she even want to? The regular reader knows that it is more than likely that love will be found; very few Mills & Boons end with the lashing out of a pickaxe and an explorer hidden in an icy grave to be slowly crushed by a glacier.

My concentration on the Arctic Mills & Boons doesn't mean to imply they shy away from other types of explorer. There are adventurers of the Amazon and the African savannah, though they are far more likely to be hot-footed and quick-tempered. As a general rule, the temperature of the explorer's chosen destination will reflect the temperature of his heart. The safest bet is probably a botanist obsessed with the Cotswolds, but even this will mean his heart is sometimes overcast or muggy.

But what of Dain Ransome. What does his name suggest?[9] He's no Saxon or Dracon, or even a Dagan Carmichael, lead lothario of *Rash Intruder*. But Dain has something more than a name; he has wisdom, camera equipment and an eye for a volcano.

'The speaker she was to listen to was Dain Ransome, just back from the Antarctic, and according to the background information she had looked up on him, a man with a large wanderlust of his own. With a background in geology, he was respected as a scientist and had written several dozen papers of a learned specialist nature . . .'

The dear reader does not need to worry her pretty little head over such things. They were learned and specialist, that's all you need to know. He is a wise man, possibly so wise he believes he can be pig-headed in the cold of the frozen wastes.

'. . . and a book on volcanoes . . .'

Thankfully, not all his books are learned and specialist; some of them are books on volcanoes, though that's not to say they aren't learned and specialist books on volcanoes.

'. . . which she gathered incorporated a lot of first-hand knowledge, and some pretty spectacular photographic close-ups of volcanic activity he had taken himself.'

If the reader was initially uncertain what kind of man Dain is, his fearlessness is no longer in question by this point. He is not scared of molten lava, he'll go right up close and stare into its hot eyes (unless he was using a zoom lens and a helicopter) and he has a vaguely artistic side, which comes out with high temperatures. There is even

---

9 According to the online Urban Dictionary, Dain means 'super ultra fantastic', 'a state of wonderfulness', but it also means 'a large doodoo head'. I am not sure that I trust the Urban Dictionary.

more to him than that: he has knowledge beyond the knowledge of men who work in financial institutions or florists. They would know little of Antarctica, unlike Dain, who 'is one of the few people who it could be said knew the region fairly well.'

Can an explorer who knows a region fairly well ever exchange the love of a region fairly well known for a woman like Kerin? It seems the thing he does not know fairly well is the ways of women. Can that heart melt, or at least defrost? I'll leave it up to you to find out. If you don't want to bother, then you can probably guess it is likely to be yes.

Love rivals

Mills & Boon is not without romantic rivals of its own. The publisher remains dominant on the shelves in seaside towns, but squint hard enough at the spines before you and other publishers' crests can be spied.

Harlequin was a rival, and is now united with Mills & Boon, a truly globe-smashing love empire. Sadly I have unearthed very few of their titles and buying them new from source is against my rules, as well you know.[10] But it was while looking at the piteous collection of Harlequins, almost hidden behind the wicker baskets laden with Mills & Boons, that I discovered a little more about the once enigmatic Betty Neels, arbiter in the Norwegian versus Dutch sex debate.

'Benedict van Manfeld needed Cassandra Darling – at

---

10 Only one book I write about was actually purchased by mail order, and at full price too. After three years of waiting and hoping to find it in a cardboard box in the corner of the British Heart Foundation, I caved in. I am not proud.

any rate, he needed her temporarily, as a nurse.' This signalled the return of Betty Neels into my life, without explorers, but with a new publisher and in the company of doctors and nurses in the book *Cassandra by Chance*.[11] It also signalled the return of the Dutch. *Cassandra by Chance* takes us to Holland and into the arms of other Dutchmen.

A pattern was forming. I have not yet found *Sister Peters in Amsterdam* or *Nurse in Holland* or *Surgeon from Holland* or even *Nurse Harriet Goes to Holland*, but Holland must have been viewed as a powerful marketing tool by Canadian publishers Harlequin, as I'm assured of their existence. Before Holland had become the country to love in, Betty's Dutch books had gone under slightly more torrid and alluring titles; *Nurse Harriet Goes to Holland* was once *Tempestuous April*, while *Nurse in Holland* was originally *Amazon in an Apron*. So where did Betty's Dutch obsession stem from?

The Harlequin Romance novels offer the reader no clues to the life of Betty. The front page, where Betty's biography might have sat, is occupied by the exciting news of the arrival of Harlequin Presents. This was a new line for 1974 that would include Anne Mather's *The Pleasure and the Pain* and Violet Winspear's *The Honey is Bitter*.

While Harlequin titles don't fear being racy, they lack the pointless extraneous detail of gingham tablecloths, cracked teapots and full-on recipes for Italian pasta dishes that the Mills & Boon author excels in. The best they can manage is the occasional advice on desserts: 'By way of afters she made a queen of puddings, adding homemade jam with a lavish hand.' Surely the reader needs to know more than the

---

11 *Cassandra by Chance* is the most expensive romance book I've bought. £2 from the Barnado's in Edinburgh.

dolloping of jam if they are to make a queen of puddings? OK, my Elizabeth Graham lasagne with 'tomato paste and spices that recalled the unique flavour of southern Italy' did not turn out perfectly (the melancholy made it slightly bitter), but at least I had some idea how to make it. Hardcore fans of *Withnail and I* watch the film and have a drink every time the characters drink; perhaps hardcore romantic novel readers could make a pudding every time the characters make one.

Betty and the Dutchman

Some months later, having been somewhat disappointed with her nurse capers, I came across Betty Neels again. This time I was inland, in a Help the Aged in Leicester. Leicester had previously offered very little of interest in the charity shop romance sections, though it had always been excellent for scientology and Westerns. If I wanted to know more about how Xenons might affect Tom Cruise, Leicester town centre was the place.

This Midlands city offered me Betty Neels again, but a very different Betty Neels. She had conquered the Dutch medical romance and the Arctic explorer romance, and now she was taking on the mighty Christmas vicar genre: 'All the village presumed that Margo Pearson was to marry George, but unexpectedly meeting Professor Gijs van Kessel decided her.' True to her specialist nature, even in the setting of Dorset vicarages Betty finds room for a Dutchman.

The Vicar's Daughter finally answered my Betty Neels queries by offering a biography. The real Betty married a Dutchman, not a Norwegian. Thus the personal love quandary is resolved. I still haven't read *Midnight Sun's Magic* but I shall presume that Annis also ran off with her Dutchman (just to avoid arguments in the Neels household). Betty was a nurse, though we are not told about any dalliances with Arctic explorers. Her Dutch husband may be an Arctic explorer, we are not given those details. Some questions about Neels are answered, but through the initial answers she only becomes more enigmatic. Betty Neels, you are like quantum physics; each answer only creates five more questions.

According to an online biography, Betty was inspired to start writing by a lady in a library bemoaning the lack of romantic novels, but to be honest I struggle to believe this. I have spent a reasonable percentage of my life in libraries – I like the hush – and there have been some shelves lacking content. I have found a lack of books on cosmology, the language of bees' dances, and spinal manipulation, but the one section that creaks and aches under a burden of books is the romance section. The librarian without love cycling in spinster fashion to her lending desk and poring over printed dreams of romance is one of the clichés of the profession; it wouldn't be a library without large-print love books.

Love bloomed over a mangy hoof

'Rose nodded ruefully as she gazed at the patches of eczema all over the dog's body.'

What has a dog's skin condition got to do with love?

If you don't want to fall into the clutches of lighthouse-keepers, Arctic explorers or mutated scientists, then you can always bury yourself in the simmering cauldron of lust that is vet romance. Highlights from the Avalon career romance series include *My Fair Lady Vet*, *Vets at Cross Purposes*, *Vets at Variance*, or, if you dare, *Rogue Vet*, featuring a vet who doesn't follow the rules when it comes to cats with weeping sores.

I found *Vets at Cross Purposes* by Mary Bowring quite rightly in a PDSA shop. It has sexual tension, rural intrigue, and most importantly a good level of pharmaceutical accuracy. I don't know the correct pills for a problematic pony with aching joints, but I sense that Mary revels in her research. *Vets at Cross Purposes* is a ménage à trois over the operating table. How can you treat distemper when your ex-fiancee is trying to deceive your new employer?

'When at last he began to talk he made no mention of the party the night before. Instead he spoke professionally about the treatment he was going to give the horses at the stables . . . "He is in a certain amount of pain from the arthritis. I'm going to give him some phenylbutazone which, as you know, is a wonder drug for horses."'

David Langley is a damn good vet and, I'd hazard a guess, a pretty satisfying lover too. Mary treats her readers to more than just love in this book. Although they might just have chosen this novel because it was the last romance on the shelf and have little knowledge of vets and their ways, by the end they will have had their heartstrings twanged *and* be able to speak knowledgeably in a waiting room.

Page 169 stands out for featuring romance around a discussion about the aforementioned drug phenylbutazone, whilst also dealing with politics and the problems of Britain being part of the EU: 'Soon it [phenylbutazone] will be banned . . . Just because in certain European countries horses and ponies are food-producing animals, it is maintained there is a risk of medicinal residue being passed on to humans.'

Why? Because of the French and other continentals who indulge in horse meat as a lunch treat; what nag-consuming madness. Not content with eating horse flesh, something the British have always found hideous, the French will also be causing more arthritic pain in our equine friends.

David reveals that this is nanny-nation nonsense; he has taken the drug himself and it did wonders for him. This is the most medicinally and politically specific passage that I know in Mills & Boon as a whole, not just in the vet genre, and it seems a fitting place to leave the publisher.

Can the pious love their gynaecologist?

'The doctor healed her heart, but who would heal her soul?'

Have we still not found the romance genre to suit you?

Could it be that you want your love story to be more gynaecological? I do not mean more blue or intimate in scenes of intercourse and genital description, but quite literally, in the world of the gynaecologist's surgery. Are you a Christian who ponders just what steps should be taken if you feel a fondness for the man who takes charge of your smears?

Prepare yourself for the visceral intensity of Christian Gynaecological Romance. 'The nurses wiped the splashes of blood on Joel's face and neck, then stepped back so he could look inside the uterus with his special light and speculum.'

Sign of the Speculum is the most eyebrow-arching title of any book I have found. It was a gift, and although I was glad to receive it in the furtherance of my collection, there are some people who may find it a rather odd present. When the title is mentioned in conversation for the first time, it creates a mixture of wincing and wide-eyed astonishment. When my wife saw my well-thumbed copy of *Sign of the Speculum* on the bedroom floor she let out a gasp: 'You can't call a book that!' I am not sure I disagree with her.

'This is the story of a woman who fell in love with her gynaecologist. It will introduce you to the fears, the thrills, the problems and the unique adventures of the hidden world of male doctors and their female patients.' The author, Jessyca Russell Gavor, has also written *How to Help Your Pharmacist Help You*, *Shadow of Love* and *The Faith of Jimmy Carter*. I believe she is on a mission. This mission is to introduce us to her Christian beliefs, tackle medical quandaries and show how you don't have to have sex in a novel about romance. It is a big mission. The novel is currently unavailable, leaving Christian women in love with their speculum handler in a quandary. Jessyca thanks her editor, Henry McQueeny, for allowing her to avoid sexual encounters, as this would be against her biblical beliefs. I have checked Leviticus and failed to unearth a law that forbids the writing of occasionally rude fiction, but in reading it I have been reminded that if a man sleeps with an animal, then both the man and the animal must be stoned to death. Poor donkey; I don't think it was a consensual act.

There can be only one. And maybe the odd sequel

If it's not gynaecologists you are after, then maybe eternal swordsmen are what you need.

Did you enjoy the Highlander movies, with their immortality, bloodlust and swordplay, but felt they lacked enough time-hopping extreme sex? Karen Marie Moning knew you felt like that and so has authored *The Kiss of the Highlander*, *The Touch of the Highlander* and *Dark Highlander* amongst others. The series is well-reviewed by the *Romantic Times* and *The Contra Costa Times*, and they pack lust into tartan.

'It had just been made excruciatingly clear to him that the human male brain and the human male cock couldn't both sustain sufficient amounts of blood to function at the same time.' This is Adam Black. As it is not a Mills & Boon book he does not have to bear a name like Sabre Valiant, which is a pity. Though perhaps Adam Black is brief and forbidding enough.

The Dark Highlander series offers it all: the glistening muscles of a fantasy blacksmith, copious sex, and patterned Scottish cloth when necessary.

'Adam arrived at 735 Monroe Street prepared for the woman to be skittish. After all, she'd run from him earlier, obviously intimidated by his overwhelming masculinity and epic sexuality.'

When warriors have traversed centuries they have had a lot of time to master satisfying intercourse between sword fights with other almost immortals, so their sexuality will usually be epic. The poor husband of the Karen Moning fan, with his average lifespan of 72, will never be able to compete, especially as the last decade can be plagued with erectile dysfunction and prostate problems.

'Far too many things to lose, Gabby thought glumly. Her virginity. Her world. Her life.' And once you've lost your virginity to an immortal highlander, it is very difficult to go back.

Do not get confused with Michele Sinclair's *Highlander's Bride* or *To Wed a Highlander*; these are just normal highlanders, without immortality but still with big pecs and lack of shirt.

What have we learned?

- How to make lasagne with melancholy
- The French eat horsemeat and, because of that, horse knee problems in the UK will increase
- Don't give up on cold-hearted vulcanologists; sometimes they just take time and a little dog death
- Love – just another of the brain's chemical imbalances that leads to irrational impulse buys and occasional murder

---

Further reading

Hot Boss, Boardroom Mistress by Natalie Anderson
Beloved Intruder by Patricia Wilson
Last Wolf Standing by Rhiannon Byrd
Crash by J.G. Ballard
– well you won't feel the benefit of pretty romance if you don't dabble in a bit of hideous car-accident-fixated sex.

An Interlude with the People's Princess

I have read one love story that does not end happily, and it is a true story. Rather than chronicling the first few weeks from unpleasant initial meeting to clinch, it deals with the last twenty-four hours before death. It was also found in the PDSA shop, but there are no vets here.

The book was inspired by a woman who kept the publishing industry, as well as the tea towel, commemorative plate and hairdressing industries, very busy in life and in death.

The whole nation was in love with Diana,[1] so she is one of the few people who would be considered worthy of a book dealing with her last twenty-four hours.

After her death, publishers knew that they must leave a dignified time for grieving before filling shop tables with

---

1 I say the nation was in love with her; the month leading up to her death saw the newspapers revelling in front-page stories about a princess whoring herself to a man who was swarthy. The nation was disgusted with its blonde princess, then it started weeping after her unfortunate death, perhaps as much out of shame at itself as pity for the dead and bereaved. Some commentators say it was her death that saw Britons finally revealing their emotions, but it was more a nation finally outing itself as hypocrites.

glossy memories. So they had a minute's silence after the news of her death on Radio 4, then called their jacket designers and hacks.

With *Diana: The Last 24 Hours* by Allan Silverman, Diana joins Elvis Presley, Marilyn Monroe and Abraham Lincoln in the select group considered either worthy or profitable enough to have their final day scrutinised and collated into loose fact and conjecture.

Allan was an investigative reporter for *Rolling Stone* magazine and also author of *Rock Hudson: Gay Giant* and *Sinatra: Rat King*, which might suggest taste and decency aren't his strong suits, which is itself probably best if your work requires you to muse over a warm corpse.

Allan somehow manages to piece together exactly what happened in those last hours of Diana and Dodi Fayed's lives. The intimate details within the book either mean that MI5 were constantly monitoring the princess and Allan had a mole, or that he has psychic powers. His tale is one of 'hedonistic pleasure', 'dilettantes' and 'love nests'.

'Diana has placed one of her teddy bears on top of a mound of fancy cushions. In the marbled bathroom the lovers have hung their two peach-coloured towelling his and hers robes side by side.' If you're going to fill a book with just twenty-four hours, then you'll need to follow the romantic fiction rule of 'excess extraneous information engorges chapters'. But does this detail mean something more? Is Allan ruminating on the fact that their gowns were hung side by side? Doesn't it perhaps mean that they were most definitely in love? Or does it mean that hooks for dressing gowns are normally side by side?

There is a love poem inscribed in silver from Dodi and a gold cigar cutter to him inscribed 'Love Diana', but these are not merely precious metals: 'The metals may be seen as implying the marriage of the moon and sun. Diana is the lunar goddess, and Dodi the solar king.'

This book may not be reliable reportage, but *Diana: The Last 24 Hours* is a Mills & Boon for those who have been waiting for one that ends in unfortunate death.

6

New Age

[(or X)]

Just imagine, that's what John Lennon asked us
to do. And Jewelle St James did just that.

Alan Twigg

Keep an open mind, but not so open your brains
fall out.

Anon

Some sort of energy . . . or a ghost . . . or magic elf . . . or something

The books discussed in this chapter win second place in the
'books I have flung furthest across a room in umbrage'
competition.

As the grip of religion has weakened its incense-swing-
ing hold, minds have become open to all manner of
preposterous propositions that gladly mix druidery, dance
and crystal-licking. I've been kept awake into the small

hours at music festivals by loud voices waffling on outside my tent about earth energies, the memory of water, and how we only use ten per cent of our brains. According to the droning diablo juggler and his paraffin-infused stilt-walker pal, psychics are the lucky ones who have trained the other ninety per cent of their mind, and it seems that bit is for ghost chattering. I have come to realise there is some truth in this, and that is that people who say we only use ten per cent of our brainpower only use ten per cent of their brains.

Defenders of traditional religion are always eager to quote G.K. Chesterton's 'Once you stop believing in God you believe in anything.' This presupposes that people who remove God from their life have to replace it with another blue blanket made of nettles and fertility chalk giants.[1] It's a quotation whip to flay the backs of secularists. Most of the people I've met who check their chakras on a daily basis are also keen on some god or other. Tony Blair may have come out as a Catholic, but he also mixed his Catholicism with nonsensical rebirthing ceremonies and assorted voodoo. Once you start believing in God, then you've opened up a whole elaborate casket of daft dogma, from wizards to wonky-headed star sign idiocies. And if you can persuade someone to buy a potion made from the nostalgia of bark, then selling them books should be a doddle. The charity shop shelves are rarely short of a New Age section. One might hope that the New Age shelves are so busy because many people read the books and immediately throw them into their charity shop box as their intelligence is so insulted. Sadly, I think it's more often that they are just

---

1 The Cerne Abbas Giant of Dorset had its penis turfed in during Victorian times to prevent ladies' fainting fits. It was also believed that his penis had got longer due to land slippage.

running out of shelf space due to the startling number of faith healers, fortune-tellers and fakirs who have hammered out another volume demonstrating the way to happiness via naked mountain dancing and chi tea. This means that a surprising number of my shelves are rammed with superstition, but I still can't walk through walls and my quantum leaps leave me with a bruised head. If I just keep reading through them I might be enlightened very soon.

Would you like to know How to Be a Supernatural Lover?

Want a crash course in Enhancing the Telepath Within?

Maybe you want heart-warming stories of reincarnated lovers brought back together through the mists of time and improbability?

I have walked into this vale of tears, ghost and 'self-knowledge'. I have tapped the table and tried to push the

Before reality TV was invented people had to make do with show business.

letters that would spell out a message from the other side. I have wondered if my angel is keeping an eye out for me and I know that I have not even scratched further than a cell's depth into the thick skin of the paranormal and New Age.

Whatever your desire, publishers possess an enormous advantage when it comes to peddling mystical balderdash to the public, because P.T. Barnum was correct in saying that no one ever lost a dollar underestimating the public. Or as W.C. Fields might have preferred, 'Never give a sucker an even break.'

My misspent youth with ectoplasm

One of the most important books of my youth – even more important than *The Young Ornithologist's Handbook* or *The Usborne Book of the Greeks* – was Arthur C. Clarke's *Mysterious World*, the tie-in to the must-watch programme of the day. Perhaps *Doctor Who and the Brain of Morbius* was a little more important, but only just. Inside Arthur's mysterious world, eager boys and girls would be amazed by phenomena that were totally inexplicable. There was literally no way of explaining them whatsoever – unless you applied a smidgen of scientific rigour, but then that would spoil everything, and anyway, scientific rigour doesn't come easy to a boy who wants to be on nodding terms with the Loch Ness Monster. How often did I muse on the haunting picture of Bigfoot, a snapshot from the film of this hairy Neanderthal nonchalantly strolling into woodland? How could I explain that footage of the hairy monster? Sure, my cynical adult eyes might see that it's clearly a man in a gorilla costume, but is it really? I mean, really really?

Yes, as it turns out, that's exactly what it is. The Bigfoot

Could this really have been Bigfoot, or a man with a glass eye in a gorilla outfit with a football helmet underneath to bulk it out? Only you can judge.

hoax was finally utterly debunked a few years ago when it was noted that one of the eyes of the Bigfoot in question was reflecting sunlight, something eyes don't do unless they are glass. The man the hoaxsters had dressed in a gorilla outfit with a football helmet to bulk out the head did indeed have one glass eye.

My child brain loved all this mysticism, though I was sometimes gripped by the fear that I might spontaneously combust in my bed leaving only a burnt toe and an enigma. Somehow I failed to notice that at the end of each chapter Arthur C. Clarke would almost always say, 'Well I don't really think there is any evidence to suggest that it is true.' I didn't hear; I wanted to believe.

Mothers normally hope that their sons become lawyers, property developers or occasionally organised crime bosses (that is, crime bosses who love their mums and buy them fabulous coats after kneecapping a dodgy furrier). However, the smart mother should know that all those careers are as nothing compared with encouraging your child into growing up to be a charlatan bamboozler. In terms of time invested and effort required versus possible financial gain, you'll be hard pushed to find employment that pays back as well as that of a charlatan bamboozler. The arena tours, the digital television shows, and book after book after book will leave you minted. And for every sceptic who tries to debunk you, you can offer the Liberace defence – 'I cried all the way to the bank.'

In flagrante with ghosts

'Dreaming provides essential nourishment for our souls.'

I have rarely if ever thought 'by crikey the scales have been lifted from my eyes' whilst reading books such as *How to Be a Supernatural Lover* by Sherron Mayes, also author of *Be Your Own Psychic*. If I did become a psychic I'd probably end up with a spirit guide who had had his tongue ripped out during the Spanish Inquisition.

Books often like to sell themselves with glowing reviews inside the front cover, and Sherron does just that. She has decided against putting in reviews from the *Times Literary Supplement*, the *Spectator* or the *New York Review of Books* in favour of reviews from Debbie, Alison, Sangeeta and Jon. Maybe they write for the *New York Review of Books*, the *Spectator* and the *Times Literary Supplement* but Sherron just happens to be on first-name terms with them. Sangeeta believes 'Your book is a Nobel Prize Winner.' I am not sure what Nobel Prize category that would be: science, peace or cockamamie.

Sherron's book promises to tune 'your inherent psychic powers to create a powerful bond of unconditional love', teach you 'telepathy to empathise and connect on a deeper level' and discover 'the intensely enriching benefits of psychic sex'.

Have you ever wondered if the bond you share with your partner might exist because you were together in a past life? Take another look at them; do they perhaps have the air of a seventeenth-century draper and don't you sometimes feel like an unfulfilled seamstress called Carlotta? It all becomes clear: you were Spanish frock-coat-makers in a past life. The reader discovers as their eyes glide over Sherron's sentences that physical attraction is often a delusion; the truth of why we are drawn to our future partner may have nothing to do with our twenty-first-century selves but with the souls within us that have traversed time. Dating just seems to get trickier and trickier. What's your favourite film? Do you have any hobbies? Would you like a glass of Chablis? What and who have you been in your past few lives?

The book opens gently with a series of quizzes, the type of thing that used to bulk out the pages of *Company Magazine* and that would help you decide if you were assertive enough or doing sex properly. (If your husband wants to beat you with a trowel do you: (a) say of course, that's fine, smash me in the face, I deserve it, whatever makes you happy darling; (b) question him briefly, but still let him wallop the trowel in your face; or (c) smack him in the nuts with a mallet. If you answered (a) you are not assertive enough; (b) you are a little assertive but need to try harder; (c) you are assertive.)

Sherron's quizzes deal with sensuality and psychic abilities, beginning with 'How sensual are you?'

(a) I am tactile, enjoy giving/receiving massage and making love if in a relationship.
(b) I don't enjoy being touched or touching others.

(c) I have been celibate for more than one year but still enjoy massage and affection.

Unfortunately, a 'none of the above' answer is not acceptable here. You're either celibate, frigid or sensual – there is no in between. In Sherron's current world, the variety of human possibilities can always be placed on a simple abc choice system.

And so the quiz continues with the options of YAY, NO! and hmmmm.

How self-critical are you?

(a) I often feel self-hatred and criticise my looks and how my life is; or I believe I am a bad person; or I am not aware of how I feel about myself . . .

That's a lot of ors in one option – are you evil or racked with loathing or have you forgotten to think about it? In the world of supernatural loving, these are all pretty much the same mental state.

By the time you reach the sixth level of quizzing (levels of quizzing are like circles of hell), you're ready to take on Higher Spiritual Love.

What are your views on God or spiritual experience?

The possibilities include 'I'm cynical. People who have so-called spiritual experiences are deluded and living in a fantasy world.' However, if you are the sort of person who spends £7.99 on a book entitled *How to Be a Supernatural Lover*, I believe it is unlikely you'll be ticking that box.

But is it right to be cynical about spiritual experience? Are many people living in a deluded fantasy world? Is there another dimension of existence, beyond human comprehension, where some semblance of our spirits may exist after our physical being is ash and soil? Let us examine the story of Jewelle St James.

The medieval loss of a Beatle

Sometimes it is only your past life that can explain your present feelings. This is what Jewelle St James discovered and enlarged on in her autobiographical book *All You Need Is Love*. When John Lennon died, Jewelle felt lost and emotionally traumatised, but couldn't quite put her finger on the reason why. She was not a great fan of the Beatles or of John Lennon's solo work, and she was no fan of his political stands. All became clear during a conversation with her psychic. The answer was surprisingly simple: Jewelle was John Lennon's lover in sixteenth-century Dorset. Once she knew this, her life became dedicated to finding out if this outlandish fable could be true.

Had John Lennon really once been an inhabitant of Dorset, possibly tending sheep? After much searching, spiritually and geographically, it turned out to be as true as any psychic's pronouncement. This led to Jewelle being more fulfilled and her husband filing for divorce, by now bored of forking out cash for his wife to find out if she had shagged a Beatle behind his back and before his birth (and her birth as well).

In *How to Be a Supernatural Lover*, Sherron Mayes explains what Jewelle has experienced. It seems that the spirit and higher mind are eternal, so your deeper essence will recognise the past love and draw you to this individual you used to frolic with near the castle moat. This can be proven with DNA research, apart from the fact that it can't.

'In previous lives your current love may have been your mother, father, child, lover or even worst enemy.' This alone is a very good reason for not dabbling in the world of supernatural love analysis. A relationship can really flounder if you find out that you were a Victorian prostitute and your partner used to be the lead suspect in the Jack the Ripper case. The only silver lining to that would be that your partner might have been a member of the royal family in his last incarnation.[2]

I see a tall, short, fat, thin, bald, hairy woman man in a hat or not

I'm not a great fan of the psychic medium. I see them as sucking cash from the desperate and bereaved while dancing on the graves of the dead. If someone rang you up pretending to be your dead grandmother, you'd slam down the phone and report them to the police as a nuisance caller. Put that same nuisance caller in a theatre dribbling out vague messages that could represent sixty-seven per cent of the population of the dead and we give them TV series and book deals.

'My name is Derek Acorah. I am a medium with clairaudient, clairvoyant and clairsentient gifts.' This trilogy of definitions are the three wise monkeys of the psychic world. Clairsentient means possessing the ability to hold an object and sense the energy surrounding it: 'As I hold this vase I get the sense that someone in your family liked flowers . . . or glazed pottery.' Clairvoyancy is your bog-standard seeing spirits, while if you are clairaudient, you have the ability to

---

2 Nowadays this member of the royal family is not really seen as the lead suspect in the Ripper case. The case will probably never close despite Patricia Cornwell's best efforts by snipping up a Walter Sickert painting. Walter Sickert is her favourite suspect, because he painted prostitutes and also had a deformed penis. Never trust a man with a deformed penis, though whether they are more likely to kill and disembowel I don't know, as the statistics are very hard to find.

hear voices, like Joan of Arc or Doris Stokes. In some cultures this is rightly thought of as a sign of lunacy rather than a skill.

Derek realised he had a power when he saw his dead grandad on the stairs. It may well be the most profitable meeting with a dead grandparent in the second half of the twentieth century. Would you too like to find ghosts like a professional spirit botherer? Follow Derek Acorah and you could be finding ghosts in your larder, attic and dirty laundry basket.

What do you need when you go off ghost-hunting? *Ghost Hunting with Derek Acorah* is the complete guide. Obviously it's best that you take your innate ability to pick up residual energies with you, but you will also need a torch. Derek reminds you that spirits can be mischievous and deliberately drain your batteries of energy, so take a couple of spare AAs in your back pocket. Like trainspotters, you will need a pen and paper to jot down which ghosts you've seen. Ghost-watchers can be very competitive, so hopefully you'll find some ghosts you haven't noted down before; again as for trainspotters, it's a bit dull if you keep seeing the same one. Whether it's the Onboard A Class 390 Tilting Electric Pendolino or the spirit of the young matchgirl who died of a nasty pox, repetitive sightings eventually lose their sheen. Cotton and tape are needed for sealing off rooms, and candles are required as their flickering suggests spirit activity. You will find a great deal of spirit activity in stone barns on moors, and open windows obviously allow loads of ghosts in. Some of the draughty ghosts are so powerful that they will blow a candle out. Ghosts are less likely to haunt well-insulated and double-glazed houses due to the difficulty of finding access.

The Boy Scouts may not yet have a badge for ghost-hunting, but the ghost-hunter must be prepared. On top of your tape, candle and cotton, you'll need walkie-talkies, a thermometer, an EMF meter, pendulums, dowsing rods, a camera, a tape recorder and a dog. This is not just mucking about; ghost-hunting is an exact science, except when it's tested by scientific standards, when it may appear to be a little inexact. Derek also recommends a bag of flour to sprinkle on the floor, as that detects ghost prints. Do ask permission of the owner before distributing flour all over their house, however, as the excitement of discovering the ghost of an ancient mariner soon subsides if you have to go hell for leather with the vacuuming the next day, and the woodprint of a peg-legged spirit can be really stubborn to get out.

When Derek enters a building where a really gory murder has taken place, he is often hit by 'the horror of the situation'. 'Residual energy – the more emotional or tragic the events which have taken place in a property, the stronger energies that are absorbed by the building.' The advantage of investigating a house where a gory murder happened is it is more likely to have been in the newspapers. For some reason it is often easier to pick up vivid details from the residual energy in the brickwork if you might have read about it in the local or national press. At no point would I suggest Derek is using his memory rather than his powers, or indeed that he might use research rather than just going blindly in; that would be cynical. Derek doesn't just sense gory murders; he can also sense manufacturing in the right environment. When he goes into cotton mills he can hear the sound of the looms and see the children working. Most people can sense if somewhere was a cotton mill due to the building clearly being in the shape of an old cotton mill, and the sign saying 'Ye Olde Cotton Mill', but Derek really does have the sound of a loom in his head.

Happy haunting to you

Derek's book goes on to describe 'anniversary ghosts' that pop back at the same time every year. On 19 May near Blickling Hall in Norfolk, you can always enjoy some head-less horses drawing a coach with Anne Boleyn cradling her bloodied head, which is much better than the Lord Mayor's Show or the simple act of morris dancing.

Then there's your walking-through-walls ghost and the spirit people. Spirit people are the travellers of the beyond; they can go anywhere they want. Unlike travelling folk who take human form in old vans, they are less likely to be campaigned against by small-minded councils and news-papers.

Derek also has the power to know if his cats are OK when they've gone for a long wander. Rumours suggest that the number of psychic meetings you have attended is often in proportion to the number of cats you own. Dog owners prefer fortune-tellers.

The mischievous dead in Dubai

Before moving on, a brief warning story for anyone who might learn so much from Derek that they carve out a career as an international psychic. It appears that spirit guides visiting Arab nations may find that the sun on the back of their mystical neck can lead to slips of the tongue and unfortunate forays into areas best left alone. A popular psychic was booked to appear in Dubai. Before going on, the promoter wished to give him some advice on how to deal with the audience, who he pointed out might be slightly different from the people he would normally play to in Burnley or Brocklehurst. Our psychic assured the promoter he didn't need any advice as he was a professional and knew exactly what to do. He took to the stage and looked out at the sea of burkha-wearing women who made up the audience, then pressed his fingers to his head, ready to receive messages for those before him. His eyes flickered – a message had arrived. The show was truly ready to begin.

'Has someone here had an abortion?'

Suffice to say, it was one of the shorter psychic medium performances in the Middle East. Now, have you heard the one about TV psychic Colin Fry and the message of the cheese and pickle sandwich?[3] Once you have 'the gift', the life of the psychic can become a log flume's worth of adventure, some of them even beverage based.

'It was national tea week and one of the producers of the show thought it would be a good idea to get a psychic in to do a tea-leaf reading.'

The Psychic Adventures of Derek Acorah was my next Acorah purchase. I needed something to read now my wife had banished me to the shed while she vacuumed up the self-raising flour from our sitting room carpet. *Psychic Adventures* is a florid account of Derek's most enlightening escapades in old music halls, dank cellars and on the cobbles of Coronation Street. The dead greats of *Coronation Street* still haunt the Granada studios. Both Doris Speed and Pat Phoenix, the soap's late matriarchs, come in ghostly form to rattle doorknobs and tinker with light switches as

---

3 See addendum for the full story of how Colin Fry found himself stymied by his spirit guide's insistence on the importance of cheese and pickle sandwiches in the life of the dead.

a dire warning to the producers to treat the living cast kindly.

Derek is also pretty sure he knows who Jack the Ripper, or Jack the Rippers, is/are. One of them has facial hair and is very conscious of time. So now we just need to work out whether any Victorian gentlemen grew beards or moustaches, and what sort of murderer would be in a hurry after a bit of garrotting and dissection.

Feeling the burn of the psychic mind

A well-written psychic book is also biologically and psychologically accurate. As Carl Rider says, 'The head is very much the leader of the team that makes up the top half of the body.' Other scientists might go so far as to say that the head is the leader of the team that makes up the whole body, but this is still just a theory. What if you are not able to access the magic powers in your head and are stuck with that humdrum ten per cent of your brain that the rest of the unenlightened have to stick to? There is no need to panic. Carl Rider's book will teach you how to exercise your brain so that it can hear ghosts, or spot bricks that are packed with them.

Your Psychic Power and How to Develop It is a Charles Atlas course in turning your brain into a powerful psychic muscle-man. In just 192 pages the reader will be taught psychic insight, clairvoyant seeing, tea-leaf reading and supernatural perception. Exercises include 'walking backwards', 'head watching' and 'thought pie'.

There is so much to learn from Carl Rider that a précis is not simple.

'If you notice a man fishing by a pond, watch him for a while.' Carl states that people are intensely drawn to fire, water, air and earth, but they don't know it. I think some people do know it. I am drawn to water quite frequently during the day; it has been an enormous help after spending much of my youth dehydrated. I am drawn to the earth via gravitational pull; sometimes I stop noticing that but thankfully gravity continues to work without my effort. I am drawn to fire whenever I want to toast a crumpet. I am drawn to air, particularly hot air, whenever I notice a New Age section in a shop.

There remains a world of the mind that is inexplicable. As Carl states, the phone might ring and you know exactly who it is, sometimes even before the person on the other end has started speaking! How could that be? Some may say it is because we have a finite number of acquaintances, that there are certain times some people are most likely to ring, and that we remember only the occasions we knew who it was before we picked up the phone and don't notice when this didn't happen. These people are called sceptics. They ruin everything and are not wanted in Uri Geller's front row.

If you want to know about psychic sneezing, and how the control of the sneeze may help control the mind, then Carl Rider's book makes having a cold more interesting, if a little frightening. Remember, sometimes what has just shot out of your nose is only mucus, not ectoplasm.

Coleridge's chemical beyond

Psychic mediums have had booms and slumps since the mid-nineteenth century, when two young girls discovered a couple of things: firstly they could click their toe joints, and secondly they could pass it off as the sound of the spirit world, thus turning a physical abnormality into a money-spinning celebrity generator.

The next boom was after the First World War. There had been so much slaughtering of youth that the desolate and grieving were looking for any hint that this was not the end. Ninety years on, and the psychic boom times are here again. As I've said before, it doesn't matter how much the best of the human race discover, from the mapping of the human genome to quantum mechanics; most people are hungry to be bamboozled. Bamboozle science is normally far easier to understand than particle physics.

Here is the dedication from a psychic book that is a cut above the rest, published during the middle period of psychic heydays:

'This work is dedicated to the heroes of war – those of the battlefield and those of the fireside – to all who gave nobly to the cause of truth . . . there is no death.'

Samuel Taylor Coleridge, 1918.

Samuel Taylor Coleridge, 1918? Have you spotted the peculiarity?

Surely Coleridge died in 1834, so how has he managed to pen a dedication to a book published over eighty years after his death?

This dedication is from *The 20th Plane: A Psychic Revelation* by Albert Durrant Watson (McClelland and Stewart). Albert used his psychic powers to interview the not dead, including Coleridge, who was kind enough to transmit his dedication from the plane. The interviewees are an enviable selection of the great – Shelley, Dorothy Wordsworth, Disraeli, Lincoln, Shakespeare – and the author's mother. It is through his mother that we have our initial questions about the afterlife answered.

What do the not dead see? 'It's everything we see and more.'

Is there night? 'It is a soft pink twilight.'

What do they eat? 'We absorb chemicals.'

You may still be wondering what these chemicals are, so Albert's mother gets Coleridge to answer this: 'Proteins. The liquid juice of a rice product. A beef extract made of a synthetic meat product . . . the distinction between our food and your food is one of vibration.'

As Heisenberg was exploring uncertainty and Schrodinger was pondering on the mortality of his cat, Watson was discovering the vibrating lunches of the world beyond.

There may be readers who see the prescience of Watson's protein food revelation; it does seem vaguely similar to the food tubes stocked by NASA for the space missions, and space missions might be viewed as journeys into the beginning of a beyond that might eventually reach the Twentieth Plane, perhaps via plunging into a black hole. Once we 'pass over' we become astronauts; many young boys' dreams may become true in death (sorry, 'not death'). While men of my age often dreamt as children of being astronauts, the astronaut dream is no longer a common aspiration amongst the young. Perhaps this is because they heard the story of mission commander Frank Bormann. Bormann suffered a bout of diarrhoea and vomiting on his space mission, which the crew had to clear up, bit by bit, as it floated around the spaceship. That never happened to Dan Dare and doesn't happen to Coleridge either.

So did Abraham Lincoln regret his assassination? 'No. Not half as much as Mary Todd.'[4]

---

4 Wife of Abraham Lincoln.

Albert Durrant Watson has a vivid imagination combined with literary knowledge, and although he has not contributed much to understanding the science of the afterlife, he has created a fascinating literary curiosity. He picks up a few less obvious insights from these literary icons, discovering from Coleridge that there are no trains in the afterlife, and from Shelley – who met Albert's mum at a talk he did on the Twentieth Plane – that Dorothy Wordsworth's hair colour is 'the sun burnished by Jove'. George Eliot, meanwhile, gives some writing tips for hopeful young novelists who are sitting around the table with Albert. Edgar Allan Poe pops up briefly too – so it appears the Twentieth Plane is quite a coffee salon of the erudite.

After this literary discussion we return to Albert's chats with his mother.

Is Byron with you? 'He is in the valley straightening his crooked leg.'

You mean his club foot? 'No, I am speaking figuratively.'

What is the figurative crooked leg of Byron? Just as previously stated about quantum physics, in the beyond sometimes answers merely generate far more questions.

'I am anchored here like the ships of Drake,' says Shakespeare of his life on the Twentieth Plane, before being asked, with Shelley, what he thinks of Albert's mum. She is as 'noble as the soul of Joan of Arc' in Shelley's opinion.

There seem to be no hoi polloi on the Twentieth Plane. Albert never gets through to Reg the chimneysweep or George the sewer rat killer; unlike most house parties, he is never delayed by tittle-tattlers he doesn't fancy speaking to. His mother has a strict door policy. The average soul may still be stuck on the banal Fifth Plane.

Fortunately for literary scholars, this book is still available on a print-on-demand basis from the United States. When your tutor asks, 'Just how did you come to this conclusion about Hamlet?' you can simply quote the words of William Shakespeare himself, as spoken from the Twentieth Plane: 'Hamlet was not insane. He was as lucid as the personification of all the truth in life . . . now as I said, to be or not to be is the question: shall I get myself gone or linger?'

Albert has no hesitation in pointing out facts that can be verified from the spirits' pronouncements. When Sappho says she was born six centuries before Christ, Albert states that this is correct (Sappho is actually on the Hundredth Plane, but she is speaking via the Twentieth, where there is better reception). When Shelley says that the full story of his drowning can be found in the *Britannica*, Albert states that this has been confirmed. This might suggest that the spirits are offering no more than what can already be found out by purchasing a good set of reference books, but don't forget, we have learnt things about afterlife drinks that were unavailable to us until Albert tapped in. Albert also checks his Sappho and Shelley facts to ensure he is not being duped by a con spirit who is just a run-of-the-mill ghost rather than someone famous or important or worth the effort of a seance. Many a psychic has discovered halfway through a conversation that they are not talking to Christopher Marlowe: 'Yeah, sorry, I'm a sewer rat killer, it's just you never talk to us so I thought I'd spice up my afterlife by disguising myself as the author of *The Jew of Malta*. Now, are there any pest control questions I can answer?'

Whatever you may think of Albert Durrant Watson – and as a poo-poohing sceptic I fear that these conversations

may not be the true words of deceased poets and play-
wrights – there is a lovable eloquence to what he has
turned out. It is rare to find such imagination in the works
of modern mediums, even those who have a psychic link
to your cat, dog or guinea pig.

What have we learned?

- Dead Native Americans have forgiven the British for decimating them by helping pasty psychics contact the other side
- Your current husband may only have been drawn to you because he killed you with a butcher's knife in a previous life
- If there is an afterlife and you get there, there's no milk and honey, just some kind of beef protein, so if you're debating whether to live a good life or not, it might not be worth the effort

---

Further reading

Secrets from the Afterlife by Colin Fry
The Only Psychic Power Book You'll Ever Need: Discover Your Innate Ability to Unlock the Mystery of Today and Predict the Future Tomorrow: Develop Your Innate Ability to Predict the Future by Michael Hathaway

Any books about how angels are watching us that make you ponder if the enlightenment even happened.

The Treatment of Cats by Homeopathy by K. Sheppard

7

Columnists

(or the fury of Fleet Street)

> The stupid are cocksure and the intelligent are full of doubt.
>
> Bertrand Russell

> To leave a child unsupervised in front of a television set is no less dangerous than giving it neat gin, or putting it within reach of narcotics.[1]
>
> Peter Hitchens

The cocksure invite you on a handcart ride into their hell

It was promised that once I got older I would be lazily right wing, moaning about immigrants and nodding at the *Daily Telegraph* letters page. Annoyingly, something went wrong and I find myself too left for the *Guardian* and therefore

---

1 This is still as yet untested by scientists, though there are rumours that the animal testing laboratory in Porton Down have forced calves to watch *CSI New York* in one room, while lambs were left on a whisky drip in another, though this was just for larks.

deemed insane in polite company. I have been forced to give up reading newspapers for the sake of my heart, though I do occasionally read the *Morning Star* in the Waitrose café with a croissant. The revolution will be here just as soon as I've chosen my jam. What a quandary – blackberry or apricot. When I do forgetfully pick up the newspaper lying opposite me on a train seat, the rabies returns. This happens especially if it is a Monday copy of the *Daily Mail* and Melanie Phillips' column is there.

I will not describe Melanie Phillips, as the libel lawyers will cut most of it out and I would rather have no description than watered-down fury. In 2009 she wrote a column about gay and lesbian parenting in which she stated that 'the fact is, there has been no proper research into lesbian and gay parenting'. Some people were quite cross and complained, as the fact is there has been quite a lot. The Press Complaints Commission came to the rescue: 'While the column had been phrased in stark terms – the journalist had made one claim which was prefaced by "the fact is", for example – the author's claims would nonetheless be recognised by readers as comment rather than unarguable fact.'

So fans of George Orwell will be happy to know that we live in a world where 'the fact is' means 'I believe that', where truth is opinion. John Major's England was meant to be inspired by Orwell, but the Orwell of ladies cycling to communion and warm beer, not of newspeak and choco rations. Tony Blair moved his nostalgia forward to Carnaby Street and Swinging London, before progressing with Gordon Brown's help to the depression of the early eighties. Whatever period Britain is in, the national character is really the same: constant fury, normally over entirely the wrong thing. That is where the newspaper columnist comes in.

Why be bothered by torture atrocities sanctioned by your country's government when there are so many speed cameras around that you can't drive your big shiny car at 110 mph? It's so unfair. Have you seen the new rise in children living in poverty? Leave me alone, I am trying to write an article on how wheelie bins are spoiling my view of Walton-on-Thames. All these columnists can profitably turn their daily diatribes into handily bound collections for the Christmas book market. And not long after Christmas, they find themselves in the bookshops I frequent.

Oi! It's Garry Bushell!

Today's newspapers feature less news backed up by more comment than ever before. It seems gathering news is costly, but thinking about it a bit and then writing a deliberately contrary column is much cheaper. Enter Garry Bushell, a man who has been infuriating liberal sensibilities for three decades now. *The World According to Garry Bushell* is a collection of his blogs and musings on the ills of society and them idiots in charge. There were four copies of the book in a neat row in the Marylebone Oxfam in London. It seemed an odd place to find it; Marylebone High Street is a Terence Conran/Laura Ashley sort of street. I bought the one that was £2.95. The bookseller looked at me with a hint of disdain, even though I deliberately bought a Kurt Vonnegut too to try and dilute the judgement. I stopped myself from making some statement that would make it clear that I was not a Garry Apostle: 'Oh isn't he terrible, it's a joke present for Michael Foot. I don't know why he has a go at gays, it makes me furious. Actually, I am buying it to burn it and I'll be back for the other three very soon. *Vive la Révolution!*'

Bushell is as English as Benny Hill's cheeky leer. Like many columnists seen as feeding the right-wing, right-thinking, lager-drinking know-it-all who smells of pork salt, he started on the left, training as a journalist on the *Socialist Worker*. He does not contribute to that newspaper any more.

According to Bushell, 'the far left and their allies – human rights lawyers, the refugee council and other members of the *Guardian*-reading classes[2] – have managed to stifle the immigration debate for years'. Damn those human rights lawyers. If there is one thing we should all hate, it's human rights, a ridiculous idea mainly for the benefit of blacks and lesbians and tawny scroungers pretending they lost their left eye while being tortured in their homeland. Amnesty International and all those do-gooders nattering on about global nastiness. The trouble with do-gooders is they always want to do good, bloody busybodies – Martin Luther King, Desmond Tutu, Joanna Lumley, kindly meddlers all. Why don't we have more news celebrating the do-badders and the do-nothings? It might make us feel better about ourselves.

Before you get the wrong impression, I ought to point out that I have a soft spot for Garry Bushell. Like Bushell I am a fan of the British variety act, so much so that I once worked with Bernie Clifton and his ostrich. The ostrich goosed me, but felt beaks don't smart. I also like rockney musical stars Chas 'n' Dave, who I supported, even performing real jokes, the sort that end 'I don't know, but the Pope's his chauffeur.' My other reason for liking Bushell is

---

2 When will the hacks stop saying the *Guardian* is left wing? It's more of a lifestyle magazine for people on the centre right who occasionally Tippex their Remembrance Day poppy because they want to celebrate peace not war and who own kitchens whose colour scheme must match the dish of the day.

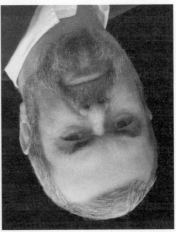

© Brian Smith/Rex Features

Only Victorian face-reading experts can know what this truly means.

my enjoyment of people who have heads that can be placed upside down and still appear almost identical.

Bushell is a well-read man. In his collected columns and blogs he quotes Churchill and Stalin, Valerie Solanas and Bradley Walsh. He energetically skewers political correctness gone mad and includes political correctness gone fictional. Reading Bushell and others of his ilk can be a fun game, and one that can actually be stretched to the reading of any daily newspaper. Read the piece, guess which bits are true, then put in a few hours of research and find out just how much, if any of the story, has a toe in the truth. So with Bushell you'll find out outrageous things about our society such as how a government quango rejected 'The Three Little Pigs' because it might offend Muslims: 'In reality, no Muslims were offended. This was another case of nit-wit white liberals taking offence on their behalf.'

Or was it? It's at this point that a little research might come in useful. Could it actually be that a publisher had its title rejected because the quango didn't deem it quite up to the standard required? Fortunately for Bushell, some mild comments were made when someone on the quango mentioned Muslims. This helped the publisher get a foothold into some free publicity with a charming bit of spin that would warm the cockles of the politically-correct-gone-mad lobby's cold hearts. You will have noticed there are no longer any talking pigs in children's TV or books, unless you open a children's book or turn on Channel Five every morning, then there are. Still, wouldn't there be more if the Muslim-loving, half-witted white liberals didn't keep messing about and crying over the smell of bacon? It's almost illegal to buy *The Tale of Pigling Bland*; the only thing that stops it being illegal is that it is not.

Those lucky gays

'Their crime was to have disturbed an outdoor gay orgy in a public park.'

What the hell! You're telling me that the law is on the side of gay public orgies?

Sometimes you really can't argue against Bushell's ire. On the face of it, this particular issue really is ridiculous. It seems that the law is on the side of men pulling each other off in leather thongs near a children's play area, and against anyone who might suggest that cottaging so openly is wrong as children run away weeping. In *The World According to Garry Bushell*, the reader is incensed to discover that a group of heroic firefighters who accidentally shone a torch on some rampant homos got themselves demoted and fined. What the hell kind of world do we live in where

the villains are firefighting heroes, and poofs can bleat invasion of privacy when they are banging away in the
undergrowth?

The law is an ass, or is it?

It has to be tough writing a column once a week, sometimes twice, so that's why the writer needs to make it easy
on themselves with a few rules. The first rule of the columnist is 'Do not research anything for very long.' The
moment you check a little background you may well find
that your story is too dull to make your readers' temples
pulse and pound. It may be a story with sides, and that is
confusing for the reader, who wants a very simple morality tale as the fried egg yolk drips onto the page below.
They are not looking for a philosophical debate. No time
for that on the 7.23 from Stevenage.

So Bushell's readers will be pleased or perhaps uneasy to
know that the world he bemoans in his column is not actually the world we live in. It seems there are some factual
errors in the piece. It appears that these firemen were not
punished for affecting the erections of the copulating
homosexuals with torchlight. The real reason that they
were reprimanded and investigated seems to be that while
on duty, they decided to take a fire engine off to a well-
known dogging area and shine their torches at the rutting
fools for a bit of a laugh. Unfortunately, 'Misuse of Fire
Engines for Peeping Tom Jollies' isn't nearly as good a story.

What makes journalistic collections so much fun is the
distance from the writing of the column to the re-reading
in book form. By the time the news is cold, it is easier to
find a few alternative explanations for the murky tales of
banned Little Red Riding Hoods and free dildos for lesbians.

Bushell's acerbic swipes at TV, the writing that really

made him a celebrity, are great fun, especially as it is much easier to check the authenticity. His attack on *Cosmetic Surgery Live*, and its televised anal bleaching, is far more entertaining and, I can vouch from having actually seen this horror show, mainly true. You never know with Bushell: one moment you're furious, the next you are agreeing with him and feeling as if you may have sullied yourself. So just as the reader agrees with Bushell about the vileness of modern telly, they find themselves sighing resignedly at a chapter titled 'Merry Winterval' – that old banned chestnut on an open fire. Every year the Merry Winterval proves that it doesn't matter how often a story is proven to be factually inaccurate or just plain wrong, if a journalist likes it, he'll sick it up again.

According to Bushell and his compadres, schools are banning nativity plays, it's impossible to buy a greetings card that says Christmas on it, and Birmingham has retitled Christmas Winterval. Once again I put this to another fact-based test and came up with a problem. You can easily buy 'Merry Christmas' cards; you don't even have to wink at the cashier, who takes you into the back room of W.H. Smith and unlocks the secret cupboard made for the illegal believers. I couldn't find a single primary school teacher who wasn't putting on a nativity play in December. Birmingham still had Christmas. Winterval was an entirely separate matter; it was a seasonal festival of shopping, as Birmingham City Council decided they needed a new angle to woo consumers into the city centre when it was a bit chilly.

As we've established, though, facts do not matter in this world, and ten years on from Winterval, the Archbishop of Wales made the headlines by blaming such things on 'atheistic fundamentalists'. If he had done a little more research, he might have realised the Winterval question was all based on a myth, but then if he took that a little further, he might have found a few other core beliefs of his coming a cropper.

Thanks to Bushell, I now know also that Muscadet is the gay drink of choice: 'Television is so relentlessly gay, it's a wonder the *Radio Times* doesn't come with a pink Versace wrap and a free glass of Muscadet.' There certainly are some gays on television, and the issue of homosexuality has always touched a raw nerve in Bushell's goat. He was never very keen on Channel 4 showing Derek Jarman films, although it seems hard to understand why it would bother him. It's not as if many *Sun* readers would be drawn to a film about a gay martyr that is entirely in Latin and broadcast at midnight. If they were, it would seem a little unfair to then be outraged – 'I thought I was just going to see a nice film about a gay martyr; I really wasn't expecting exposed cock, and so much of it. What if my television screen could be seen from outside and my house was near a children's play area and the film was on at three p.m.?'

How gay is your television?

To test the veracity of the statement 'television is relentlessly gay', I open the TV listings for the day I am writing this.

BBC 1's morning is all about buying homes. Some are under the hammer, some are to buy or not to buy. Is buying or selling a house gay? I think it would be fair to say that property purchase is omnisexual, though I would have to concede that interior decoration was until quite recently considered to be more the thing for women and gay men.

Television has certainly used this to its advantage, often employing harridans or camp men when trying to generate viewers for their primetime 'what the hell do you think your house looks like?' slots. If the daytime presenters this morning were gay, they were not so relentlessly gay that there could be any certainty.

The afternoon offers up *Diagnosis Murder* with Dick Van Dyke – a hospital-based crime show. But is it gay, or not gay? Outwardly, it is not particularly gay, BUT Dick Van Dyke was in musicals so perhaps it is a bit gay. Male nurses have often been considered to be more likely to be homosexual than many other professions too.

Then we come to *The Weakest Link* presented by Anne Robinson, a former alcoholic who has since had plastic surgery and dresses like a science fiction supervillainess. She is therefore a 'survivor', and hence her show is gay.

The news is not gay. Neither is *Holby City*, *The One Show* or *EastEnders*, though *EastEnders* has sometimes had a character who is gay, so it's a bit gay sometimes and the previous statement about male nurses being more likely to be gay than male scaffolders still stands.

Finally, I encounter *Torchwood* – oh good heavens. The main star is gay and the series was conceived by a gay man; it is therefore gay. It is also broadcast in primetime, adding further points to Bushell's gay barometer of television.

So all in all, a summer Tuesday BBC 1 schedule is quite gay.

I can't seem to find anything very or slightly gay on BBC 2, however, with the possible exception of a *Murder She Wrote* repeat, which is a little camp, and *Newsnight*, which can be a little camp if the interviews get catty. But camp and gay are not necessarily one and the same, so BBC 2 fails dismally if it is attempting to surf the presumed gay zeitgeist.

Channel 4, once home to any form of deviant behaviour according to the newspapers in the 1980s, offers very little. There's a nun movie, which in the hands of some directors could be sapphic and racy, but this one is *Black Narcissus* by Powell and Pressburger so scores zero. ITV seems to offer nothing either – *The Jeremy Kyle Show* is as heterosexual as a street fight in Buxton where a girl with vomit on her teeth is shouting 'Just leave it, Keith' as her boyfriend lunges blindly at air that has insulted him; while Channel 5's triple bill of *CSI* does little to further the cause of a gay invasion of television..

In summation, rather than being 'relentlessly gay', television sometimes has some gay men on it and an occasional lesbian during outdoor sports coverage. But again, that idea for a column doesn't sound nearly as good.

So to summarise Bushell, by all means read and enjoy the TV criticism, but take care with the politics, as most columnists take a holocaust-denial approach to writing in this area – they know the conclusion they want; now they just have to find the facts or hearsay that will back them up.

As I am now middle-aged, it would be disingenuous of me not to admit that as well as stroking my chin to Bushell, I have also nodded in agreement while reading books by Richard Littlejohn and Peter Hitchens, particularly when it comes to quotes like this:

'I spent ten years of my life working as an industrial correspondent, coming into daily contact with many senior managers responsible for running our industries. I was left with the impression that very few of them could run a bath, let alone a company with a multi-million-pound turnover.' (Littlejohn.)

'The Queen Mother has always struck me as a complete waste of space.' (Littlejohn again.)

'"Doctor" Gillian McKeith, as welcome in my living room as the Ebola virus.' (Bushell.)

'I hurt my bottom when I fell out of that wheelbarrow.' (Hitchens.)

All genuine quotations from the authors, though I may have misremembered the last one. It may have read more like this:

'Britain had been living on her Victorian inheritance, an elderly but rather grand steam locomotive, hiding her leaky valves behind shiny paint and well-polished brass.'

But just as I think, 'Why, these men are gurus and emperors who could lead us from civilisation's collapse,' I stumble on the sentence that brings my shrine-building to an abrupt halt. It's like reading a book by David Icke. Your nodding is gaining momentum as you read some of his neo-con and George W. Bush based conspiracy theories; then your head suddenly crashes into the wall of 'and Prince Philip is a reptile'. I met David Icke a few years ago when we shared a sofa on a digital TV show. Afterwards I suggested that it might be worth dropping the reptile bit, but he was quite certain that this element really was the crux of the matter.

Thus spake Littlejohn

In my opinion, the highest-paid, most ill-thought-out reactionary columnist with delusions of being Jonathan Swift is Richard Littlejohn. For the vaguely left-wing comedian with his or her own delusions of being a wannabe Bill Hicks, Littlejohn is the first port of call when looking for a rant to draw applause from a similarly leftie crowd. I was one of those comedians. Even the *Guardian* picked me up on it, though they hadn't realised that by that point I'd dropped the *Daily Mail* gags and moved on to shouting about the *Guardian*'s obsequious interviews with New Labour MPs – 'Gordon Brown meets me in the garden of Number Ten. He looks like a man without a care in the world. His skin is peachy and fresh' is one *Guardian* quote that particularly sticks in my mind. After years of fearing that the Prime Minister was coming out in boils, burst capillaries and dry patches, the *Guardian* reader's fear for Brown's skin was assuaged.

I had not thought of Littlejohn for a while when one day I was browsing in a west London Oxfam window and decided there was a book I must have: *Littlejohn's Britain* by Richard Littlejohn. There were three reasons it ended up in my bag. Firstly, it was his latest book, and it was in an Oxfam window. Secondly, I enjoyed the fact that by purchasing the book, money might go to buying a donkey in the Congo. By mere guesswork from reading Littlejohn, I have a suspicion that he is not as keen on charities that help build drinking wells in Africa as he is on those that build ornamental wells remembering First World War soldiers in Stoke Poges.

But there was one reason above all others that made this a must-have, and a limited edition. Someone had drawn a speech bubble coming out of Littlejohn's mouth on the cover that simply said 'I'm a twat'. It was written in cheerily cheap biro ink, and whatever hand had done this had etched it in with gusto. As a fan of modern art, I felt it had to be mine. I accidentally giggled childishly as I placed the defaced book on the counter. The elderly shop assistant was appalled at the defacing.

'This is terrible. Would you like money off?' he enquired.

'No, charge me more,' I merrily replied. 'It's bespoke.'[3]

Many weeks later, while performing at a gig and talking about the book, I discovered that the 'I'm a twat' had been added by someone who worked in the shop. I like it when charity and Tourette's come together. This was the same charity shop where I heard two old women angrily flipping through a multitude of paperbacks before furiously opining, 'The price of these books is ridiculous. Oxfam is worse than the Cancer.'

Littlejohn is the voice of the people, as long as they are people who like burning books and attacking the houses of paediatricians.[4] 'While the incestuous worlds of Westminster and the chattering classes were working themselves into a lather of indignation, in saloon bars and supermarket queues the length and breadth of Britain, most people were wondering what all the fuss was about. What really frightens the bien pensants is that they know millions of people in Britain think in exactly the same way as Evans.'

Have you ever chattered? Or have you managed to live a life of dignified, monkish silence, perhaps only using language for important declamations? Littlejohn has – he is no member of the chattering classes, even if his job does rely on the elevation of tittle-tattle to news. So who is this Evans that the people of Britain will empathise with as the leftists and Chablis-drinkers splutter?

Evans was the MP for Welwyn and Hatfield who demanded that 'black bastard' rapists should be castrated, and

---

3 A minor revolutionary act, but it's a start. Next time we up the ante and use indelible marker.
4 During the 'every one of your neighbours is probably a paedophile' period of British history in AD2000, a female paediatrician returned home to find her house vandalised because the angry mob, the good honest people who are not the horrid chattering classes, had confused paedophile with paediatrician.

called his opponent 'a single girl with three bastard children'. He lost his seat to the mother with all those bastards because the chattering classes of Hatfield don't like straight talkers. The people of Hatfield had obviously been smudged by the *Guardian* joss stick, tofu, Che Guevara poster mentality.

At the end of 2006, Littlejohn was frustrated by the Guardianistas again. It seems some people had felt a little sorry for the five prostitutes killed in the Ipswich area. Nincompoops. Did they not know that strangulation is just an average risk of the job, like miners getting black lung, and anyway the victims were 'disgusting, drug-addled street whores'.

I would say that reading sniffy, paranoid and delusional books by right-wing demagogues is my guilty pleasure, apart from the fact that I don't get very much pleasure out of them and I leave the guilt part of my brain to deal with that shoplifting I did when I was eight. I won't go into it now; suffice to say that dusting for prints on bon bons is harder than you'd imagine, both time-consuming and tasty.

Many years before I purchased the graffitied *Littlejohn's Britain*, I had come across his first volume of collected journalism thanks to an abscess and two fillings. My dentist gave me a copy of Littlejohn's *You Couldn't Make It Up* that had been discarded at his surgery. It seemed he didn't want it cluttering up his waiting room and ruining the view of the fish tank. I read it while stuck in a room in Pretoria after exhausting all the other options available in this South African town, which seemed to mainly be looking at big guns and shooting things with them. I enjoyed Littlejohn's book then, as the very act of reading seemed vaguely revolutionary in a town that was clinging on to old South Africa, but returning to it a decade later, while sitting in a shire, it all seemed different.

You Couldn't Make It Up begins as any collection of right-wing polemics should, with a tinge of nostalgia for a bygone age and a smearing of paranoia that 'them lot' are taking over. 'I was born in 1954, white, male and in Essex. In twenty years' time any baby answering that description will be found hidden in the bulrushes.' Littlejohn is frequently enjoyably facetious, as well as hinting in this sentence that there may be just a bit of Moses about him. He knows he is a prophet and he's ready to chisel his commandments. He will be the one who can lead us, oppressed white males, to freedom. In Littlejohn's world, we, the heterosexual white males, move with our heads bowed, ringing a leper's bell to warn the blacks and the Muslims and the state-sanctioned transvestites that we are coming. Then they may get ready to spit on us or have enough warning to hug their children's faces to their robes or sequins, for fear they may see the freakery of this vision of middle management. His regular readers nod and curse over their boiled egg and toastie soldiers, fearing that soon the PC brigade will ban them from calling them soldiers as it encourages memories of Western imperialism incurred by military force. That there is scant evidence for these truths is, as usual, not important.

'Multiculturalism means never having to say you're sorry, unless, of course, you happen to be a white man from Essex.'

Having returned to Littlejohn, I decided to repeat my Bushell experiment to collate the evidence on whether his paranoia is justified. If you'd like to attempt a similar experiment you'll need the following:

1. A notebook with a bingo-style grid on it. In each box is a fact: 'the BBC is run by loony lefties'; 'you've

got to be ashamed to be white'; 'bloody immigrants are given sacks of gold in their luxury hotel accommodation'; and so on.
2. A pen.
3. Your eyes open to look at things.

That's it, now off you go. This requires far less preparation than ghost-watching with Derek Acorah and is more likely to lead to a result.

I attempted this experiment using the words from the introduction of *You Couldn't Make It Up*. From a scientific perspective, it could never be entirely satisfactory. I was hampered immediately because, though I am a white man, I am not from Essex, I am from Hertfordshire. Whereas Essex is home to White Van Man, the white vans of Hertfordshire are more likely to have 'Restoring Antique Fireplaces Since 1983' written on the side. That said, Hertfordshire does border Essex, so I felt I should at least feel half apologetic due to geographical proximity.

I thought I would start the day by going to the BBC. On my way into London I did feel the urge to apologise to a black woman I saw. This was less to do with the guilt of history; more to do with a sudden lurch as we departed from Hemel Hempstead, that propelled me into her newspaper. Sadly, she did not curse me and remind me of my ancestors' imperialist past that led to slavery but merely smiled and said, 'That's OK.' Nevertheless, I feel I can tick the box of apologetic white man.

'Try selling a jar of home-made jam at a jumble sale and the full weight of the law will descend upon you.'

It was a Tuesday, so I couldn't find any jumble sales that would be suitable for jam-selling. Also, I fear making jam. I remember when I was a child being told by my mother, as she stirred hot marmalade, that boiling jam was the most heat-intensive goo in the known universe and should it land on your tongue it would be stripped of all its skin. So that's why I don't make my own jam. If I may cheat slightly, a few days after the Littlejohn test I was in Dorchester where I attended a fete at which home-made jams, cakes and cheese straws were openly available, but these people may have been law-breaking mavericks. I wasted a fortune on the tombola and I never did get that kitsch Teasmaid I wanted.

'It's now a criminal offence for a publican to sell a pint of shandy.'

I bought a pint of shandy at the Yorkshire Grey, though maybe the landlord had a haunted look in his eyes that I didn't notice. So I went to the Dover Castle and ordered another one, this time using all the observational powers of Desmond Morris that I could muster. A pint of shandy was placed on the bar towel without a glimmer of persecution or paranoia, apart from the moment when the barman looked at me and said, 'Sorry, is there something the matter?' I realised that I had been staring too intensely and pretended I was a horse-brass historian.

'Schools that have given up teaching how to read and write bar Christmas on the grounds that it is racist.'

I refer here to my previous research into Garry Bushell's 'Winterval' column. Not a fact. If you wish to be further enlightened about this, if you see me in a café or pub, ask me and you'll find out just how hours can drag on.

Littlejohn can be enjoyable, barbed and so misinformed that his verbal brutality is often fun. But while he has the puce demeanour of a man shouting in the back-room bar at a cockfight, enjoying the occasional taste of chicken blood as it spurts near his lips, Peter Hitchens is out in the snug bar, mumbling to himself with tearful eyes, remembering what might have been for this proud isle.

If St George could see us now

I found my first Hitchens book while wasting time waiting to disappoint an audience in Tenby. Unfortunately, the local museum had closed early due to a member of staff getting their finger trapped in a lifelike miniature re-creation of a distressed trawler. This was a pity, as I enjoy local museums; what they lack in budget, they make up for with invention, introducing vampire legend scenarios constructed from old mannequins and ensuring that even the smallest pebble discovered in the foundations of the new shopping centre is more than likely part of an Iron Age mortar and pestle set. They are also one of the few places where I can still feel young, as they are normally the hang-out of the old whiling away their time before the soup thermos can be opened, or kids young enough not to have had the excitement of learning beaten out of them. All in all, though, the early closing was a blessing, as it took me to a Barnado's shop where Hitchens was waiting.

The Abolition of Britain states its case from the outset with a gloomy cover of defeat. Buckingham Palace is under a bruised sky, its Union Jack at half-mast. This is not for the death of a monarch, but for the death of all that made Britain great. We cannot see outside the palace gates, but I imagine it is a cesspool of squalid sex and rancorous junkies urinating on a bearskin hat that lies in the empty sentry box.

Chapter by chapter, Hitchens unpicks all the features of modernity that have led to the dismantling of the once proud Great Britain.

'Comedy killed the upper-class accent, the tweed jacket and the grouse moor. It made an entire class too ridiculous to rule.' After all those decades where political comedians were told that there really was no point in mouthing off in the spotlight about the ills of society, Hitchens sees the sketches of Jonathan Miller and other polite revolutionaries as being what destroyed the aristocracy. If only all those martyrs who were either shipped off or burnt had known: they should have armed themselves with fewer pitchforks and placards and more Footlights review sketches and one-liners.

Peter is an expert destroyer of ridiculous nonsense. Sometimes he makes the task easier by making up the non-sense himself, then crushing the nonsense that only existed because he made it up in the first place. Here is how he did it when analysing Barack Obama's election victory of 2008: 'And if those who voted for Obama were all proving their anti-racist nobility, that presumably means that those many millions who didn't vote for him were proving themselves to be hopeless bigots. This is obviously untrue.'

And why is it untrue? Because you made it up in the first place, with the all-important Hitchens 'if'. If everyone who voted for John McCain did so because they get aroused by thoughts of Vietnamese torture, then does that mean that everyone who didn't vote for him isn't aroused by Vietcong torture porn? This is also obviously untrue. Do you see, I made the first bit up, just like a proper well-paid news-paper columnist.

Peter is the brother of another contrarian, the religion-loathing writer Christopher Hitchens, author of *God is Not Great*. In the United States, this was subtitled *How Religion Poisons Everything*, but the UK was not deemed to need quite such an acerbic addition to help shift units and stir up the neo-con pundits of Fox News. Similarly, Martin Rees, the Astronomer Royal, had the title of his book warning of the possible end of the world, *Our Final Century*, renamed *Our Final Hour* in the US, a century being such a long period of time that it really was nothing to panic about.

If Goebbels manufactured Stepford Wives

The intelligent design lobbyists, formerly known with greater candour as the creationists, are a devious bunch of hucksters.

If there are some very minor details in the opposing argument that have slight flaws, they will declare that the minute flaw means that everything else in the theory/evidence cannot hold water and then shout until their opponent is forced to give up arguing back. The technique of shouting over everyone else so they cannot be heard proves that the opposition have nothing to say, and thus the creationists win. They talk about 'academic freedom' and point out that though their argument is academically ludicrous, not being allowed to teach it makes it like living in Nazi Germany/Communist Eastern Europe.[5] Intelligent design proponents believe that evolutionary theory has so many gaps that it does not stand up as science and that some form of intelligent designer must have been involved to make hummingbirds so pretty and bacteria propel themselves.[6] And by the way, none of this has anything to do

---

5 Obviously if you're a holocaust denier you wouldn't use Nazi Germany as that is an example of a nation that to you was on the right road, pootling in its Volkswagen to outright genocide.

6 Intelligent design propaganda has frequently used the example of the supposed irreducible complexity of the flagellum, a sort of propeller possessed by bacteria. Unfortunately, research has discovered it's not as irreducible as the average pope might have hoped. See *The Flagellum Unspun* by Kenneth R. Miller.

with religion; it just so happens that they are also fundamentalist Christians – it's one of those spooky coincidences.

And so we arrive at the work of Ann Coulter. I should explain that up until this point in the writing process I have not touched a drop of alcohol, but that the next passage will be written under the influence of a selection of beers and spirits. It is the only way.

If you are decent or kind or humane, you may have avoided the work of Ann Coulter; if you are lucky, this may be the first time you have become aware of her existence. She is a strange character, considered by some to be an intellectual, should an intellectual be someone who avoids all rational thought in favour of each evening devouring a big steaming dish of her own prejudice and then spewing it out in the face of a public hungry to chomp on her discharge. Sorry, I told you I'd been drinking. If you are the sort to disagree with Ann Coulter, you will find her a preposterous, ridiculous character, more suited to being a life model for a cruel Disney villainess than a political commentator. The only problem is her books are best-sellers and her opinions are regurgitated across the States as fact. I have a copy of one of them. Thankfully, this took some hunting down; it is not found in many of the charity shops of England. I had to order this one, which I know is against the rules, but it was only 50 pence and I got a deal on the postage by also buying a book about my inner fish.

Ann Coulter, who has laid her stall out a few times before, lays it all out again in the opening paragraph of *Godless: The Church of Liberalism*. 'If a Martian landed in America and set out to determine the nation's official state religion, he would have to conclude it is liberalism, while Christianity and Judaism are prohibited by law.'

Have you been to the United States of America?

Did you see any evidence of religion?

Time to make another of my bullshit-spotting bingo cards, I think.

I am trying to work out in just which part of the church-saturated acres of America this fictional Martian of Coulter's imagination has landed. Even the supposed homosexual and deviant cities of New York and Los Angeles are not short of churches, Jesus-heavy billboards and cable channels screaming with money-grubbing evangelists. More than any UK-based shock journalist, Coulter relies on her reader avoiding hard evidence. She may be a lawyer, but her avoidance of evaluating all the evidence suggests that it is a good thing that she gave up her practice and replaced it with showing off to the right-wing hordes like Eva Braun dancing in crotchless pants in a bunker.

Coulter's book is a stunning treatise on supposed demands by liberals that all women must have constant abortions, whether pregnant or not, and how evolution is an idea almost as mad as Copernicus declaring that the Earth might orbit around the sun. If Ann had her way, there would be no cures for cancer, smallpox or rickets, because those cures all involve science, and that can surely only be the work of liberals. She seems to dream of a time where parents never got close to their children because they'd be dead by spring.

'From Marx to Hitler, the men responsible for the greatest mass murders of the twentieth century were avid Darwinists.' I grit my teeth as another idiot who clearly has never read any books by Charles Darwin, as that could sully her argument, tears into this kindly man who made his son play the bassoon to flowers to find out how they might react. I don't believe Ann Coulter has so much as played a kazoo to a daisy.

My A-level history course covered the Renaissance and the Dutch War of Revolt, but despite that, I still have an inkling that the appalling treatment of Jewish people didn't spring up in Europe after the publication of *On the Origin of Species* in 1859. If any part of Darwin's book influenced Hitler's thinking, it might have been the discussion of how pigeon-fanciers breed pigeons, so if we must lay the holocaust at the door of something other than the Nazis' manipulation of a population via their prejudices, then maybe it is time that the pigeon-fanciers took their portion of the blame. Hitler forgets to name-check Darwin in *Mein Kampf* when talking about oppressing the Jews. He does name-check someone else, though Ann forgot to mention this: 'Hence today I believe that I am acting in accordance with the will of the Almighty Creator: by defending myself against the Jew, I am fighting for the work of the Lord.' Oh no, don't tell me the Lord was involved again. If he's not careful he's going to start getting accused of being an accessory in some of these murderous incidents.

Ann Coulter is the type of personality about whom people say 'If she didn't exist, you couldn't make her up or rather you wouldn't make her up.' Much like Richard Littlejohn, this underestimates the power of the human imagination. Read William Burroughs, watch John Waters[7] or listen to Diamandas Galas[8] and you'll discover just how much the human brain can make up. If Ann Coulter did

---

7 John Waters' *Pink Flamingos* is about the filthiest people alive. Many people who have heard of it but not seen it shiver and say, 'Oh God, I hear Divine eats real dog shit at the end of the film.' She does, but there are many other things to startle the eyes, such as the chicken killing and fucking scene, the man doing a dance with his sphincter muscles, the egg man, the insemination scenes, etc. I was a very surprised teenager when I first saw this. When Divine is asked her political philosophy she replies, 'Kill everyone now.'

8 An operatic vocal terrorist.

not exist she could still be invented, by Ralph Steadman in a very bad mood.

Ann is nice and loose with her statistics and edits quotations with judicious scissors to make sure they do what she wants them to: 'Nearly half the members of the Supreme Court – the ones generally known as "liberals" – are itching to ban the references to God on our coin and in the pledge of allegiance.' This is the same liberal Supreme Court that gave George W. Bush an election he didn't win and the world the worst US president in history. The bloody liberals.

In the candy factory of the mind

When debunking evolution Coulter quite rightly points out that there are no transitional fossils. I use the term 'quite rightly' in much the same way as Melanie Phillips uses the term 'the fact is'. There are many transitional fossils, but yet again, that ruins the article in the same way that the statement 'there is evidence of gas chambers, no, there really is' can spoil a sunny afternoon for a holocaust denier. Ann is unhappy with transitional fossils because as yet there isn't one with the head of a sparrow, the body of a bonobo and the legs of an iguana.

Coulter's arguments against Darwin are many and varied; it is problematic to choose my favourite. If there is a mechanism of evolution via natural selection she does not understand why a worm does not evolve into a beagle – stupid lazy worms. She is also outraged that when Darwin went to the Galapagos islands there were thirteen species of finch, and now, a good 170 years on, there are still only thirteen species. Evolution is too darn slow for a neo-con to believe in. My favourite today – and it changes daily – is

One of the many transitional fossils that does not exist
according to Ann Coulter.

'No matter what argument you make against evolution, the response is, well you know it's possible to believe in evolution and believe in God. Yes, and it is possible to believe in Spiderman and believe in God, but that doesn't prove Spiderman is true.' I am beginning to think she doesn't know what she's talking about. I'll leave it up to you to pick the Spiderman argument apart.

There's nothing new to wishing it was yesterday

Angry swipes at society's decline don't change over the years; it's just that yesterday's cesspit always appears so much more fragrant to dive into. Since polemic has been written down on papyrus, philosophers and historians have been yelping, 'Sweet Zeus, the kids nowadays, isn't everything awful,' as you will discover if you read a little Juvenal.

Go back forty years and you can discover Arnold Lunn and *The Cult of Softness*. Sir Arnold was the author of many books, including *The Mountains of Youth*, *The Story of Skiing* and *The Swiss and Their Mountains*. He was also an Olympic skier, inventor of the slalom and a believer in Franco being the correct victor in the Spanish Civil War. He was a real man, in a way a lanky hippy or nicotine-stained beatnik would never dare dream of.

Lunn remembers a happy conversation with a Francophile: '"You are ready," I said, "to fight, and if necessary to die, to save Spain from atheistic Communists."' It appears to me that Spain was saved from atheistic Communists and enjoyed the attentions of a fascistic regime instead. But what do I know? My knowledge of the Spanish Civil War is mainly gleaned from a little George Orwell, *Pan's Labyrinth* and the songs of the Manic Street Preachers. I have not been able to find a copy of Lunn's *Communism and Socialism* (Eyre and Spottiswoode, 1938), but I suspect it is not a glowing report on these movements.

The Cult of Softness lays into the usual entourage who gather around the putrefaction of a once noble society – the atheists, the intellectuals and the BBC. Lunn is joined in this battle by co-author Garth Lean. Together they call to arms all Christians, urging them to unite 'in a militant counterattack upon the enemies of faith and reason'.

Amongst these enemies is the avant-garde, the group of artists who create sentences such as 'we foindle and funkle, we bonkle and meigle and maxpoffle, we scotstarvit, armit, wormit, and even whifflet. We play at crosstobs, leuchars, gorbals, and finfan. We scavaig, and there's aye a bit of tilquhilly. If it's wet, treshnish and mishnish.' This is 'Canedolia' by Edwin Morgan, and it makes Lunn cross, fearing that such nonsense will addle the brain.

Arnold Lunn suspected that the English were becoming a nation of pansies. No longer were we the explorers, adventurers and killers of colonials that the British once were. The signs of degradation, such as over inch-long hair on men, women without corsets, and Little Richard, were all acid to his eyes. Once Britain could proudly say that our musculature and bench-pressing ability were the envy of the world, as long as the world believed our self-aggrandising poetry and paintings. Even at the beginning of the twentieth century, when we were still spinning the classroom globe and giggling at how much was ours, things were not all Scott of the Antarctic. Seventy per cent of the men of Manchester were deemed too unfit to be soldiers in the Great War, with a similar picture in industrial cities around the island. Despite this setback, most of the malnourished managed to get to France once it was realised that they were fit to fight if they could muster the energy to get over the top of the trench for long enough to take a bullet in the chest. Yet this is not the past that Arnold Lunn recalls.

Lunn's least favourite nation of Western Europe still remains popular with the indignant moralists of today. There's always been something wrong with the ghastly Dutch and their boastful gays.

'Sexual perversity was a recurring topic at the conference, which ended yesterday. Twice a Dutch author announced he was a homosexual.' Hush hush, Dutchman, what you do in the privacy of your life is your own disgusting business. Say what you like about the Dutch and their progressive society, which was a haven for errant scientists and philosophers from across Europe; they will always be seedy and dirty people in the eyes of 'the moral majority', with their narcotic cafés and window-dressing of prostitutes under red lights. It would simply be too

terrifying to consider that any enlightened thought on matters sexual or narcotic might improve society, as before you
know it British teachers will have to teach more sex education, and we all know where that'll lead – streets of
terrifying shame.

Mind you, it's not just the Dutch that Arnold thinks we
should fear: 'As the *Daily Telegraph* (14 February 1964)
writes, "taught by Malinowski and others, we tend nowadays to admire the unrepressed and easy sexual mores of
Polynesians and other primitive peoples." We may copy
them if we please, presumably, but only at the risk of sink-
ing to a Polynesian level of culture.' Sadly, it seems that level
of depravity may already have been reached, if my few
nights on St Mary Street, Cardiff, are anything to go by.
Arnold and the *Daily Telegraph*'s fears may have become
reality, but without managing to maintain a level of culture
equivalent to that of the Polynesians. I know of a Welsh
cameraman who photographed the Vietnam War but said
no to capturing Friday night on St Mary Street: 'At least in
Vietnam you had some idea which direction the missiles
would come from.' No one knows from what direction a
bottle of blue drink may be lobbed in Cardiff.

As well as the Dutch and organised deviants, there are
other constants for the umbrage manufacturers of the twentieth century: 'Thousands of ordinary people are deeply
concerned about the influence of the BBC on the homes
of Britain.' In Lunn's time, the BBC was the place where
Play for Today glorified errant youths, Dennis Potter deliv-
ered his smut, and documentary-makers ingested LSD.
Lunn, the author of *Towards a Quaker View of Sex*, is disappointed that the BBC should allow all manner of authors
to peddle their wares without proper checks and balances
in place. In 2009, columnists are still obsessed with the

BBC and its mind manipulation of the population, though this outrage is now increasingly driven by the journalist puppet's desire to please his masters, who are hungry to burn up the TV licence and let their more expensive smut and political bias control the living room.

However much you hope that there was a time when everyone was happy and not looking over their shoulder at who was getting more than they were or spreading syphilis, it appears life has always been rubbish.

What have we learned?

- We have been going to hell in a handcart ever since handcarts were invented
- Young people are ghastly, especially if they are not from around here
- Neat gin versus unsupervised television, we still can't be too sure which is really worse for a five-year-old, but stop the experiments now
- There are good reasons for worms not to turn into beagles, but check your garden every morning just in case

---

Further reading

Londonistan by Melanie Phillips
Help! Mom! There are Liberals Under My Bed by Kathrine DeBrecht and Jim Hummel
50 People who Buggered up Britain by Quentin Letts

An Interlude with Roger Moore's Youth Gang of Wasteground Urchins

Are there as many clubs as there used to be in my childhood? I'm not sure. In the seventies, children were chomping at the bit to get a regular newsletter and a badge. Now, in these times of bedroom computers and DVD players, shiny badges have lost their kudos. Although I was a typically club-mad child, I somehow missed one that appeared in 1977 – I was probably too busy celebrating the Queen's Silver Jubilee or mourning Elvis Presley's death.[1] The club in question was called the Crimefighters Club, and membership of it meant that you'd receive a newsletter, a badge, and the chance to meet Roger Moore. You

---

1 Not being alive when JFK was assassinated, I have had to pick other deaths to always remember where I was when I found out about them. I heard of Elvis's death as I lay on my bedroom floor putting Spitfire stickers into my RAF Hendon sticker book. When John Lennon's death was announced, I was in after-school art club having just stabbed Robert Boughton in the hand with a craft knife. Craft knives were banned after that. I also once stabbed Adrian Chorley in the face with an ink pen when he was bullying me, but no one famous died that day.

would not definitely meet Roger Moore, but you were one step closer to hearing his eyebrow arch in person. Roger Moore and the Crimefighters is a series of books that demonstrate the level of adoration Moore had by the late seventies. The first Crimefighters I encountered was thrown at me while I was on stage. This was not due to a shortage of soft fruit and other projectiles; by this point rumours had got round that I had a thing for second-hand books of a particular ilk. While others have hoped for underwear or tight clingfilm wrap of some drug or other, I was happy to find myself catching books about otters and motor caravanning.

Forty years ago, Moore had already been Simon Templar, James Bond, and Sean Flynn in *The Wild Geese*, and he was yet to be Ffolkes, the bearded misogynist obsessive knitter and adventurer in *North Sea Hijack*. Such was his fame, in fact, that he was only available for a cameo at the end of the first Crimefighter novel, entitled *The Siege*. Even in print and in the imagination of an author, Moore's hectic schedule meant he could only drop in for a few lines.

'I'm Roger Moore.'
'I know,' said Bonnie, her face burning.
'You kids did pretty well,' he said.
'And Dalek,' said Darren.
Roger grinned. 'Yes, and Dalek. So I've got an idea to form a club called the Crimefighters for kids like you. Do you mind if I pull up a chair and tell you about it?'

Dalek is the name of Darren's dog. I presume this is because the book was written by Malcolm Hulke, best known as writer of *Dr Who*, as well as *The Avengers*. Hulke saw *Dr Who* scripts as a critique on the nature of power and he was a member of the British Communist Party. His Crimefighters novel also tackles dictatorial African regimes.

> The other two men who made up the government were General Chibambo, who commanded the army, and Police Commissioner Mumbo who was in charge of law and order. Both Chibambo and Mumbo were chubby, fat men, and chosen for that reason.

The joy of the first book in the series is the cultural references within it and the world outlook that places it in 1977 and nowhere else (OK, possibly late 1976 or early 1978). A popular theme for action adventures of the time was the crazed African dictator who had risen to power once the British loosened its empire grip. This seemed to be the plot of TV action series *The Professionals* every other week, though it might be that I've just seen that one episode over and over again. Race issues, in fact, appear with startling frequency. For instance, the book's hero, Darren, refuses to believe that a young black girl he meets could have a father who has met the Queen. The first time I read this I laughed, but in 1977, as the National Front were experiencing one of their brief swells, Malcolm Hulke is teaching the children: 'Black people don't meet the Queen, they drive buses and work in hospitals. They're all right because my dad says so, but they don't meet the Queen. I bet your dad hasn't even met Dickie Davies.' To which our young black heroine, uninitiated in ITV's *World of Sport* and its moustachioed, Mallen-streaked host,[2] replies, 'Who he?'

---

2 Catherine Cookson's Mallens; the streak suggests evil in their demi-Heathcliff manner.

The idea went down well, and further adventures were spawned, such as *1,001 Shoplifters, Crook Ahoy!* and *Deaths in Denims*. *Deaths in Denims* was penned by genteel British actress Dulcie Gray, who was delightfully upper crust in numerous British films and TV soap *Howard's Way*. What is she doing writing of deaths in denims? As we shall find out imminently, there was more to Dulcie Gray's imagination than her actorly front might suggest, but we'll deal with eyeball necklaces in the following pages.

8

Horror

(or ANIMAL HORROR DEATH)

Nature red in tooth and claw.
                    Alfred Lord Tennyson

'Eaten? What the hell do you mean eaten?' Alan
Mason screamed. 'Inspector, people are not
eaten in their beds in the middle of Kent.'
                    Spiders, Richard Lewis

The animals and me: the horror of angry toads

Why must scientists meddle? Their darned inquisitive
minds and dabbling with rays and genes and mutants and
potions and microscopes have led to a world of giant bats,
psychotic cats, rabid rats and a whole zoo of bone-crunch-
ing mammals, bugs and crustaceans.

I was brought up in a time of terrible horror.
Fortunately, it was not the horror of war or plague or leprosy or gulags or oppression, horrors that have blighted so

much of human civilisation. That's not to say there wasn't a hint of genuine horror hanging over our 1970s heads, of course: fear of the unions was so extreme that they were satirised in the Carry On films, and rumours of the impending nuclear holocaust[1] filled children's minds with images of mushroom clouds, mutation and Marxism. But the real plague of horror spouted forth from the seventies horror fiction market.

The decade was a boom time for *The Mayflower Book of Black Magic Stories*, Alfred Hitchcock's *Things That Go Bump in the Night* and gaudy books from the New English Library, purveyors of anything that could be cheaply bound and placed in a carousel.[2] While youths failed to get into the X-rated films of Hammer Horror by putting on a gruff voice and their grandfather's trilby, they knew they could still indulge in the delights of the genre via the medium of sleazy paperback.

Pan, bringer of death

> You'll never feel safe in your bath again.
> *Slither*, John Halkin

Flesh torn from bones? Check. Flayed eye sockets spewing blood and jelly on to ruptured skin? Check. Someone gets nude before being dipped in acid? Check.

That's the checklist of the horror novels of my youth –

---

1 Carl Sagan summed up the nuclear arms race as 'two men up to their waists in petrol, one with five matches and one with seven'.

2 While the first LP purchase of other generations may have been *Rolf Harris Sings Children's Favourites* or *Rock 'n' Roll Party*, my friends all wanted a copy of *Sound Effects of Death and Horror* so they could dance away to the sound of slicing pendulums and rats' dungeons.

outrageous gore, sex, and more outrageous gore. My introduction to the genre had come via the melancholy
wretches of Edgar Allan Poe, but before I could descend
too far into a well of absinthe, I found one of Herbert Van
Thal's many volumes of the *Pan Book of Horror Stories* in the
rotating bookcase of a Dutch relation. You may be wondering whether a normal child would be drawn to a cover
of a rat perched on a skull. By the age of nine I was so
obsessed by horror that I had a sheep's skull, found in a
Somerset field, on the table next to my bed. I had placed
a candle on top of it and made sure that some wax dripped
into the sockets, just like in the films and on the black-
magic-based paperback covers. My sisters were reasonably
certain I would grow up to be a serial killer, but my pickle
jars still only have onions and the occasional cabbage in
them.[3]

Once I had found my first *Pan Book of Horror Stories* they
seemed to appear in every second-hand bookshop I walked
into, and I loved them.

As I approached eleven years old, the morbid designers
at Pan grew up with me, rejecting pen-and-ink sketches of
skulls and replacing them with mocked-up photographs of
unsightly ends or new zombie beginnings – an obviously
rubber dead head with a scattering of clearly plastic cater-
pillars and bugs crawling on it, or a glass-eyed bearded head
in a bucket.

The stories were sometimes magnificent, and sometimes
run-of-the-mill spooky tales with a nasty twist at the end.

---

3 Jeffrey Dahmer, the Milwaukee cannibal serial killer, kept bits of his victims in jars as
sexual keepsakes. He was found sane by an American jury. I don't know exactly where
the line between sane and insane is, but I reckon once you've taken out someone's
lungs, made a slit in them, and then had sex with the offal, it is a little bit mad.

Occasionally Herbert offered up intriguingly incongruous pieces such as John Lennon's 'No Flies on Frank' from his nonsense collection *In His Own Write*, or Frederick Treves' description of Elephant Man John Merrick. The most surprising was a story by Dulcie Gray, who you may remember as the author of *Death in Denims* from the Roger Moore and the Crimefighter series. Dulcie, for those who are not obsessed by either early postwar British cinema or TV soap *Howard's Way*, was an actress best known for playing the most English of upper-class ladies, frequently next to her husband Michael Denison, who would be in tweed and cravat. Her story involved lurid, ugly torture and eyeball-threading performed by a simple, dribbling child brute. Presumably when your acting career is mainly about playing delightful old ladies in headscarves, there has to be an outlet for those darker thoughts that haunt you. In Dulcie's case, that outlet just happened to involve writing about eyeball jewellery: 'When the police came, he was sitting calmly on the floor of the living room, making a necklace for the matron of the home, from eight humans' eyes, six trouts' eyes, two cats' eyes, and assorted coloured beads.'

Hidden in a garage somewhere may lie paintings of beheaded rotten corpses created by Celia Johnson, or leather statues of priapic devils fashioned by John Le Mesurier. Who knows what unspeakable horrors might have been perpetrated by the British acting fraternity who portrayed on-screen decency?[4]

---

4 The police probably. They would have known if Jack Hawkins had been involved in ghastly slaughter.

When big mice go bad

One day, I grew up. Not properly – I still can't grow an effective moustache – but enough to turn my back on my hideous horror collection. Fortunately, a return to another seaside town reminded me of one of the great sub-genres in publishing, and all it took was a cover portraying megalomaniac ants.

This thrilling sub-genre of horror hit its stride in the seventies, and has since made up a significant proportion of my current collection. The vengeful beast genre required CPR after a decline in animal attack fiction in popular culture during the sixties, but luckily James Herbert was on hand with the defibrillator. Herbert was the perfect horror author for the pubescent reader. Stephen King may have been the king of horror for those who thought they knew best, but younger readers wanted to make sure that in their books there was an emasculation of a PE teacher with a pair of garden shears, or a neo-Nazi investigator hanging by the neck from a nail in the door. For them, James Herbert was the choice. His first book, *The Rats*, started the rise of the novel nasty. Packed with hideous mutilation, it was critically savaged but a huge publishing success. If you have not read *The Rats* you were not born between 1954 and 1976. After *The Rats*, horror fiction was changed, and like a horde of atomically mutated rats from a canal, out poured the savage animal novels. No longer did the marketing people have to think up a catchy hook line for their books. Gone was the 'a hideous death lurked unseen in the river/abbey/well' rubbish, to be replaced by the much simpler 'in the tradition of *The Rats*'. Merely to suggest a book would be a bit like James Herbert's was a masterstroke of salesmanship. The publisher was saying: 'There'll be gory mutilations from vicious creatures in this book too, so you'll probably like it. Although we can't guarantee the commentary on social deprivation that Herbert slips in; we might add a little more nudity to make up for it.'

James Herbert is the lord of the modern gory pestilence novel, though the enormous success of Peter Benchley's *Jaws* cannot be discounted either. Benchley was influenced by Henrik Ibsen's *Enemy of the People*, while Herbert shows influences of H.G. Wells.

The modern psycho-animal-on-the-loose novel probably started with Wells' *Food of the Gods*, which, unlike *War of the Worlds*, was sadly never turned into a rock opera by Jeff Wayne. In those times, there was much talk of the world becoming overpopulated, whereas Wells' title offered a vision of a world where things were getting oversized. It doesn't take long for overpopulation to happen, though, if rabbits are getting twenty times bigger. The scientific meddlers have invented a formula, Herakleophorbia IV, to create chickens so gigantic that family buckets would need to be the size of quarries. Unfortunately, the magic formula ends up scattered all over the place and soon everything from wasps to giant princesses is running amok.

So when you read about the whole killer-crabs-on-the-loose-in-Wales genre which began with *Crabs on the Rampage*, don't forget that its true fathers are Wells and Ibsen, and that's why the Crabs subgroup of the sub-genre are classier than you might think.

How to make your field mouse psycho

The animals in these books are very rarely psychos of their own making. To stem vigilante attacks on spiders, worms and crabs, most horror authors make it clear that the animals are not naturally crazed. They are usually the result of man's silly dabbling, but once the silly dabbling is over, the nightmare begins, and it's very likely to be 'a nightmare as old as time and twice as terrifying', whatever that means.

As with previously discussed romance plotting, the killer animal narrative has a specific and oft-repeated pattern. Once manipulated, the animals become power-hungry, and there is seemingly nothing that can stop them. The danger of the beasts is ignored by top brass, who are then eaten for their arrogance while the mavericks try to take control. Although there are *some* things to stop the animals, it will take a lot of trial and error, death, and sex with a pipe-smoker before the unstoppable can be stopped.[5]

Even after the ravenous debacle, there are frequent hints that the bestial horror hasn't had the abrupt extinction that the high-fiving survivors imagine. At the end of *The Rats*, the creatures are destroyed, but somewhere in a greengrocer's basement or sewage pipe, one lone mutation survives, and it is giving birth. Crabs, too, are wont to keep coming back.

Any beast will do

The beasts-that-go-mad-or-grow-huge-or-are-poisonous-or-just-plain-evil genre normally reflects the neuroses of the time. For some time during the late 1950s, the predominant reason for animals going awry and slaughtering

---

5 If horror stories are vaults of truth, then when an unstoppable force meets an immovable wall, it's whichever one can catch the common cold that loses out. This allows the scientists to say, 'To think, we tried everything from lasers to H-bombs, yet it turned out the immovable creature could not survive something as simple as the common cold. Who would have thought it?'

nubile teenagers and moonshine-drenched hobos had been some secretive nuclear testing. Then as the Cold War cooled down, the reason for mutation moved from the nuclear to the more ecological, such as scientists pouring a vat of green goo into the water supply or a greedy corporation turning cows into cannibals in a bovine version of Soylent Green. As yet, the melting glacier climate change terror novel has not achieved its full potential, but as the climate change movement keeps gaining momentum, the defrosted-killer-woolly-mammoth genre will surely set the horror fiction shelves alight: 'The Proboscideans had slept for four thousand years, but only now man had destroyed the sky was it time for the mammoth to rule the earth.'[6] That's the first line, not sure where to go with it after that.

Printed horror fiction revels in lurid taglines. Unfortunately they are not always biologically or anthropologically accurate. For instance, 'Out of earth crept mankind's oldest nightmare,' declares the back of *Spiders*. Now I am not an expert on hard-wired fear or Cro-Magnon horror, but is mankind's oldest nightmare really the spider? According to Carl Sagan's *Dragons of Eden*,[7] the oldest nightmares are of falling, the dark, and snakes. Spiders may be man's *most common* nightmare, but only since the invention of the plughole and drainpipe.

The back cover of *The Bats* keeps it nice and loose, avoiding the possibility of anthropological errors: 'and with the bats came death'; while *The Cats* reverts to the Herbert-clinging sales pitch 'In the tradition of *The Rats*.' *The Bear*

---

6 The tagline from my work-in-progress horror novel *Die Mammoth Die!*.

7 I realise this is not my first namecheck of Carl Sagan, but when you are immersed in Mills & Boon and Hell's Angels thrillers, your mind starts to hanker for books by well-read, humanitarian astronomers.

starts to dabble in the horror of height: '18 feet of gut-crunching[8] man-eating terror'.

Curiously, many of the animals that wish to take over the Earth are exactly the same animals that an old woman might swallow if she had a niggling problem with a fly. As far as we know, the fly the woman swallowed was not radioactive, but if it were, this might explain why it affected her judgement to such an extent that she eventually attempted to swallow a horse, obviously killing herself.

Only the General Synod can save us now

Occasionally the giant beast is a little more enigmatic than a normal animal gone haywire or enormous (or both). 'What is THE THING?' asks the back of *This Creeping Evil*. This is a Christian monster horror novel set in Portsmouth but found in the damp basement of another Notting Hill second-hand book palace. It is a novel where the protagonists fear blasphemy as much as they fear ghastly death at the hands or tendrils or sucking thing of the thing.

What is the creeping evil that 'some had imagined usurped the throne of God'? On the cover, the thing that comes to Portsmouth is pictured as giant poo with eyes and a long wiggly arm. I have spent a Friday night in Portsmouth, amongst the mass of drunk, shouting hotheads smelling of blue drinks, and have to concede that yes, they did occasionally look like a big poo monster.

What begins as a 'poo monster in Portsmouth' horror ends up fitting more neatly into the collection of booklets found between a font and a collection tray. 'As I said, I

---

8 I have never eaten haggis, but from looking at guts in a butcher's window, I'm not sure they are crunchy.

came up against an unclimbable mountain of business morality which belied Christianity, and an employer–employee relationship which was the negation of Christ's second commandment.' There is also much talk of the glory of the navy and the brilliance of commanders and crew alike. How did this happen? The author Geoffrey Bennett's previous life, before he devoted himself to books of adventure, was spent as a commander in the British navy – and one who warned of the growth of the Soviet navy at that. *This Creeping Evil* is a poo monster allegory that tells you to put Christianity in your heart and be alert, as this devil that rises from the sea may be a beast that cuts you down with a hammer and sickle, or with its permissiveness, or maybe it just wants to consume the Union Jack, crumpets and other things that made Britain great.

Geoffrey, formerly Sea-Lion, his pen name when in the navy, doesn't want to risk readership missing the allegory, so he includes a brief preface. He admits that past works may have been escapist adventures, but the time has come to put his writer's imagination to some use. 'Hence this book, which some may read as a macabre thriller during a single evening or a train journey. Others will realise that it has a deeper theme, one dealing with a vital problem of today.' Sea-Lion and Arnold Lunn may well have seen eye to eye on moral decay, but I think Sea-Lion would have been more fun to hang around with; a naval yarn is so much more exciting than a skiing tale.

Like *Dixon of Dock Green* and prawn cocktail in a tin bowl, *This Creeping Evil* is a reminder of a past time, a near-mythical England not yet tainted by punk rockers and regional accents on television. Characters have names like Albert Evans, they live on Acacia Avenue and end up featured in the *Daily Clarion*. The world is populated by people like Ted, eyewitnesses lacking command of the English language, which makes this a safe read for those who don't wish to wallow in the grotesque. Something horrible happened, but fortunately 'Ted's vocabulary was insufficient to do justice to it'.

So, ultimately, reportage of the giant shapeless monster that consumes Exeter is less specific than we might wish, as the survivors that our narrator relies upon are simple folk who do not possess the words to paint the full picture of horror. One witness, Daisy, spends almost as much time describing *The Seventh Veil*, the first film of the double feature on the night of the attack, as she does the attack itself. She is saved from death because she is lured from the cinema by a seedy gentleman with a flash car: 'An' then I sees as it's movin' towards the power station – sort of slitherin' towards it as you might say. An' it was quiverin' shakin' sort of like a jelly – or maybe since it was so dark, I should say a chocolate blancmange. Do you like chocolate blancmange, Mr Delaney?'

A dry, naval commander's sense of humour runs through much of the novel. The narrator, Tom Delaney, will stop himself, correcting facts, or apologising for not introducing himself earlier on. For a few chapters the narrative becomes that of his wife, who he occasionally apologises to for interrupting and popping back into his own narrative.

Tom is a middle-aged man who likes things traditional, doesn't care much for modern music, enjoys a good glass of wine and decent grub, and generally represents the hoped-for readership of decent people with umbrellas and brogues. After investigating this shapeless thing 'to the extent no one can describe the shape of something which is always changing shape', he returns to his wife: 'I'll not dwell on our meeting. When a husband and wife, whose marriage is a happy one, have been separated for two years, there is much in the days that follow the reunion which can compare with a honeymoon, and the details of such a period in the life of any couple are too personal to place on record.' Such coyness would have no place in the racy, groin-thrusting horror novels of the mid-seventies, but *This Creeping Evil* was first published in 1950, and it would be some time before sex was invented.

After the destruction of many towns and cities in England, the people gather in their churches and, upon departure, discover their faith has destroyed the creeping evil. As our hero says to his wife, 'It won't be long now, my dear, before with God's help, we shall build Blake's new Jerusalem "in England's green and pleasant land".'

This Creeping Evil is most definitely not in the tradition of *The Rats*.

Bees like Zulus

The Swarm – 'a masterpiece of chilling terror that just might come true' – is the only beast-based horror novel I own that has a glossary by revered sociobiologist Edward O. Wilson. In this case it is taken from his book *The Insect Societies*. Even if you are not swayed by the slightly limp tagline, you are safe in the knowledge that by the end of the novel you will definitely know what melittology and eusocial mean. Melittology is the study of bees and eusocial is too complex to go into here.

The creatures' presence is felt long before their first official sighting: 'Anxious to preserve the mood of their brief idyll, John Wood had put off telling Maria about the bees . . .' If there is one thing to stymie romance, it is bringing up the subject of killer bees, especially if the

partner in question has previously suffered from anaphylactic shock.[9]

In a chart of animal horror novel authors based on the
research they conduct into the mind, body and hive of their
chosen creature, Arthur Herzog, author of *The Swarm*, takes
the number one position. In his book there are diagrams
including a graph representing spectrographic analysis of
toxic bee venom and a figure showing the distribution
and spread of the adansonii hybrid in South America.
There are also some very attractive equations involving
time and mass. The inclusion of equations in any animal
horror novel adds an academic level that can be a welcome
relief from arterial spurting and dripping incisor descriptions. They serve to add education to the bloodshed or tidal
wave of anaphylactic shock, though the author may still
take a detour from vigorous rationalism.

'I have this funny, unscientific feeling that the bees could
have won if they'd wanted to.'

$$S_0^\infty \, y^{a-1} \, e{-}y$$

This he converted to

$$Pr(W > w) = \sum_{20}^{k-1} Pr(X = x) = \sum_{20}^{k-1} \frac{(aw)^x e^{-tw}}{x!}$$

And this emerged after many formulations as

$$O^2 = M''(o) - y^2 = a(a + 1)\beta^2 - a^2\beta^2 = a\beta^2$$

A bee-based equation. I've forgotten the value of X
so that doesn't really help.

---

9 Kenneth Halliwell witnessed the death of his mother from a wasp sting; despite this early
setback he grew up to become famous in the world of literature. Sadly, it was by hammering to death his critically acclaimed lover, Joe Orton.

The bee does of course instil fear in certain people. The easily panicked will often be seen foolishly running about swatting at the air and crying in flower gardens. However, it is far rarer to see anyone swatting at a worm. Most worms, when discovered by humans, will either be ignored or sliced in half. As anyone who has been taught by a biology teacher seeking a pupil's attention knows, both halves of a worm live on after being sliced in two. Eager psycho gardeners are keen to demonstrate this whenever turned soil uncovers an earthworm. But be warned: the worms will get their revenge on gardeners and sadistic children in . . . *Worms*.

Worms – 'when the nightmare ended, the real horror began' – takes quite a time to get started by horror beast novel standards. It spends most of its first thirty pages mulling over one man's dying marriage rather than any death by soil-burrowing slitherers. The unfortunate man in question is James Hildebrand, who attempts to enjoy the Norfolk coast as his uptight and ungenerous wife derides him or powders her nose. By page 42, however, we get a hint of the horror to come as author James Montague describes the first ugly worm horror: 'a dead rat was suspended in the water, head up, tail down, its paws on the surface almost as if it was praying. It was covered in worms.'

Fortunately, just three pages later we're plunged into the real meat of the story. Hildebrand's wife is struggling like an insect in its final death throes after he has impulsively crushed her with some loose coastal concrete. The worms may not have killed her, but they are ready to sup and savage once the rot sets in. 'The head of a second worm appeared from my wife's nostril. Unable to control myself, I cried and stepped back. My foot trod on the fire and a cloud of sparks blew across my wife's corpse, turning into black specks against her eyeballs. I fainted.'

Worms, despite its skull-with-worm-in-eyehole cover and promise of unrelenting horror, is not really a member of the savage-beasts-take-over genre. It is about wife murder and guilt, and ends with false imprisonment and hints that the seagulls are going to eat more babies next, but it is not 'in the tradition of *The Rats*'. Despite this, they are still awkward little bastards.

'The worms are not going to like this,' I repeated.

However enigmatic and lackadaisical these seaside worms are going to be, the next worms up are properly psychotic.

Toothy worms spoil shampoo

If you find yourself wanting a more vicious and bloody worms-gnaw-human-skin narrative, then John Halkin's *Slither* offers visceral feasts, some sex, and a warning of how animals might get revenge if slaughtered and utilised as fashion accessories. Beware those mink overcoats; the mink may be next to seek revenge, and I'm thinking of getting rid of my leather shoes in case the cows get irradiated and tetchy.

Slither was the first book in a trilogy, to be followed by *Slime* and *Squelch*. If number of copies available in charity shops is the marker for popularity, then *Slither* was the outstanding success of the three. Halkin's publisher, Hamlyn, made the female models on the books' covers go through some of the more interesting shoots of their careers. The cover girl of *Slither* merely has to lie with her head in some soapy water, staring up in the last

moments of agonising death, her face covered in bur-
rowing lizards and bleeding holes. *Slime*, on the other
hand, requires the model to be topless, covered in toy
slime, surveying the horrifying worms in her hands.
Squelch goes for a cartoon instead, possibly due to the
number of models on strike due to topless plastic bug and
slime abuse.[10]

If one sentence might give you the gist of Halkin's work,
it is: 'They had to cut the strap of her bra and hold her
breasts apart before Aubrey could get a grip on the worm's
neck.'

TV cameraman Matt is nearly devoured by worms in
a sewer; fortunately, they just eat one cheek and a couple
of fingers; oh, and an ear. Luckily, his buttock skin makes
a good alternative cheek. Nevertheless, as with many books
in this genre, the health of his marriage is questionable,
because he is disappointed with his wife's ageing process.
He may have a botched cheek and be short of a few fingers,
but it seems her hips have expanded slightly.

After headlines such as MAMMOTH WORMS EAT
TV MAN IN SEWER – GRUESOME NEWSREEEL
SHOCKS NATION dominate the papers, worm panic
seems to die down. In fact, it turns out the worms have
pretty skin, ideal for making belts. 'She shivered, and then
fingered the worm-skin belt she was wearing with her
simple brown dress. "What if one day they take it into their
heads to start skinning us?"'

Due to a slippery shower curtain that she can't get a grip
on, Matt's wife is eaten by worms that pop up through
plughole. But that's OK as Matt is having an affair with

---

10 Having recently found a copy of *Squelch* in a hospice shop in Bury St Edmunds, I discover the original cover was a woman with a worm eating out her eye.

Fran, the woman behind the worm-based clothing line. Her hips are not as big, and she has small breasts; mind you, her neck is freckly. Later, she gets much of her leg eaten. This may or may not be punishment for her freckles or an imperfection we never knew about. And that, in summary, is the story of how the worms avenged themselves for being turned into an accoutrement.

Remember, it's not just slithery beasts that want to take over the world; sometimes even our favourites can be driven towards a nasty streak.

'I only have one question to ask you.'
Inglis leant forward in anticipation.
'Have you subjected the animals to intense heat?'

Yes, he has, and now the cats have got vicious and a naked boy leads them, his brain turning feline. An Arab man, an ageing prostitute, a potential rapist and a fully fledged psychopath all die at the talons of *The Cats*. It is 'in the tradition of *The Rats*'. So remember, do not cook your cat. That seems to be the message of the author, Nick Sharman.

What's in an ant's mind?

Occasionally I risk buying things from internet auction sites. That's where I found the pristine promotional sick bag for Herbert Lom movie *Mark of the Devil*. It is still pristine. I'd rather be sick in my own shoe than sully this collectable. One of my two a.m. impulse buys was 'box of terrific horror novels and Betamax videos'. Amongst films such as *Possession*, where an alien creature that may be the embodiment of the id lurks and screws about, was *The Ants*, 'the shattering novel of insect horror' by Peter Tremayne. It tells us of ants chomping their way through explorers and natives. Unfortunately, this book has no dedication or reference to sociobiologist Edward O. Wilson, despite the fact that he has made many keen observations on the altruism of ants over the last few decades. It seems *The Swarm* was a rare example of research rigour in animal horror novels. Edward O. Wilson has written at length about ants' hard-wired behaviour patterns and willingness to sacrifice themselves for the greater genetic good. He has written very little about the evil inner monologues and malevolent plotting of leader ants. Peter Tremayne has, and he knows how hungry they are for sinew and flesh: 'A few moments later there lay in the clearing a glistening white human skeleton.'

Jane Sewell has popped into the Brazilian jungle to say hi to her dad. On arrival at the tribal village he has been hanging out in, she discovers very little, apart from lots of gleaming skeletons, every morsel of sinew and blood stripped off their body. 'She bit her lip in perplexity.' What could achieve such hideous but impeccable results in such a short time? With 'blood singing in her ear', Jane finds the bones of her father. Tremayne makes identification simpler by giving her father cavities, a distinct difference to the skeletons of primitive natives, who have nicer dead teeth. A boat returns to collect Jane, but unfortunately the crew appear to have been eaten as well, with the last dying word of the final crewman to succumb being 'Formiga.' This is rather perplexing for Jane, as it is the word for ants.

Consuelo de Silva Xavier cares nothing for a horde of people dead; all she worries about is that this may affect her social life. 'But Jose!' she exclaims. 'You promised that I could attend the party at the Rozinantes' place this weekend.' Consuelo is full-figured, much younger than her husband whom she cuckolds. In keeping with the conventions of the genre, it can be confidently predicted that she will die smothered in ants as a punishment for her arrogance; the question is when. She is finally consumed by the perpetually peckish ants within the last few pages of the novel. If only real life was a horror novel, all the cruel people would die from a beast's bite or claw and the good people would live on, only vaguely saddened by the death of another of life's greedy disappointments.

The Ants' finest moment comes on the last page, when the reader travels into the mind of the ant commander. 'Soon the soldier ants would be strong enough to match the puny man things who felt themselves masters of the earth and lords of the future . . . now the ants were evolving, storing knowledge as men did, and forming ambitions . . . the ambition to be masters of the environment. The general rubbed its antennae together. Soon. Soon . . .'

What Peter Tremayne lacks in precise entomological detail is made up for with his knowledge of ancient Celts, his specialist subject. He has written Celtic fiction and authored *Wales – A Nation Again: The Nationalist Struggle for Freedom* and *The Cornish Language and its Literature*. Not surprisingly, he is a big man with a beard, and for these books uses his real name of Peter Berresford Ellis. Man cannot live off the royalties from Celtic fact and fiction alone, though, so that is why Peter Berresford Ellis becomes Peter Tremayne. He has supplemented his income with tales of terror more awesome than you can imagine. So awesome, in fact, that they require exclamation marks: *Zombie! Snowbeast! Swamp! Nicor! The Morgow Rises!* Each title screams, 'Are you man enough to enter these pages of fear?' and occasionally it also screams, 'What is a Morgow?' Obviously a Morgow is a legendary monster of Cornwall – a monster of Celtic proportions – and it may represent the fight for Cornish nationalism. I don't know, I haven't read it.

And so the beast novels go on; from bears to dogs to spiders to cats, there are few animals that have been unsullied by the minds of horror authors.

Sex and death and sex

As with the attack pattern of beasts, using the mind of a sociobiologist, one can begin to find a pattern in the wildlife-gone-wilder horror epic. That is not to say there won't be occasional mavericks, such as worms, that will stray from the path and create an awkward peak in your graph or an unsuspected shaded area in your Venn diagram.

From my study of this genre – and remember, this is particularly focused on the seventies and early eighties period – these are the behaviour patterns I have found.

The public that are mainly baying for more ants/bats/crabs/cats books are in their teens. If they are not in their teens, when they decide to read these books their minds revert to teenage desires.

Just as autism is predominant in men, so is the love of horror fiction. This does not rule out women reading these books, but it is true to say that the male mind is more drawn to things that are horrible. If you pick up weekly women's magazines, they may deal with real-life tales of psycho husbands and nasty accidents, but men's positively revel in photos of dead men in giant snakes' bellies and hands that have had the tendons pulled out by a lathe. This might be because of the damage done to male esteem after boy children are told they are made from slugs and snails and puppy dog tails.

Much of this audience is also hooked with a hint of sex,

or at least female nudity. This should be placed as early in the book as possible, or maybe even on the back cover. Something akin to 'When Jilly Somers' naked body with smashing breasts was washed up on the beach, everyone thought it was just another run-of-the-mill drowning; that was until the starfish started crawling out of her brain'[11] should do the trick.

These books are also popular amongst men whose marriages have got stale and so they:

a) like to go into their sheds where they pretend to mend some shears whilst reading passages of lust from horror novels believing that's how their married sex life once used to be;

b) revel in imagining their wife being devoured by a giant lobster on their next trip to Teignmouth; that'll serve her right for making fun of his espadrilles in front of that young pretty girl at Thomas Cook last spring.

Now we know that these books are mainly bought (probably) by teenagers or middle-aged men, it's perhaps unsurprising that sexual intercourse is rarely guilt-free in the horror novel. Sometimes it is almost without guilt when the coitus is interrupted by the discovery of a mangled body. This normally saves the couple from going all the way and so means that the author doesn't feel it necessary to have them killed by a group of accidentally moral slugs.

The sex before ugly death is usually adulterous, so we know that the in flagrante couple deserved it. If they had continued having comfortable suburban sex under their

---

11 This is not as yet my opening to *Starfish of Blood*, but it might be.

nylon/cotton-mix bed covers, all would have been fine. But their surreptitious canoodling in the outdoors meant it was open season for the irradiated alligators or chemically enhanced alpacas.[12]

Robin Evans, author of *Croak*, another book from my internet auction box, is a little left field when it comes to opening sex scenes. *Croak* is a tale of toad mayhem[13] and so begins with sweaty toad sex. Some male toads wake up in Gloucestershire, hungry for spawning. 'Throughout the long winter months of inactivity their testicles had suddenly grown. Now they were swollen, crammed to bursting point with semen.'

Never in the history of the BBC Natural History Unit, or any other natural history unit, has the coupling of toads been so explicit. 'The stagnant water was thick with males, their bulging eyes glazed with sexual greed.' If Hieronymus Bosch was ever asked to paint a 'toad orgy in hell' canvas, then this would[14] have been it. 'The uncoupled males were demented with frustration. They struggled and kicked. They lunged and grabbed at a leg, a head, a neck – any exposed part of the female. Before long, several of the females were engulfed in a wriggling web of lust-crazed males.'

At this early point in the novel, some men who have popped into their shed to pretend to mend their shears have become confused, forgotten that they are actually reading

---

12 As far as I can discover, there are no alpaca horror novels. The nearest is the Push Me Pull You of *Dr Dolittle*. It's a pity, as fluffy animals are far more entertaining when rabid or insane. See the film *Night of the Lepus* – 'Look out, there's a herd of killer rabbits coming this way!'

13 The toad sadly has a bad reputation, mainly because it has knobbly skin. In the Middle Ages it was seen as the witch's friend, but on the up side it was liked because it could cure warts.

14 I should really have put 'might' rather than 'would', as it seems very presumptuous of me to declare what a Bosch toad sex orgy hell picture would look like. I still reckon it would be a bit like this.

about toads, and are briefly engulfed by a guilty thought that they might secretly be aroused by amphibian pornography.

Robin Evans follows the rule that declares nothing should be left to the imagination. Every detail must become more detailed so no reader can ask the question 'But why?' or 'Tell me exactly what sort of house this kitchen would be found in': 'Clutching his two containers of spawn, Terry Gellner hurried across to the kitchen entrance of their single-storey three bed-roomed house.' Later on, Terry's eyes start 'dancing behind his spectacles' as the spawn jars are opened. We'll leave him there, eyes dancing and ready for spawn.

As Shakespeare might have said if he had written plays about giant stoats

Another good rule for beast horror is to elevate your manuscript by commencing with a classical quote, preferably from William Shakespeare. John Halkin's *Slither* kicks off with 'The worm is not to be trusted . . . there is no goodness in the worm' from *Antony and Cleopatra*. Peter Tremayne's *The Ants* offers the reader some *Merchant of Venice*, while *Worms* chooses a little *As You Like It*.

Robin Evans loses some marks for his introductory quotation. He could at least have used something from the Bible. 'And I heard a voice in the midst of the four beasts And I looked and behold, a pale horse. And his name that sat on him was Death. And Hell followed with him' (Revelation 6: 7–8)[15] might have suited a toad melodrama,

---

15 I mainly like this one as Johnny Cash speaks it at the end of 'The Man Comes Around'. Should you wish to hear more of Johnny Cash reading the Bible, there is an 18-CD set of *Johnny Cash Reading the Complete New Testament*.

and Revelation is generally a good one to cherry-pick quotations from if you are writing anything with a sense of doom. What the author declares by quoting Shakespeare or the Bible is 'I have read things, you know; just because I have written a book involving genital mutilation by crows, doesn't mean I can't quote the Bible', while to the casual book-buyer, a quote from the Bible subliminally suggests that the book they are holding may be as good as the Bible.

Robin Evans, however, chooses a very different prophet for his opening: 'There's a killer on the road, his brain is squirming like a toad' from 'Riders on the Storm' by Jim Morrison, revered by many confused people as the finest rock poet of his generation. Rather than suggesting that Robin is ridiculously well-read, it merely suggests that he is an occasional Goth who perhaps once went to Père Lachaise cemetery and poured Jack Daniels on the Lizard King's grave in the hope that he would rise again like a leather-trousered zombie. I think he actually used the quote because it had the words 'toad' and 'killer' in it. A quick check of the Bible suggests very few, if any, toad references. The writers were more interested in frogs on the whole. Shakespeare offers only 'I had rather be a toad, and live upon the vapor of a dungeon than keep a corner in the thing I love for others' uses', which doesn't really fit in at all, so Robin Evans can't be blamed for resorting to Jim Morrison.

In another similar convention to that of romance, your horror hero must also possess a name that the reader might wish they had themselves. These names are particularly important, as they often open the chapter.

'Jack Dawson clenched his teeth together angrily.' (*The Web*.)

'Harry Kaminsky was a tall thin man.' (*Amok, King of Legend*.)

'Dan Mason leaned back contentedly on the Victorian rocking chair.' (*Spiders.*)

'Jose Joaquin de Silva Xavier was worried.' (*The Ants.*)

'Cliff Davenport sat with his back to the wall in total darkness.' (*Night of the Crabs.*)

Cliff Davenport may not be the most prepossessing name on the above list, but his name is more important than Jose or Harry or Jack, because he is the lead in the most important, exhilarating, nasty and long-running series of novel nasties I have ever come across in Weymouth, and I believe that would still stand if I had found them in Dorchester.

Guy N. Smith – the pipe-smoking emperor crab of the macabre

Guy N. Smith is the author of *The Sucking Pit*, *Return of the Werewolf*, *The Plague Chronicles*, *Deathbell*, *Satan's Snowdrop*, *Slimebeast* and *Wolf Curse*, as well as *The Walking Dead* – 'Hungry, seductive death beckoned from the black depths of the sucking pit.' Most importantly, he is also the author of *Night of the Crabs*, *Crabs on the Rampage*, *Origin of the Crabs*, *Crab's Moon*, *Crabs: The Human Sacrifice*, and *Killer Crabs*. In the world of devouring sociopathic crustaceans, he is peerless. I believe if you are not converted by the end of this chapter to the crustacean genre, as I was when I first opened a hungry crab horror spectacular on the beach, then you have some crab-horror-loving part of your brain missing.

Smith is more than a prodigious author of gut-tearers; he is also an expert pipe-smoker, winning a British pipe-smoking competition, and a writer for *The Countryman's Weekly*, which on the day I looked at it included finding a new ferreting partner, a moral dilemma over shooting a roebuck, and beatings with lurchers and terriers.

Guy N. Smith is the only horror author to demonstrate that avoidance of the Radio One Roadshow in a seaside town may lead to death by pincer. He is also the author of *Writing Horror Fiction*. This guide reveals just how hard he pushes himself when he states, 'Your novel must not be less than good.'

Guy's crab epics were published by the esteemed New English Library. As I viewed the cover of my first Crabs novel in Weymouth, so soon after seeing a few cracked open in a fish shop, I knew I was in for quite a ride. The cover of *Night of the Crabs* is laden with promise. It shows a vicious crab, dripping with blood, standing atop a splintered 'Danger. Keep Out' sign. This crab will not be following man's rules.

Crabs on the Rampage goes for a similar scene, although this time the crab is bloodier and straddling a broken 'Private. No Fishing' sign. This crab doesn't care about the territoriality of the *Homo sapiens* angler. By *Crab's Moon*, the facetiousness of these mutant crabs has gone beyond mere sign vandalism; its cover star is attacking a postbox. What hope is there when even Her Majesty's venerated postal service is disrespected by an angry carapace wearer?

Night of the Crabs has no pretentious quote from a great work to open it. Guy N. Smith does not need to elevate his work with Shakespeare, Milton or Exodus; he knows his words can stand without the crutch of the classics. He merely requires a dedication, the simple 'To Jean, who has to put up with it all.' We are left to wonder what 'it all' is; the mind does boggle at what a spouse must have to go through as her husband churns out another few thousand words of seaside devilment.

Night of the Crabs begins with sexual tomfoolery. Julie and Ian go for a swim. Julie has a figure that would make any man want her 'badly, really badly'. But before they can get to a cove for a night in flagrante, they are devoured. 'He fought to free himself from whatever it was that had hold of his left leg that could only be compared with a pair of garden shears with serrated blades, biting deeper into the bone with every second.' Ian and Julie don't really deserve to be slaughtered as they are not as morally bankrupt as those who are usually consumed or torn apart first. Sure, they are thinking of briny sex before marriage, but they are not having an extramarital affair.

Professor Cliff Davenport is a pipe-smoker; he is also the uncle of Ian, the crab-consumed young man. He will be our hero for the next 115 pages. Although the first in the series is the only book in which the victim is related to our hero, they nonetheless all feature early death, of course.

Crabs on the Rampage avoids commencing with sex hindered by death; instead, a birdwatcher by the name of Ike Ballinger meets a bloody end while out ogling bitterns: 'Blood spurted from the wrist stump, a scarlet salute to the king of crabs, rich wine spurting into the wizened, lusting face.'

Crab's Moon returns to form and sees a hater of the Radio One Roadshow but lover of immoral sex meeting his fate at the end of a crab because his loin lust leads to an extramarital affair. The lesson is clear: avoidance of caterwauling DJs can lead to death.

On each occasion, Professor Cliff Davenport is soon dragged into the fray to conquer the crabs.

In *Writing Horror Fiction*, Guy N. Smith suggests the writer base his characters on real people. Cliff Davenport is a pipe-smoker; so is Guy N. Smith. Cliff understands the ways of the wild; so does Guy N. Smith. In later novels, Cliff has his hand replaced with a hook after a crab-munching;

Guy N. Smith does not have a hook, but I bet he's dreamt of having one occasionally when whittling a beating stick with a penknife. When I see Cliff Davenport, I see Guy N. Smith, but apparently I am wrong. Guy N. Smith admits that he based the lead character in *Werewolf by Moonlight* on himself, and he is also Sabat from his Sabat series, but the real man behind Professor Cliff Davenport remains a mystery. Guy also tells the prospective author to watch out all around him for characters. He once attended a wedding where a man walked in late wearing a black fedora; sure enough, Guy N. Smith went on to write *The Black Fedora*.

Night of the Crabs is Professor Cliff Davenport's first duel with giant crabs. By page 33, after an incident with the RAF and the first scratchmarks of giant crabs observed on the rocks, Cliff meets his future wife, Pat Benson, recently divorced from a rotter. This means she is morally clean; though divorced, it is the fault of the bounder. She is not a slut; she should not die.

'His eyes were already on the dark-haired, petite girl who sipped tomato juice, a wistful expression on her face. She was wearing a cotton blouse above a tartan skirt, and he saw the outline of her small, firm breasts.' Breast description is a vital part of understanding the character's destiny. It is the mammary equivalent of the art of the Victorian physiognomist. Pat's breasts are small and firm; she is clearly a woman of dignity. Women with flabby, undignified breasts that lollop around are more than likely sinful or prostitutes. They are devious or fools or both. No hero of horror is ever disappointed by the topless view of their paramour. If they are, it is de rigueur for that paramour to die, especially if she has used a bra to suggest her breasts are not what they really are. As we know from Halkin's *Slither*, losing control of your hips can also lead to being consumed.

Pat demonstrates a rudimentary knowledge of crabs and has noticed the strangely gigantic crab scratchmarks on the shore. Guy N. Smith is a traditionalist and does not have Pat and Cliff entwined on the first night, but they both rise late the next morning. 'Most of the other guests had already breakfasted and departed by the time they sat down and made a start on their respective melons.' I cannot deny it, 'respective melons' does bring forth my English Carry On sensibility, and I am sorry for it.

The reader is not allowed to get overly familiar with the main characters, and Guy will wherever possible give them their full names: 'Cliff Davenport and Pat Benson were walking out towards the shimmering sea.' Despite this, there is soon familiarity between Pat Benson and Cliff Davenport. The combination of the Welsh coast, a good B&B, nephew death and mutation fear can often act as a lubricant to love.

> 'What a beautiful night,' Pat remarked as they passed alongside the barbed wire fence. 'If only we didn't have to worry about giant crabs!'
> Cliff pulled her close and kissed her.

Before long, sex raises its salacious head, as Pat Benson and Cliff Davenport can no longer control their libidos. For Cliff, who has only recently lost his nephew, and Pat, recently divorced from a cruel man, this is their interlude: 'Nothing else mattered . . . not even the giant crabs.'

In *Writing Horror Fiction*, Guy N. Smith advises the new horror author that sex must be written about with subtlety. To reveal all is to ruin the erotic mood. Here he dwells on the enigmatic nature of Pat's pudenda. The moonlight highlights her white thighs and 'the darker triangle of soft fluffy hair between them seeming to withhold secrets from him. Secrets of men who had lain there.' And so the reader sees Pat's vagina, and indeed all vaginas, as a recording device of past conquests.

To deviate away from Guy N. Smith's crabs series, *Cannibals* is one of his gorier works, and his image of the female cannibal beasts stands out as one of his finest creations of grotesques. Any arousal that occurs in *Night of the Crabs'* sexual musings will be vanquished by *Cannibals*: 'Their girths were the thickness of ale barrels, with sagging breasts overhanging them, bulbous flesh and nipples that resembled spreading cancerous growths. Their thick thighs were separated by a tangled undergrowth of pubic hair, as thick and wiry as the hair on their heads.' I'll spare you the rape scene that follows a little later.

Moving on, and despite *Crabs on the Rampage* commencing with the death of a birdwatcher, Guy N. Smith's writing develops further into the world of the nasties (as they were called during the bleeding-gut-laden eighties). Ike Ballinger's entrails 'flopped out' and are then ripped into bits. Surely that would be enough for Chapter One. But Guy N. Smith knows that by 1981, the competition in the horrors is stiff, and so ups the ante with two more ghastly demises before Chapter Two. Lorna Watson muses on her child born out of wedlock due to a sojourn with an Italian waiter. Watching her son Rodney splashing in the sea, she ponders on his existence: 'You're just the unlucky bastard out of possibly scores who might have spawned in a nympho's cunt.' Fortunately, Rodney is horribly killed by the crabs, blood spurts and his eyes burst. Lorna dies too. What a relief: the bastard and the bastard spawner are dead, saving them from lives that could never have been fulfilled due to the Mark of Cain of immorality.

Later, there is a heroin-smuggling subplot involving a squat-featured man. Like sagging breasts, squat features suggest evil or waywardness. Will Lo Chee survive until the end of Chapter Six? I'll allow you to read *Crabs on the Rampage* to find out. But of course he doesn't.

Having dipped into a couple of stories of seaside attacks, you might want to take a break by turning to the skies, and Guy N. Smith's *Bats Out of Hell*. Professor Brian Newman is another inquisitive scientist, so he accidentally creates a new deadly virus. It will all be fine, of course, as long as the virus doesn't escape the laboratory, where it is safe behind glass. 'But glass is too easily broken.' Or should you prefer 'a winged nightmare of swarming terror', then Guy N. Smith's *Locusts* offers up a feast worthy of his Crabs tales. By this point in the author's history, no longer is 'in the tradition of *The Rats*' required to sell a book. 'By the author of *Night of the Crabs*' is quite potent enough for the carousel. Guy's own methods have developed too, and he thanks Chris Hemmings from the Centre for Overseas Pest Research for allowing him to use information from his publication *The Locust Menace*, so the reader can be certain of the biological accuracy of this work.

'However, at that moment Alan Alton had more important matters to attend to than Uncle Fred's crate of best-quality Pennsylvanian peaches.' And that is Alan Alton's first mistake. Alan is in a marriage that is beginning to founder, partially due to his wife's lack of understanding in country matters such as boys collecting bugs. Ironically, it is her son's bug-collecting that leads to the book's first hideous creepy-crawly confrontation. His wife, Sheila, and son, David, find themselves at the mercy of bugs, though not locusts, but grasshoppers. Or do they? 'It's teatime, David. The grasshoppers' teatime. Run!' Sheila and David run, but the grasshoppers, 'fiddlers of death', make it clear that their end shall be soon: 'We're going to kill both of you, crawl over you in our thousands, into every orifice, drive you mad, suffocate you.'

Just as it appears that the end is definitely upon them, Alan slaps Sheila across the face, and wakes her up from what is revealed to have been a nightmare. Unfortunately for Alan, Sheila and David, once the true ghastliness of the secret cargo of Pennsylvanian peaches is revealed, it will be anything but a dream. The first victim is an annoying tramp called Mac. From his introduction in Chapter 3, we suspect he might not make it beyond a few pages, and before we know it 'they were wriggling alive in his stomach'. The next victim is Steve Emmerton; he is fat, so deserves death as he is too lazy to diet and blames his glands.

Guy N. Smith is a one-man factory of the macabre, and he knows exactly what he is doing. He is a technician of gore, thrills and rural infestation. What Mills & Boon is to love, Guy N. Smith is to dismemberment. Just as Mills & Boon books have an almost mathematical pattern to their structure – from that first angry encounter with the agrarian hero that our metropolitan madam will loathe for a few chapters, to the final clinch by the forge – so Guy N. Smith knows exactly where his readers want to be taken, when they want death, when they want pipe-smoking philosophy, and when they want sex.

What have we learned?

- One day, after a brief bout of radiation or genetically modified maize, your hamster may rise up and take over the world
- The Welsh coast is very good for crab spotting
- Ants are plotting, don't squirt washing up liquid on them

Further reading

Monstrous: 20 tales of Giant Creature Terror
The Sucking Pit by Guy N. Smith
Scorpion by Michael R. Linaker
'a seething swarm of flesh-searing claws and death-dealing venom seeking out human prey'.

9

Religion

When Steve found tubes in Justin's bedroom, he realised his son had been sniffing cannabis.
Occult Explosion, David Marshall

Repent all ye who have danced to Donna Summer

My family tree grows vicars like acorns. Until the generation before me, there was a preacher or two on every branch. Below my Adam's apple I occasionally detect a dab of white, like a genetically inherited dog collar made flesh. The family home had all sizes of bibles secreted within, some with gold inlay and tainted leather, others with charming childish images of Daniel in the den of lions. Sadly, I am the glitch in the family matrix, as somewhere along the line I forgot to believe in any gods. I was confirmed at school, but that was mainly because it allowed you to take some lessons off and the confirmation tutelage mainly consisted of sitting and eating cake while the chaplain played 'Yes! We Have No Bananas' on his piano. Fortunately, atheism is at its most fashionable now. It is a rare moment when I am accidentally fashionable, and it is rather discomfiting. I was years out with that Greek fisherman's hat and way too early with the duffel coat.

Despite my godlessness, I remain drawn to any specialist religious bookshop, which is lucky, as some of the most peculiar philosophies of lifestyle and brimstone have been written invoking the name of Jesus. Let us start with diet, and a book I found in a broken furniture shop in Glasgow.

Are you looking for the perfect diet? When you think of the lean and muscular that you envy, who springs to mind?

Keanu Reeves? Too thin.

Lance Henriksen? Too old.

Vin Diesel? Too bulky.

There is one man whose figure, like Goldilocks' perfect porridge, is just right. He is the subject of iconic paintings that adore his physique, sometimes even when he is blood-drenched, torn and in the throes of death. He is not merely revered on paper, but also fetishised in multicoloured sun-pierced glass around the world. If you want the perfect body, don't purchase *The Cambridge Diet* or *Rosemary Conley's Hip and Thigh Handbook*; you need to consult the master. The question is, what would Jesus eat? And it is answered in *What Would Jesus Eat?* by Don Colbert. Don is also the author of *The Bible Cure for Weight Loss* and *Muscle Gain and Deadly Emotions: Understand the Mind Body Spirit Connection That Can Heal or Destroy You*.

What Would Jesus Eat? sets you on a nutritional journey laid out two thousand years ago, when meat was green, salty and likely to confuse your belly into convulsions, and the taste of honey came with the likelihood of a few swollen sting holes. It will tell you how to get a waistline like Jesus, and which seeds are the most delightful when it comes to aiding contemplation.

'Would Jesus eat this? We need to ask this question often. Jesus certainly did not eat processed, high-sugar, high-fat, high-salt, low-fibre foods.' This demonstrates the Messiah's incredible willpower, as well as the lack of availability of any of these foodstuffs. There was a long wait for the Walnut Whip in biblical times.

As well as asking themselves the big question regularly, followers of the diet are encouraged to remember a couple of key Bible passages to help them say no to dessert: 'Do you not know that you are a temple of God and that the Spirit of God dwells in you? If anyone defiles the temple of God, God will destroy him. For the temple of God is holy, which temple you are.' (1 Corinthians 3:16–17.) Should I have my apple crumble and custard rejected in such a way I will say nothing, but I won't be inviting that superior son of a bitch back for dinner. Just say no if your God doesn't think you should have pudding.

According to Numbers 11: 31–34, God punishes those who are gluttons. In ancient times he punished them with death by plague; now he punishes them by leading them into TV chat shows and documentaries that engender loathing and derision.

The Good Book and the not so good ones

The Bible may be 'the Good Book', but there are many other books that aren't quite as good but that can still come in handy.

The Bible has been a rip-roaring, trillion-copy success for the book trade. It's in every hotel bedside drawer and available in thousands of different versions, from pop-up to

Aramaic. You'd think that the sheer numbers in print would have kept hungry Christians satiated, but fortunately, the Bible is open to a very broad range of interpretations – from Marxist to Fascist to Amish – and thus religious book-shops are stacked high with guidance.

Discover how a Christian university realised through experimentation that disco music made pigs deaf and mice gay, and why John Denver danced with Satan. We will also find out who appears to be the most closeted gay-hating religious maniac (while avoiding libel of course). We may not find out very much about the Church of Scientology; they have the most muscular legal department and more Hollywood A-listers than the Church of Latter-Day Saints.

Is God right?

> I think God prefers atheists; at least they don't keep
> bothering him all the time.
>
> Dave Allen

The world of theology is rife with debate, but one of the great perplexing questions has often been overlooked by popes, bishops and cardinals. What does God do when women pray, if indeed it is anything at all?

The answer is at hand, in a book usefully entitled *What God Does When Women Pray*. This was my first foray into the potent world of Christian politicising. Discovering this book felt like a revelation from the scriptures, as if God was shining his light on me. This was because the cover is so shiny that the Oxfam tea lights were reflecting off it and dazzling my eyes. The cover sparkles. It is an alluring shiny mottled purple with the title boldly shouting in a sizeable font.

The exterior artwork is so magnificent that I feared what-ever lay within could not live up to it.

I was wrong. Until I read this book, I had never imag-ined that getting cancer could be a gift from God. I was also enthralled by the idea that the deity of the Abrahamic faiths might be gender specific when it comes to prayer response. And if he is, is he also as right wing as coiffured and wealthy evangelists seem to imagine? If God is more Che than Pinochet, would Billy Graham and Jerry Falwell want to spend their afterlife on a harp-heavy cloud of equality rubbing shoulders with soil-fingered potato pick-ers? Would they possibly prefer picnicking with the Manson family in Hell?

Sadly, Evelyn Christenson's *What God Does When Women Pray* errs more towards the Republican god than the Socialist god. According to Evelyn, with your prayers to God, you can make sure that the ghastly liberals and left-ists, with their 'we are going to force you to be gay and not allow you to shoot elk in the neck with an Uzi' agenda, will not reign in America. How does she know that God is on her side? She knows because she has collected the evi-dence that surrounds her. God is constantly popping in to remind her that she is loved by him.

Take this anecdote, for example. Evelyn arrives alone in Japan, her body clock is twelve hours off and she is happy not to have jet lag. 'I wrote in the margin of my Bible beside Nehemiah 1:5: "5/23/93. Arriving in Japan. Feeling amazingly good and every need taken care of. Our God is an awesome God."' God watched over Evelyn and ensured she did not have jet lag. If you have experienced jet lag on your travels, you now know why. You are not loving God enough and he doesn't give a jot about you feeling drowsy and sick in Brisbane or Bangkok or wherever else you are doing your sex tourism. I can't help feeling that a God who remembered to make sure that Evelyn didn't feel too groggy on landing should tie a bit of string around his finger to remind him to sort out future Rwandan genocides or another Thai tsunami. Perhaps if he spent less time dealing with the marginal discomfort of praying air travellers on landing, and more curbing violent death and rape, then sales of *The God Delusion* might subside.

For Evelyn, prayer is also a political tool. While in South Africa she writes of meeting a teacher who was saved from necklacing[1] by the power of prayer. It seemed he was at a funeral with fifty thousand others when a group of white people decided that he was taking his pupils off to teach them how to bomb their schools. Fortunately, just before he was horribly killed, the police stormed the funeral . . . and this was all because his prayer chain had tugged at the hem of God. Miraculous indeed; as historians have often noted, it was extremely rare for the police to storm any large black gathering during the apartheid regime.

'The then powerful Communists were taking young children off too, giving them small bombs to put in their lunch buckets and teaching them how to blow up their schools. (Several mothers pleaded with me to get their young children out of prison for destroying their schools with those bombs.)' Try as I might, I cannot find any evidence of a mass of children blowing up their schools during the eighties. As far as I know, even Communists were keen on their children getting a vague semblance of education before the glorious revolution. Could it be that Evelyn

---

1 Necklacing is a pretty word to hide an ugly deed, much like the delightful names that explosive devices are given – daisy cutters for instance. It involved the placing around the neck of a car tyre, which was then set on fire.

© Advertising Archives

With images like these it's amazing that Hartlepool ever stopped confusing monkeys with continental invaders.

will believe any old nonsense if it's about those dastardly Communists like Stalin, Mao and Lionel Stander?[2] Perhaps like the fuller versions of the Bible, *What God Does When Women Pray* is in need of an Apocrypha. Mind you, the use of children in atrocities is always a handy way to dehumanise your enemy – I've heard that during the Great War, toddler fricassee was thought to be the main dish on the Hun menu.

'Prayer is the only answer.'[3] The secret of prayer in *What God Does When Women Pray* mainly seems to involve

---

2 Lionel Stander was a Hollywood actor blacklisted by the House Un-American Activities Committee for being a Communist. He is now best remembered for playing Max in *Hart to Hart*, but unfortunately some people confuse him with Ernest Borgnine. He said of *Hart to Hart*, 'I'm in a television program that is always among the top 20, that's shown in 67 countries in the world, helping lobotomise the entire world.'
3 Though sometimes you are allowed to give chemotherapy a go as well.

sucking up, which must be very dull for God. After all, even the biggest Hollywood star must ultimately get bored with non-stop praise. (Perhaps just once, Jack Nicholson would like to be in the audience of the Oscars without the host saying, 'And hey, look who it is, it's Jack!' as the whooping begins again with a horrible sense of déjà vu.

'Dear Jesus, my heart is exploding with joy at what You did for my prayer life. Thank you that I was born on this side of the BC/AD hinge of time . . . oh Dear Jesus, words cannot describe my gratitude to You! In your awesome name, Amen.' Rather than a heartfelt, poetic imploring to a man who has touched your heart and steers your life, this seems to resemble the fake testimonial on an advertorial for hair-plugs, stay-sharp cutlery or anti-ugly pills: 'Dear Dr Gorgeous, you shall never know how you have made my life full again with your anti-ugly pills. My face is no longer a car crash but a rose garden, or so I am told, as your untested pills seem to have the side effect of making me blind.'

Praise the tumour

Prayer takes many forms, and Evelyn explores them all. For example, what is the power of solitary prayer? Evelyn offers a few examples.

The reader is told of the cleaner of a poorly attended Swedish church. For thirty years the cleaner prays that the church will be full, and yet it is usually empty. Then one day, thanks to the miracle of prayer, God fills the church. Perhaps a poster and leaflet campaign might have been more immediately effective. It is lucky the cleaner's prayers concerned church attendance rather than a life-threatening blood disorder, as three decades just isn't a quick enough response time for arteriosclerosis.

Religion rewards the believer with a very different logic to the hellbound secular population, as the story of Nancy demonstrates. She had been praying for her husband's salvation and her prayers were answered in a rather mysterious way. Did God paint a sky so beautiful that Nancy's husband could not resist being drawn to the Gospel? Did he part a sea to help him out of a traffic jam? No, he used the system of tumour-giving. 'God allowed me to have cancer and go through chemotherapy for a year. One month ago he [her husband] received Christ!' I know that it is not really the done thing to question God, but honestly, God, are you sure the best way to lure a man to the righteous path is by blighting his wife with a great big tumour?

The 'not quite as good as the Good Book' book of Evelyn includes many tales of people falling down things, fracturing things or getting an unsightly pox and then God eventually clearing up the rancorous sores or smashed ankles (at approximately the rate of the healing process sometimes), though it never quite explains why God shoved them down a crevasse or covered them in pox in the first place.

So what does God do with corporate prayer? This is the issue dealt with in Chapter 4. Sadly, it does not include the pleas to heaven of scurrilous, devious companies like the shamed Enron and all those other cloak-and-dagger organisations that have slid into shame under a fog of lying accountancy and the trickle-down effects of greed and fraud.[4] Instead, the chapter deals with setting up corporations of pray-ers to pray together, as it seems God can be

---

4 Kenneth Lay, one of the shamed CEOs of Enron, announced that 'God's got another plan right now' after being convicted on six counts of corporate fraud and conspiracy. Despite this, God was never indicted in the Enron case.

pushed into action by mob rule. Some miraculous case studies prove its effectiveness: 'The Lord heard and the kidney stone was passed that evening.'

And so it goes on. Evelyn is saved from molestation by imprisoned deviants in San Quentin jail thanks to a telephone prayer chain, from a hurricane in Brazil and from a Democrat election victory. Did God create sexual deviants/hurricanes/Democrats just to make sure people prayed to him in the first place? He seems like a lonely neighbour deliberately throwing dog excrement into your garden to force some sort of conversation. He is then happy to have been noticed when you go round and say, 'Could you stop throwing your Great Dane excreta over our fence', even though you were red in the face with anger, so he stops chucking the poop over the fence. Until he wants you to notice him again.

If you want to keep praying, then do, but remember, in all that time you spent on your knees or on your telephone prayer chain, you could have built an orphanage or maybe bombed an abortion clinic instead.

Hey baby, Jesus is cool

God is For Real, Man is a book filled with good intentions. The author is Carl Burke, who also penned *Treat Me Cool, Lord*. You probably get the idea: this is Jesus for dudes, hipsters and convicted criminals. I have never been a dude, hipster or convicted criminal, but I like it anyway.

Carl was a prison chaplain, and realised that the disenfranchised, broke and broken found the Bible dull and square; even the King James Version. He took it upon himself to liven up religious texts with the language of the sixties, to prove that a good story is a good story, however it is told. Gather up your tambourine players, unsheath your ponytail, here is the word of the Lord. This is Psalm 23 reinterpreted for the felon and recidivist.

> The Lord is like my probation officer,
> He will help me.
> He makes sure that I have food
> And that Mom fixes it.
> He helps her stay sober
> And that makes me feel good all over.

That's now a psalm with real relevance, not merely laying us down in green pastures but also reminding the parole officer to help keep mamma off the gin.

Then there is the story of the Good Samaritan, an important tale with a lesson worth learning, but one which might not appeal to the youth of today, who would have no interest in hearing about raiment stripping and Jericho. The Good Samaritan is thus transformed into 'A Cool Square Comes to the Rescue'. Who would think a square could be cool? I didn't until I read this. I'm not sure if I'm completely convinced, but I'm certainly sure that the square is cooler than the squeak and the hood who pass by the beaten man. If I am honest, I don't know what a squeak is. I hope I'm not one. The cool square helps the man who was left beaten and bruised and 'puts a couple of Band Aids on, gives him a drink and a lift in his car.'

Parables are one thing, but how does Carl describe the creation of the world, without the popular 'and the earth was without form and void'? With a play, that's how. The foreboding monologue of Genesis is replaced with a chat between Gert and Sam, a slightly more grown up version of *Sesame Street*'s Bert and Ernie. While Bert and Ernie deal with the difference between 'near' and 'far' or 'loud' and 'quiet', Gert and Sam deal with the biblical version of how something of infinite density and no mass went bang.

> SAM: One day God said, 'Guess I'll make a world.'
>   First it didn't look like much, just a bunch of goo
>   like comes on the roof on hot days.[5]
> GERT: You mean like a glob of tar or somethin'?
> SAM: You got the idea, girl.

Goo is actually a cornerstone of the creationism-for-children argument. Avid creationists, the extreme Christian version of the avid Darwinian, hold up a lump of goo and tell the children, 'Scientists say we come from this, urghhhh, but we know we come from God, which is a much less gooey beginning, so we win.' Later on in life, those children will find out that whether you believe in God or not, there will definitely be some goo involved in the act of creation.

Despite the late sixties Haight–Ashbury lingo, Carl doesn't let things get too wishy-washy and liberal with the creation story:

> SAM: God looked at everything he made and he says,
>   'How about all that? Not bad for a few days' work.
>   Seems like somethin' is missing. Let's see, what did

---

5 *Goo* is also the title of one of Sonic Youth's best albums, though purists curse it for being melodic and on a major label. If you are ever asked your favourite Sonic Youth album say *Confusion is Sex*, despite it not being very good. Then say you are really into free jazz nowadays, even though it is actually rubbish.

we forget? Hmmm, I know, we needs a man to run
the thing, we can make him somethin' like us and he
can give all the animals names and keep them in line.'

It's reassuring to see that even in hippy/beatnik times,
animals are for whipping and eating. After all, why would
God have made them so delicious if he hadn't wanted man
to eat them?

God is For Real, Man has many advantages over the Bible.
It is considerably shorter. At just 144 pages including glossary, you could read this and *Mohammed is the Big Daddy* in
one long sunny afternoon.[6] The book also has cartoons by
Bill Papas.

The titles of the stories are far more beguiling too. Why
read about having a mote in your own eye when you can
read 'When You Ain't So Hot Yourself'? Would you prefer
Judas's betrayal of Jesus or 'A Stoolie In Jesus's Gang'? Advice
to a sluggard (Proverbs 6: 6–19) or 'Don't be a Lazy Bum'?
Paul and Silas in the Philippian jail (Acts 16: 16–40) or
'Thrown in the Hole for Helpin' a Girl'?

You know your Gideon is ready for the trashcan now.

Carl Burke's Jesus is an altogether more muscular character than the docile, doe-eyed carpenter of so many
interpretations. Witness the resurrection, or rather 'When
Jesus Busted Outa the Grave': 'After Jesus busted outa the
grave, he met two of his gang on a road. Man! Were they
ever spooked and surprised.' He is also a blaxploitation hero
up there with John Shaft and Sweet Sweetback. Meanwhile
the two Marys, mother and Magdalene, become two gals.
It will be a while before a pope summarises the Virgin

---

6 Unfortunately, *Mohammed is the Big Daddy*, my hip version of the Koran, is having problems finding a publisher.

Mary as a gal; then again, it might be a while before a pope properly acknowledges the AIDS crisis in Africa. I think the gal thing might come before that.

God is For Real, Man might not convert you, but it is impossible to condemn a book that calls the feeding of the five thousand 'Some Lunch, Huh?'

Disco infernos lead straight to hell

As some religious authors wish to heighten the coolness of the Christian faith, others wish to remind their flock that some of youth's foibles should not enter into the world of the believer. The worst youth foible? Pop music of course, the filthy bastards.

Fortunately, I have not spent too much of my life listening to heavy metal music and so have avoided shooting my brains out after hearing 'Cradle of Filth' backwards or brought on a nosebleed by overzealous headbanging to Lemmy. I have also never found it necessary to sew Led Zeppelin patches on to a dirty denim jacket that smells of athlete's foot. Nevertheless, I am a great fan of heavy metal, not so much for the musical quality but for its ability to bring out a feisty autism in religious fundamentalists who re-rig their turntables to play LPs backwards and use abacuses to carefully tally every mention of evil secreted in a songsheet.

Since Cliff Richard first hugged Billy Graham, he has been trying to prove that the devil hasn't got all the best tunes. With 'Wired for Sound' and 'Devil Woman', he showed many people that he was right.[7] Despite that, it still seems that most pop music *is* the devil's music, hellbent on

---

7 You may well think I'm being facetious here, but I'm not. I think the late seventies period of Cliff is pretty good.

dragging its listeners into drugs, suicide and orgies, whether played forwards or backwards.[8] You may be surprised to hear just who makes the evil list.

Shakin' Stevens was once headlined as 'the new king of rock' in the *Daily Mirror*. Reporting on his concert, the paper said, 'Halfway through the performance the atmosphere sweats with buttoned-down sexual excitement, cascading over the guy on stage, who does things with the microphone as sexually explicit as the law allows.'

Pop Goes the Gospel by John Blanchard doesn't approve of Shakie. It is a small, unassuming book by the standards of fire-and-damnation publishing. I nearly missed it as my finger trailed along a charity bookshelf in Bury St Edmunds within the shadow of the cathedral. Fortunately, after my almost ignoring it, the book fell open in my hand and I discovered that the first shock rocker wooing his fans into Hades was not who I might have imagined. Wales's answer to Elvis seemed like such a nice young man when I was growing up, but Blanchard doesn't think so. Is Satan lurking behind that green door? In Blanchard's view, Shakie is one of the many who are dancing with the devil and inviting sex into the lives of the young and impressionable.

Jethro Tull, the folk band involving a man balancing on one leg while blowing into a flute, are 'bizarre and loaded with sexualism'. Donna Summer, Pink Floyd, Olivia Newton John and, obviously, Led Zeppelin are all named and shamed. It is the hypnotic effect of the repetitious nature of rock music that worries Blanchard and his co-authors:

---

8 Judas Priest were taken to court for causing the suicide of two young men who listened to their music. It appears that if their song 'Better By You, Better Than Me' was played backwards you could hear the words 'Do it. Do it.' Really this can only be heard if someone says, 'Hey, doesn't that sound like "do it".' In their defence, the band played the whole album backwards and pointed out that you might also be able to hear 'something smells fishy' and 'Look Ma, this chair is broken.'

'Quite apart from the erotic elements and simulated orgasm, "Whole Lotta Love" has about as much variety of sound as a pneumatic drill.'

Within the book dwells a fear that these musicians are really on a mission to scramble the minds of their audience so that they become Satan's slaves, when I was always of the view that they just wanted to be on *Top of the Pops* and drink champagne from crevices. It is not just nasty rock and camp pop that is to be feared, though; even Christian pop is dangerous and wrong. Blanchard worries that 'vinyl blasphemies' are lurking in the record collections of committed Christians. *Pop Goes the Gospel* is a collection of childish shrieks and wide-eyed stares of confusion mixed with some pretend science and finger-waving.

Daily Mail TV critic Herbert Kretzmer's statement 'songs, in short, have become the new pornography' is used by Blanchard to succinctly illustrate his major concerns. I think porn shop clientele might be a tad disappointed if their request for porn at their local stockist merely yielded *Now That's What I Call Music 43*. Pornography is really the new pornography. Last century's postcards of women with their pubic hair on show is this century's two shaved women and a man with a sex manufacturing machine on the internet.

'The lyrics of "Bohemian Rhapsody" include the statement that Beelzebub has a devil set aside for them.' Here, the author has confused the lyric as narrative and the lyric as 'things I did today and demand you the listener believe in my rhyming agenda'. If I've got it the wrong way round, the song also includes Freddie Mercury's confession that he is a murderer, which may be of interest to the Metropolitan Police Lyrical Investigation Department.

It is one thing to fear what a song says when played forward, but it is when the lyrics go backwards that the gates of hell really swing open. Backward masking is the purported insidious machination that manipulates your minds, you dead pop zombies. Play any song backwards and you'll more than likely find that 'it's fun to smoke marijuana'[9] and 'I am Satan'.[10] 'The concept is frightening, particularly as there are scientists who claim that subliminal messages (including those inserted by backward masking) can be received, stored, unscrambled and impressed on the mind *without the knowledge of the listener.*' Blanchard doesn't feel it is necessary to tell you which scientists. I thought I would ask a scientist who is an award-winning author and has studied the subject. This is what Simon Singh said to me:

> For years I have been lecturing and demonstrating this incredibly powerful yet utterly meaningless effect, otherwise known as the observer-expectancy effect. Play the music backwards and initially the audience hears nothing at all except garbled noise. But if I prime the audience and build up an expectation (i.e., show them the words that they are supposed to hear) then virtually everyone hears complete phrases. The effect is shocking. We hear things that don't really exist, simply because our brain has been primed to hear specific words. It is a clear demonstration of how we can fool ourselves and why science is important in achieving an objective view of reality. Cheerio.

Hmm, should I have edited out the cheerio?

---

9 Queen's 'Another One Bites The Dust'.
10 From the Doors' 'Break On Through'. More of these can be found at http://jeffmilner.com/backmasking.htm who has put them up, forwards and backwards, for fun, not as a dire warning that hell is coming and it's walking backwards.

The chapter titled 'The Filth Connection' quotes dirty rockers in their own dirty words, from Debbie Harry and Mick Jagger to Frank Zappa and Johnny Bristol. That's right, that seedy sex guzzler Johnny Bristol, you know, from Johnny & Jackey?[11] Again, it seems, ostensibly Christian events aren't exactly blameless: 'The difference between a Slade concert and many Jesus rallies is negligible.'

Blanchard asks the question that no other Christian I know has asked: 'What happened to the hyssop?' And don't think you can justify your compilation tapes with the words of the Bible, either: 'Those who justify their musical activities purely on the grounds that musical instruments were used in Old Testament worship could find the same justification for putting tassels on their clothing, asking God to purge them with hyssop, walking about Zion and waving bits of dead ram.' I have never waved a dead ram at a Morrissey concert and now I wonder if I should have done. I might have waved my hyssop, though, as it appears to be a collection of perfumed twigs, and in those early Smiths days, many of us brought our talcum-dowsed twigs to pay homage.

In Blanchard's world of Satan, Donna Summer is one of the horsemen of this beat-per-minute apocalypse. Her first record, 'Love to Love You Baby', earned her the title of 'the first lady of lust', although since then she has claimed Jesus as her saviour and put her foot in it with her core gay audience by declaring that AIDS may have been sent by God to punish those with unruly sex lives.

David Bowie, meanwhile, is castigated for saying, 'Jesus Christ was a strange boy himself.' This is in fact considered even worse than John Lennon's description of Jesus in his

---

11 My lack of knowledge of Johnny Bristol shows the gaping hole in my grasp of Motown. 'If I Could Build My World Around You' and 'Your Precious Love' are amongst his many hits.

surrealist book *A Spaniard in the Works*, where he calls him a 'little yellow greasy fascist bastard'. Most readers might consider it a little strange to be the child of a god and a virgin who does wine tricks, but Blanchard has decided to take Bowie's words as an insult rather than a statement of the bloody obvious.

Blanchard makes the meaning of life clear as he underlines Ecclesiastes 12: 13: 'Fear God and keep his commandments, for that is the whole duty of man.' Doesn't seem like much of a life to be constantly living in fear of a deity, but it will do for some. Personally, I'd rather listen to 'Touch Me, I'm Sick' by Mudhoney, as long as its hypnotic beat doesn't make me turn to sacrifice again.

Counting the fucks in Slayer songs

I had gone to a Balham antique fair – well, junk shop with affectations and delusions of grandeur – looking for a music box that played the Harry Lime theme from *The Third Man*.[12] I didn't find one. I did find David Marshall's *Occult Explosion: An Investigation into a World of Dark Forces* (Autumn House, 1997), which examines in depth the Beelzebubbish world of headbanging, occultism and excessive cider drinking.

David Marshall, or rather Dr Marshall, is described as an investigative journalist with 'a first degree and a Phd'. What his degree is in is not considered of any importance to the publishers, while he has obviously not investigated the conventions used by people with PhDs – it's not considered the done thing to call yourself a doctor if you have one, I

---

12 It was to replace the music box I already have that has taken to playing the Harry Lime theme too slowly.

hear.[13] In a medical crisis I fear he might be as much use as
Dr Hunter S. Thompson. In fact, Dr Hunter S. Thompson
might actually be more useful. If I was in an accident involving my fingers and a circular saw, I would probably prefer a
bottle of Chivas Regal and some high-strength marijuana to
a reading from the Gospel According to Matthew.

'If we do not take spiritual warfare seriously, the horrible things this book describes will continue to happen,'
writes Jennifer Rees Larcombe in the introduction, suggesting that we might be in for a religious war caused by
Nickelback. The book was born out of the unpleasant
news that a teenager had committed suicide. Dr David
Marshall, however, knows that this was not suicide. Not
only that, he also knows who the murderers were: 'Hard
rock, heavy metal, kerrang and rave music.' I'm not much
of a fan of raves: I don't appreciate chemically altering my
brain to such an extent that I hug strangers and enjoy blowing a luminous whistle, but were these really the shrill,
overly sweaty murderers of a young man?

In Chapter One, 'Tripping Into Rave', a picture is
painted of the young suicide as a smart boy who was 'well
built with a pleasant disposition'. Apparently, his mother
died when he was thirteen and he had a problem with
communication; could these factors also have come
into the equation, as well as Black Box, or Adamski, or
whatever the popular repetitive musicians of the time were
called? Dr Marshall then uses this melancholy story to take

---

13 For an enjoyable romp into the world of pretend doctors, read Ben Goldacre's account
of Dr Gillian McKeith, the celebrated nutritionist who sieves your poo and tells you it is
full of bad stuff. How dumb a world do we live in that Channel 4 has churned out so
many series with this woman in which we are meant to be enlightened when we find out
that just eating Mars Bars, 57 packs of crisps and anything that is served in a bucket
may not be good for you.

Watch out God, this man is after your congregation.

the reader on a trip that includes sniffing cannabis and accidentally thinking you're gay.

The numerous joys of reading rock-loathing Christian doctrines include the autism with which they catalogue the lyrical minutiae of songs. Vivienne James, at nineteen years old just the sort of person that could be manipulated by Metallica, Slayer or And You Will Know Us By the Trail of the Dead, analysed twenty-six heavy metal magazines including *Raw* magazine to aid the momentum of the anti-rock movement with actual facts. In Issue 117 of *Raw* she found '310 references to death, 107 references to drugs, 44 references to Satan'. The magazine also contained an interview with Glenn Benton of the band Deicide,[14] in which he said that he wanted 'to kill all Christians'. What neither Vivienne or Dr Marshall has noticed is that Glenn Benton is also ridiculous and hilarious, and hopefully financially secure because he'll find it hard getting a day job with that

---

14 Deicide means to kill God.

tattooed upside-down crucifix on his head. Speaking of which, if you ever think organised religion is a little dotty, then just how idiotic is Satan-worshipping? If you've not experienced it before, just paint your room black and pretend you're fourteen years old and no one understands you and no one will understand you because you won't let them and smoke banana skins that you've dried on the radiator because you've been told that it will get you high and pierce your nipple with a sewing needle that's been sterilised over a match and watch your nipple fill with pus then watch as it starts leaking when you're trying to chat up that girl with dyed black hair and a lip ring who laughs in your face instead. Then you'll understand.

The rock-will-kill-you genre relies on having no sense of humour and believing that every tuppenny pronouncement from a lead singer is a heartfelt call to arms to evildoers. Yes, David Vincent of Morbid Angel, I am sure you would 'kill somebody not think twice about it'. It's just you haven't got around to it yet. I imagine Dave has also, as stated in his songs, had sex with Katie Holmes, bench-pressed three hundred pounds and drunk 112 Black Russians without even being sick, yeah!

Though godly metal experts are good at counting rude words,[15] they are not so good at getting facts straight, unfortunately. Dr Marshall rails against the lyrics of the Bends. It seems there may have been some confusion between the name Radiohead and their album *The Bends*. It is tricky on an album cover; two different phrases, which

---

15 According to campaigners against *Jerry Springer the Opera*, it contains 3,168 mentions of the word 'fuck'. How did the writers, Stewart Lee and Richard Thomas, manage to fit so many in? In the accounting system of Christian Voice, a minor but vocal gathering of fundamentalists, if a choir of fifty sing 'fuck' as one, that counts as 50 fucks. This is how they manage to get the cunt quotient up to 257.

one's which? For a long time I was a huge fan of the band Pet Sounds, though later I decided the Joshua Tree were an even better outfit.

Meanwhile, Goth outfit Bauhaus are described as a heavy metal group. The Goths shall be angry tonight. And if those who daub eyeliner on to their eyes like icing and wear black lace gloves think they're angry now, they should wait until they see what *Occult Explosion* has done with the Manic Street Preachers: 'In their song, "A Design", released in 1996, the group Manic Street Preachers included these two lines: "we don't talk about love / we only want to get drunk" and before we die laughing at their stupidity, let's admit that many people answer the question what is life for along similar lines.' Dr David fails to notice that the song is called 'A Design For Life', that it's about celebrating the power libraries can give and that the Manic Street Preachers are criticising exactly the same viewpoint as he is. This man is no Paul Gambaccini, Mike Read or Tim Rice.

This is also a book that takes Mr C seriously. You remember, the chemical-eyed jittery dancer who jumped about shouting 'Es are good'. Apparently to many he is a New Age philosopher. Dr David informs us that C's band, 'the shadowy gang of spaced-out mystics called the Shamen, are modern-day equivalents of those in past centuries who have talked with the spirits'.

Dr Marshall froths so much that the froth occasionally interferes with brain mechanisms. 'In the album *The Damned Patti Smith*, a band titled Gloria sang, "Jesus died for somebody's sins but not mine".'[16] The album is *Horses*, the singer is Patti Smith, the song is 'Gloria'.

---

16 Damn, I hope I've got a good proofreader or my facetiousness is going to look pretty lame.

Ozzy Osbourne, unsurprisingly, is declared a mischief-maker for Hades. This was before he was redefined as the world's cuddly heavy metal dad figure. The Institute of Bio Acoustics Research was brought in to evaluate 'Suicide Solution'. Apparently, in court, when Osbourne was being sued for mind manipulation of young people, representatives of IBAR said, 'If you concentrate, you'll hear a heartbeat moving quite fast. That's designed to key into your own heartbeat and make it move faster.' They also discovered the sort of subliminal messages you might expect. The IBAR sound a very interesting group. I would like to have heard more about their work, but in searching for them I have only found them referred to in relation to this case, suggesting that they may not be quite such an official scientific organisation of acoustic research.

As you will have noticed, the majority of books in this chapter have dealt with Christianity, and so some people may feel there has been an unhealthy focus on Anglicans. Sadly, most other religions just aren't as well catered for in the charity shops and jumble sales.

I have found surprisingly few fun books on the Muslim faith. That said, a visit to Buckfastleigh in Devon led to the purchase of *Teach Your Children to Love the Prophet Muhammad* by Muhammed Abdu Yamani (Dar Al Taquwa Ltd., 1995). It is much easier to meet your required word count with a book on the Prophet Muhammad, may Allah bless him and grant him peace, because every time the Prophet, may Allah bless him and grant him peace, is mentioned, you must write afterwards, may Allah bless him and grant him peace. I think that's why I chose atheism; it really cuts down on the rigmarole even if it does increase the hate mail.

Scientology books seem to appear regularly in the Midlands, and L. Ron Hubbard's *Dianetics: The Evolution of*

This is how I remember the Scientology view of the mind. Lawyers, please note, I may be wrong, it's just what I remember, okay? Let's not get silly about this.

a Science has one of the most entertaining illustrations of what makes up the brain I've ever seen. The brain's complexity is summed up with images of springs, gyroscopes, apples and martinis teetering on candlesticks. I imagine that the Church of Scientology wouldn't be too happy about letting us publish it as they can be quite sensitive – so here is a version drawn by me.

The problem with Scientology is that it takes itself so seriously that its recourse is to call the lawyers. I highly recommend you pop in and have a personality test. They will find out what is wrong with you and normally find a cure. I think the cure is usually the embrocation of Scientology.

What have we learned?

- Don't look at cancer as a disease, look at it as a gift
- Jesus didn't eat marshmallows or squeezy cheese
- If your pig can't hear you then get rid of its Slayer records

Further reading

The Lie: Evolution by Ken Ham
The Road to Hell: Everlasting Torment or Annihilation by David Pawson
Why There Almost Certainly Is a God by Keith Ward

10

Thrillers

(or men's books)

> But why don't you ask me how I feel? I was
> lucky enough to love one woman the way a man
> can and she died of leukemia! Leukemia! I saw
> Hiroshima with my own eyes and I married a
> woman who died of leukemia. That's why I
> became a cop! I hate physics!
> *Phyllis*, E.V. Cunningham

Women Beware! These Books are for Men and Only Men

As someone who was brought up with two older sisters, I have never feared the feminine side of literature. From an early age I was as happy reading their *Bunty* annuals as *2000 AD*, or at least I was happy to read *Bunty* annuals if I côuldn't find my *2000 AD* annuals. Ours was a house not groaning with manly literature; there were few novels of war and aggression, angry jockeys in a Dick Francis, or scarred rhino hunters in a Wilbur Smith. The most frightening images that might have suggested manliness were the covers of Tom Sharpe novels, and they were just large-breasted women and tribesmen sketched like a saucy seaside post-card. Having my head buried in a horror novel or a Terrance Dicks adaptation of *Doctor Who and the Keeper of Traken* kept me away from the action of war novels involving beer-jug-laden fraüleins and ugly, barking tank commanders. But what of men who fear they may be emasculated should they find themselves holding the wrong novel, a novel for ladies, for instance; how can they ensure staying true to their gender in the reading room?

How does a man know if a book is meant for him and not the lady reader? After all, imagine the shame of a man on the beach with his mates, reclining in a deck chair enjoying Noel Streatfeild's *Ballet Shoes*, only to have his masculine friends turn on him, laughing uproariously as they explain that it is a book meant for girls. The man skulks off, hurls *Ballet Shoes* in the bin and decides never to read another book. Later, he is convicted of killing Darcey Bussell in a rage to try and redefine his masculinity. And what of the suburban housewife? How does she know which novel will appeal to her husband's hedge-trimming, driving-glove-wearing manliness?

She knows he likes to read great literature so chooses a book that has won a prize. What if, too late, she discovers it won the Orange prize, an award for lady authors? The husband will feel slighted, as if his wife has been questioning his masculinity all these years. Vases are thrown, hedges are cut angrily and inexactly, a cat is thrown over a fence. This is the modern problem of gender confusion and reading, two things that the majority of the population had little time for in earlier centuries.

One day, back on my favourite beat of the Nicholson

Street charity shops of Edinburgh, I found the solution in a box under a table in the British Heart Foundation. In the late fifties and beyond, someone found a way to avoid all this hullabaloo. One publisher knew how important male pride was in publishing, and that publisher was Odhams. The solution was simply to tie together three testosterone-laden novels and wrap them in an omnibus series crudely – beautifully – entitled Man's Book. Imagine: the wife looks to the bookshop shelves and there she sees words that cannot be misinterpreted. It is a book. It is for man. It is Man's Book. Her husband is a man and he will be glad.

'The Man's Book service is unique. It was the first, and remains still the only book service catering exclusively for the rugged reading tastes of MEN!' declares the cover blurb. It's an invitation. It's a threat. Are you really man enough for Man's Book?

Each volume introduces us to the men who have toiled to create books for proper men; they are 'the MAN'S BOOK Men!' Douglas Warner, author of *Death of a Tom*, is 'a talented bachelor' and 'a happy wanderer through Europe in his Dormobile caravan'. Donald Mackenzie, author of *The Genial Stranger*, enjoys life hugely, 'from kippers to Cadillacs; he hates pomposity and Spanish gin, and, understandably, policemen!' He also asserts that he is 'not a psychopathic'. Donald Gordon, author of *Flight of the Bat*, is retired, but pursues his life work – 'how to prevent collisions between aircraft' – while Jerrard Tickell is 'a gay and charming companion who roves the world in tankers'.

The titles add to the certainty that these are books with an XY chromosome. *Subsmash! Deadly Welcome. Sex Trap. Appointment in Zahrain. The Predator.* Although for sheer manliness with a hint of the enigmatic, *Temptation in a Private Zoo* wins hands down. The cover illustrations meanwhile show guns, cleavage, Nazis, sou'westers, machine guns, gorillas, test tubes, anti-tank guns, and more cleavage, this time with a Nazi cupping it.

The whores!

The cover illustration for *Death of a Tom* seems to have been sketched by Enoch Powell after a night of haunted dreams. A white woman, the strap of her dress falling from her shoulder, recoils from a razor-blade-wielding bug-eyed psychotic negro.

'Horncastle stood at the top of the stairs. He did not think about his wife. The whore, he thought, the whore, that whore has done this to me.' Douglas Warner takes us into the whore-heavy mind of a 'ripper'. Detective Inspector Wyndham goes in search of the psychopath, finds out that there are toms and there are toms, meets some hookers with hearts and some without, and some who used to have them before they were cut up. It is certainly a man's book. Endearingly, Warner dedicates it to his parents.

The reader also learns a thing or two about how to judge what class someone is. To read the *Telegraph* rather than the *Mail* or *Express* suggests snobbishness, but if you say Bordeaux wine rather than Bordeaux, you have revealed the truth of your state-educated upbringing.

'The lamplight shone on his face, greasy with sweat, saliva and blood, as a group of Coloureds swung out of the tube station.'

In the same collection as *Death of a Tom* is *Phyllis*, a stealthy, brooding cop melodrama of sex, intrigue and nuclear fission. When a policeman loses his wife to leukaemia, he is destined to hate physics for ever more. Annoyingly for physics hater Detective Thomas Clancy, he must make love to a crazed physicist's girlfriend or it could spell the end of the world. *Phyllis*'s author, E.V. Cunningham, suffers the indignity of being given no biography on the back of the book. No vintage jalopy racing or stag-hunting for E.V. This might be because he was actually Howard Fast, who had worked for a variety of Communist newspapers and also won the Stalin Peace Prize; yes, there was a time with so little irony that there could be a prize linking Stalin with peace. Manly men of the sixties would be far from sure that a Communist was capable of writing manly things. That said, it should be noted that titan-toothed banjolele-strumming George Formby was awarded the Order of Lenin by Stalin. Behind every genocidal despot their lies a man giggling under his moustache at the leering antics of a Lancastrian . . . perhaps.

Back to *Phyllis*, where Detective Clancy is forced to visit lectures about 'light as a particle' where 'bricks emit neutrons'.

I don't know about you, but I feel strongly that there are not enough macho thrillers set in the world of particle physics. Now that Dan Brown has tackled the masons and the Vatican, can't he have a go at the Royal Institute Christmas Lectures and the plotting deviants who may lie behind them?

Clancy, meanwhile, has to go undercover as a physics lecturer. 'The subject of my paper for that day was the meaning and origin of high-energy cosmic radiation.' With ten days' rapid physics cramming and the submersion of his cancer-based science hate, he makes it through.

Speaking as a fan of Nobel prize-winning, bongo-playing safe cracker Richard Feynman and spy bomb thrills, *Phyllis* is the pinnacle of Man's Books for me. It just goes to show what you can get if you give a Communist a chance. Think how many more novels there might have been about wave particle duality and infinity density and no mass if Joseph McCarthy hadn't been so scared of the conjecture of Communism.

The final story in this particular triumvirate of man lit is *Wind Along the Waste* by Ewart Brookes. It is the tale of sibling rivalry over a woman between trawlermen. I don't have many rules in life, but one hard and fast one is that I don't read love-triangle books involving trawlermen (unless they are background characters, obviously). I shall merely flick the book open and whatever sentence is on the page will suffice:

'Why is it you sparkers always work up a fug that could be cut with a knife?'

Enough said. That particular volume was published in 1963. Throughout the sixties, the compilations follow roughly the same pattern, or at least the job lot I bought at the British Heart Foundation in Edinburgh follow the same pattern. I might be totally misinterpreting this. It might just be that the deceased man whose wife donated all these after his heart attack was obsessed with prostitutes and Nazis. There may be a whole other world of Man's Book that has never tainted my mind. Stories about feuding florists or meditations about coming out by teenage boys with a secret crush on their history teacher, perhaps. I have not found those.

In 1960, one typical Man's Book contains *A Twist of Sand* – 'an old man's legacy of a lost island . . . a top secret U-boat, mistrusted even by the Germans, hunted to death in a burning sea'; *My Shadow, Death* – 'battered and bleeding, waiting for nightfall'; and *Appointment in Zahrain* – 'it was their only chance, thirteen men beyond hope, condemned to execution by the Amir of Zahrain'.

Another favourite of mine from 1963 is the compilation of *The Liberators*, *The Genial Stranger* and *The Unquiet Sleep*. *The Genial Stranger* gives warning to avoid the suave who appear to accidentally spill drinks. *The Liberators*, meanwhile, is the tale of adventurer Harvey Landon, who, 'with a murder rap hanging over his head', gets embroiled in a South American plot to usurp a dictator. But it is *The Unquiet Sleep* that will draw you in. Firstly, it is this story that warrants a cover illustration of a seemingly buck-toothed gorilla and a microscope.[1] This is far more enigmatic than the usual man with swastika being shot, or bloke in a vest carrying a scantily clad girl. Yes, this is a tale of prescription drugs and the evils that may lie within. It begins with a government department conundrum: 'The ministry of Social Welfare was decidedly an odd one. It wasn't pensions and national insurance, and it wasn't health; and it wasn't housing and local government. And it wasn't labour.'

To someone used to any book that involves experimentation and animals (mainly those involving killer crabs obviously), *The Unquiet Sleep* is a disappointment. My mind has been weakened by the thrills of the nasties of the seventies and eighties. The author, William Haggard, provides a pleasant government department thriller for another pipe-smoking gentleman to amiably read on the 7.42 from Aylesbury to Marylebone, if he's finished the *Times* crossword over breakfast. The women of Haggard's imagination are symmetrically correct: 'She wasn't flaunting too much of a good thing – he hadn't himself gone transatlantic – but she had everything where it ought to be . . . wow.' And the experimental monkeys have incongruous names: 'The

---

1 A Penguin edition of this novel has a photo of a dead monkey with a syringe in its arm: even better.

simian, near-human gestures sickened him. Ermyntrude was an addict.'

Sex rears its inquisitive head

Luckily, by the late sixties, Man's Books were becoming more tempestuous. In a world where free love was being both celebrated and reviled, Man's Book had to catch up. By 1969, the compiled books were *The Gunner*, *The Predator* and *Sex Trap*. No more genial strangers for men now.

Before the reader has even got to the start of *Sex Trap*, author Bill Turner turns a trick that means we know we're in for a sweaty, seedy ride into worlds we dare not go as we're too busy tidying the shovels and jars of weedkiller in our toolshed. Bill takes us by the hand into London's recesses where urbanites pay for their kicks, by dedicating *Sex Trap* 'to the ladies of Bayswater, Notting Hill and Soho'.

Yes, lads, put down your *Stag Movie Review*, this is a tale that will definitely be prostitute and death heavy.

The first character we encounter, Crowgill, is a tough man, the kind of man who doesn't use a kettle, for a kettle can hide dark secrets such as poison or excess limescale. Crowgill 'liked to see what he was going to drink, boiled or not.' After some mundane musings on why the rim of a coffee tin always gets gunked up with coffee powder, Bill Turner twists our heads when the reader discovers Crowgill has just committed a gruesome murder. But who in London can solve this murder? No one it seems. The London police just aren't good enough, and so Louis, a young lad from Yorkshire, is sent to the capital. He is not a fan of London's fancy ways. Bill Turner himself was born in York and contributed to the *Yorkshire Post*. If there's one thing Yorkshire men don't like, it's people who aren't from Yorkshire and people who think London might in any way be better than a Yorkshire town. London doesn't even have a Viking museum, and their Ripper wasn't as good either.

'London: there's too much of it for a start, Louis decided.' Louis is also infuriated by the London Underground. It's just too complex to change lines, what with the stairs and signs and arrows system. He goes undercover, playing the part of a tough nut, even if he is a tough nut who is constantly confused as he attempts to change from the Piccadilly to the Northern Line. Fortunately he has been given expert advice on how to play the part of the hardened villain and blend in with the average commuter on the tube. 'Remembering Vic Grange's advice, he tried to keep his mouth open all the time in order to simulate a sneer.'

Louis then spends a hundred pages or so sneerily finding out just what London is: a seamy, sweltering hell pit of perverts. Transvestites and psychopaths are exactly what a good honest northern copper needs to bait his sex traps. You won't find a transvestite in Ilkley Moor; they don't have that sort of thing up there.

By 1970, a Man's Book trilogy included James Leasor's *They Don't Make Them Like That Anymore*, John Morris's *Fever Grass* and Anthony Dekker's already praised *Temptation in a Private Zoo*. This last title contains everything real men want, from sex, death, and the oft-forgotten bear-baiting to catering advice on classy dining. As this sentence demonstrates, ill-chosen confectionery can sully a soirée: 'It was a pity about the After Eight mints.'

Richard Streamer has been invited to an exclusive weekend in Bear Garden, an Elizabethan country mansion. The invitation is vividly pink. This disgusts him – it seems so feminine and is definitely not a man's colour. He attends anyway. He likes cars and girls (of course), particularly the lead girl in this tale, called Rainbird. 'The rest of the girl was as exciting as the promise of her face. She wore not only a headscarf in the same colour as the car, but an entire trouser suit in the identical shade.'

Men love to have all their accessories matching. Poor oppressed new men rarely mention it due to the political correctness brigade or feminists or lesbians or something, but they really would like their wives' headscarves to match the chassis of their Ford Capri. The reader must make an early decision as to what sort of woman Rainbird is. As we know from the bestial horror genre, this is best done via breast examination. Rainbird's breasts are 'pert'; this makes her initially acceptable, but the espionage/intrigue can occasionally play tricks with mammalian preconceptions. Certain women are drawn into subterfuge precisely because their breasts do not give away that they may be deceitful, though they frequently return to morality in the final throes of plotting. 'Right now he found it intriguing to watch the way Rainbird's breasts trembled in unison a split second after the E Type took each bump.'

If Jeremy Clarkson wrote thrillers . . .

Is the idea of breasts moving in unison so very odd? Later the reader discovers that Rainbird has a 'jaffa firm bottom', as opposed to a kiwi fruit firm one, which again might suggest betrayal.

If there is one lesson to be learnt from *Temptation in a Private Zoo*, and there may well be more, it is that 'invitations to weekends at stately homes with free prostitutes, brandy, oysters and bear fighting very rarely come without strings attached'. In the case of this private zoo, angry

Germans who wish to discredit Jewish businessmen run the whole shebang. Things explode, people die, breasts remain pert. Now that's a man's book.

Like E.V. Cunningham, Anthony Dekker remains a mystery, with few autobiographical details on the back cover. Whereas E.V. may have been without them because of hints of Communism, Dekker is apparently a thirty-nine-year-old newspaperman who wished to remain anonymous. This rules out Woodrow Wyatt and Bill Deedes.

Unleash the swords and biceps

Not all men want their sex and violence in a fictional here and now. They want their violence to be dealt out by a biceps-bulging arm holding a weighty sacred sword, and their sex to involve the lightest of loincloths. The author to provide this is John Norman. On this occasion, I am ashamed to admit that my total recall of book purchases flounders. I am pretty certain I was still on the Nicholson Street beat, but which charity shelf laid Gor before me? It may have been the Your Local Hospice shop. One thing I can be sure of is the shop also had a Second World War novel which boasted a fulsome quote from holocaust denier David Irving praising its veracity. You don't see that so often now.

John Norman is the author of *Tarnsmen of Gor, Outlaw of Gor, Priest Kings of Gor, Nomads of Gor, Assassin of Gor, Raiders of Gor* and nineteen other novels ending in 'of Gor'. He is the creator of the entire Gorean universe. He previously penned *In Defence of Ethical Naturalism: An Examination of Certain Aspects of the Naturalistic Fallacy, With Particular Attention to the Logic of an Open Question Argument.* Who would imagine that a professor of philosophy could turn with such ease to swordsmanship and bare-breasted encounters?

It seems so much easier to sense when a fantasy or science fiction novel is rubbish than a boring novel about divorce and attempted suicide set in 1950s Brooklyn. I can drag my eyes across page after page of melancholy, pensive and painfully slow drama and say at page 43, 'Crikey, this is rubbish,' only to be roundly lambasted by the others in the train carriage or cocktail party who tell me that it is a classic of its kind and has won some prizes and that I must be an idiot not to understand a book that so brilliantly holds a mirror up to the death of the American dream in the ghostlands of the suburbs. I only need to read one or two choice sentences from the fantasy genre to make up my mind, and it is much more fun.

'I had never forgotten her, the beautiful, olive-skinned, green-eyed Talena, so stunningly figured, such fantastic lips, the proud blood of Marlenus of Ar, Ubar of Ar, Ubar of Ubars in her veins.'

It's the Ubars, Mubars and Tubars of fantasy novels that put me off, in the same way that much cheap science fiction thinks that in the future legislation will be brought in by some letter-X revolutionaries that will demand that most names involve the letter X or a Z if necessary. The words 'such fantastic lips' seem incongruous in the world of slaves, priest kings and tarnsmen; it is just one step away from 'the proud-blooded warrior queen from the line of Tarsus of Korsus, Morsus of Brosus and Toxus of Moxus stood regally, her dark flaxen hair ennobling her angular face that dared to be looked at. He could think only one thing: "Smashing knockers."'

But apparently I would be an idiot to dismiss John

Norman. I am the philistine, not him. According to Gorean fan literature, Norman has used his background in philosophical and classical education to populate the Gor landscape with fully realised versions of Graeco-Roman, Viking and Native American cultures as well as asking and answering important philosophical problems. '"It's possible," said Samos, "that it is an image you love, and not a woman, that is, not a person but a memory."'

If John Norman's final intent is to give us a classical education in the guise of fighting fantasy, his publishers don't seem to be giving that message out with the cover design. *Hunters of Gor* (1980 edition) is adorned with a bowman in a bobble hat, or Gorean equivalent, clasping an unconscious and barely clad blonde with a well-manicured bikini line. The celebratory fortieth-anniversary reprints of the Gor saga have dispensed with any extraneous cover details. The modern cover is a simple photo of a naked manacled woman from neck to ankle. If only Soren Kierkegaard's publishers had put something like that on the cover of *Either/Or*, maybe he would have been more popular and less derided in his lifetime.[2]

One may debate whether John Norman has an obsession with the slave girls of his imagination, though Chapter One seems to offer a clue. Here is the first description of the slave girl on page 8: 'She was clad in a brief bit of diaphanous scarlet silk. Her beauty was well betrayed. Her collar, a loc collar, was yellow, enamelled. She was dark-eyed, darkhaired.' She does a little taunting with her body in that way that women in brief bits of diaphanous silk so often do, then before you know it Norman has occasion to describe her again at page 11. 'In her brief silk, the two-handled bronze

---

2 'Existentialism isn't a philosophy, it's more a bad mood' (anonymous quote).

paga vessel beside her, knelt the slave girl, waiting to be summoned. She was dark-haired and beautiful.'

One thing the reader knows for certain now is that she is definitely in a small patch of silk and she is dark-haired. There is as much certainty in this as there is in knowing that Don Estelle definitely was in a pantomime with Jim Davidson. But what if the reader gets to page 15 and has forgotten all that information because thoughts of being a warrior and having your own nearly naked slave on a chain distracted you and you started pencil-sketching your imagination? John Norman decides it might be best to go through it all again on page 16. 'She was very beautiful in that bit of slave silk . . . she was slender, dark-haired, dark-eyed. Her eyes were wide. She had exciting legs, well revealed by the slave-height of her brief silk.'

Is this repetition a literary exercise? Is it meant to represent the narrator's obsession with hair and diaphanous silk? Was John Norman consistently distracted by a yapping dog outside his window as he attempted to write this chapter? Or is he just so familiar with his readership that he knows that if he bogs them down too much in plot and conversation they'll expect a little treat of a slave girl description to keep them going through the boring bits? Don't worry, readers, the sexy girl is still there. Only the experts, philosophers and Norman himself can know. The 'of Gor' series remain the finest 'modern-day professor falls into past mystical world and fights with swords and girls' books currently available. The internet abounds with discussions about what they mean; having only read two and hidden them away at the back of my collection shed, I do not believe it is my place to add to the debate.

Overall I don't trust books with enigmatic titles such as *The Memory of Geography* or *The Music of a Forgotten Song* or

'Hark Ye!' Said the Plague Man. I like it when books declare just what they are. The reader knows that *Crabs on the Rampage* is about precisely that. That's why I like it when a book about a thing that kills is called *The Killing Thing*. I imagine the publisher's discussion with the author, Kate Wilhelm, was a simple one:

> PUBLISHER: What's your book about?
> KATE: This scientist invents a big thing that goes on a killing spree.
> PUBLISHER: Shall we call it *The Memory of Forgotten Blood*?
> KATE: No. We shall call it *The Killing Thing*.

With so many Man's Books to read, however, *The Killing Thing* remains no more than a cover to me.

Morrissey's shaved idols

By the early seventies, books that were aimed at the men's market cut back on titles even as lengthy as *Death of a Tom* or *Sex Trap*. Titles were now approaching the monosyllabic – *Chopper, Mama, Suedehead*. As surely as newspaper journalism feeds off paranoia and fear of change, publishers have been quick to make a buck from the latest youth tribe to grace the front page. Mods, rockers, ravers, bikers, skinheads, teds, and beatniks have all been celebrated, sensationalised and vilified in cheap paperbacks.

For middle-aged manly loins no longer stirred by espionage or police thrillers, youthsploitation was a welcome arrival. Youth culture was a creation of the mid-twentieth century. Until then, most youths died before they made it to thirteen from some sewage-based pox or pustule-ridden nastiness. If they made it to fourteen they went off to the factory to lose a hand in a pulping machine and eventually sell pencils from a mug. Life wasn't much of a life in the old days. But after the Second World War, the next generation outrageously decided that there should be a moment in their life between cradle and grave that should be fun, and thus the permissive society grew and outraged those who were angry that they hadn't had any.

The first wave of youth culture novels told of bedsits, coffee bars, sensual dancing, chunky rollneck knitwear and abortions. For all their straight-from-the-fridge, be-cool-daddio varnish, they were still about the trials and tribulations of young love and the obstacles in the way of it, whether these were prudish parents in fear of greased hair, or a switchblade and bicycle chain. Then, as the fears grew, as the switchblade wielders mounted up on the beach, the pulps dealt out increasingly vicious action. Could you take the full-blooded tension of being embroiled in a skinhead knife fight or a Hell's Angel bike chain mashing?

Richard Allen's skinhead books have been copiously covered before, and are now deemed bona fide classics of the New English Library dangerous-spitting-youth-in-rebellion genre. Unlike many exploitation novels, he is given rigorous critical examination by some. 'The hetero-sexist manner in which Allen depicts adolescent sexuality IS objectionable, but the fact that such sexuality gets depicted at all IS worthy of note,' writes Stewart Home in his essay *Gender, Sexuality and Control: Richard Allen, Mick Norman and Other New English Library Youthsploitation Novels of the 1970s*.

According to Stewart Home's website, this is the aim of his work: 'I have attempted to continually reforge the passage between theory and practice, and overcome the divisions not only between what in the contemporary world are generally canalised cultural pursuits but also to breach other separations such as those between politics and art, the private and the social.' Could Richard Allen, author of *Bootboys*, *Skinhead Girls* and *Suedehead*, ever have imagined he would come under such academic scrutiny?[3] Allen wasn't a skinhead, or an Allen, he was James Moffat, a heavy-drinking journalist who ghosted numerous books and became surprisingly popular when he delved into the skinhead youth culture genre when he hit middle age. He has hovered in my mind since I was a teenager first facing abuse from skinheads as I traipsed around in my cardigan with my string-tied books, but his novels are treasured, so rarely appear in the charity shops. Sometimes those who seek, especially if they seek shaved-head kitchen-sink knife-jabbing novels, don't always find.

Unlike Richard Allen, Peter Cave was still a young man when he wrote his Hell's Angels novels.[4] The Angels were not just confused or angry kids; they were big greasy men with a lust for fighting and fucking around great big bonfires. My first Peter Cave was found on a small bookshelf in a lifeboat station in Staithes, once home to Captain Cook. I put fifty pence in the collection box, bought a pint in

---

3 There is something far more joyous in scrutinising low-brow culture than in examining the high-brow. The incongruous mix of writing about post-Freudian analysis within the context of oedipal mother worship when it concerns Jess Franco's *Bare-Breasted Countess* is so much more entertaining than reading another academic analysing T.S. Eliot's *The Waste Land*. Then again, I would say that; look at the book I'm writing. For film enthusiasts, *Necronomicon* magazine included 'Deep Throat: Pornography as Primitive Pleasure' and 'Marco Ferreri: Sadean Cinema of Excess'. I'd just watch the films if I was you, or read a book about string theory.

4 Peter Cave, the author of *Chopper* and *Mama*, is not the same Peter Cave who sometimes 'explains what physicalism is, why he believes it to be true, and how it can be defended against a range of criticisms', who is a philosopher, which is a pity.

the seafront pub, and settled down in this rural seagull-squawking idyll, ready for my mind to revel in gang fights as my body remained in picture-postcard beauty. Peter Cave's *Speed Freaks* portrays a battle between the two things Middle England most fears – hairy bikers and the men who ride fairground dodgems. 'The enraged fairground workers could fight just as dirtily as themselves. Boots smashed into Angel ribs, steel bars across Angel skulls.'

Readers of the New English Library biker books may have been disappointed if they ever decided to give up their day job and take to the A43 full throttle. 'The novels of Peter Cave are as far removed from the reality of the British bike scene as Westerns are from the reality of riding the range . . . the truth is stranger still,' explained Maz Harris, Hells Angel MC. But as *The Devil's Rider* (another Hell's Angel epic) illustrates, these novels were not intended to be read by those it portrayed. Halfway through the novel, the sleaze and motor oil is punctuated by a thick cardboard advert, not for a Triumph or a Suzuki or a leading purveyor of German military helmets, but for the Prudential. Where better to remind accountants of their own mortality than in the middle of a novel celebrating violence and death.

'Like a moth to a naked electric light bulb, or a junkie to his nearest "fix", a Hell's Angel always gravitated towards the nearest possible fight, or the quickest possible sex . . .' From the outset of *Chopper*, the reader has been warned. Get ready for the ride of your life, every day on the 7.34 from Reigate to London Waterloo. You're not on your way to another day behind your desk at the chartered surveyor's; you're taking a journey into the mouth of Hades . . . then on to the double-entry bookkeeping until five, when the blood can spurt.

'She had stripped off and was busy helping screwball Sam

to do the same. Mudso and Frenchie had contented themselves with removing their jackets and unzipping their jeans. Just two more volunteers were needed before the show could commence.' With the amount of sex Peter Cave's Angels have, you would think they spent most of their lives taking a postcoital snooze in a lay-by. The Hell's Angels novels are the manliest of all manly books; read two in a row and you'll arrive at the office smelling of motor oil, sweat and rust.

One for the chaps

Glasgow is the home of the cowboy thriller. I don't know why so many Glaswegians want to pistol-whip a man in elaborate chaps, but their charity shops have almost as many Western novels as seaside towns have romantic fiction, in my experience. There is something about the gait of a Glaswegian on a Saturday night that has a suggestion of *Shane*. You can also see people thrown out of bars with a momentum that suggests saloon swing doors.

'Chepete was spewing out a strange mixture of Canuck French and Cree blasphemy as he sat up, blood spilling from clenched teeth and down the corners of his ghastly grin.' With the exception of the 'Canuck French and Cree' the rest of this sentence could be as specific to Glasgow as it is to the old West.

I prefer my cowboy tales sung in three-minute bursts by Johnny Cash, but if the battery runs out on my iPod, I can turn to *Fast Gun* by Walt Coburn, a Western from Barnado's, or maybe Imperial Cancer Research, in Glasgow's West End. You know where you are in a Walt Coburn horse opera. Chapter One begins, 'Bryce Bradford had ridden a long way', Chapter Three with 'Bryce Bradford smiled grimly',

Chapter Four with 'Bryce Bradford shoved past.' Bryce goes on to push geldings, get up before sunrise, and carry a black satchel. If Bryce doesn't open the chapter it will be Jack Quensel caught behind a bolted door or gritting back a low moan of agony. Chapter Eleven takes the unusual step of opening on the slow grin on the leathery face of Wade Applegate, but it soon becomes apparent that his slow grin is caused by looking at Bryce Bradford.

And incidentally, why do publishers need to put 'The End' at the end of these books? We know, you know, we've run out of pages. Do publishers like Trojan believe that I'll keep reading all the way to the back cover blurb, turn the book around and start at the beginning again, trapped in a book loop that means *Fast Gun* is never-ending, so I won't need to buy another Trojan book and they'll go bankrupt due to their readers' stupidity?

What have we learned?

- After Eight mints are not considered as luxurious at a bear-baiting event as its seventies adverts might imply
- Nazis sell books
- Man's Books have sadly been replaced by *Nuts* and *Zoo* magazine, which combine nudity and nasty pictures plus some bar-room jokes without the burden of narrative and with the aid of copious glossy illustrations . . . which is a pity

---

Further reading

Punk Rock by Richard Allen
Kiss the Boys and Make them Die by James Yardley

11

Self-help

Skirt length should be short, but within the
normal range for where you live.

Margaret Kent

Humanity likes to boast that we are the best of the animals
because we have self-consciousness, but with this comes
self-disgust, paranoia, and waves of existential angst.
Fortunately, authors, talk-show hosts and quack psycholo-
gists have ruthlessly exploited our innate mental weaknesses
with self-help books, which promise to foist the power of
YOU upon us. What is the power of you? Read enough of
these books and you'll see it is the power to be lured to read
anything that says YOU loudly enough. Any chemical or
mental addiction can be cured with an alternative addiction
to manuals. Suffer from narcissistic personality disorder?
Then tuck in to Elaine Payson's *The Wizard of Oz and
Other Narcissists: Coping with the One-Way Relationship in
Work, Love, and Family*. Need to manage your anger? Then
it's got to be Thich Nhat Hanh's *Anger: Wisdom for Cooling*

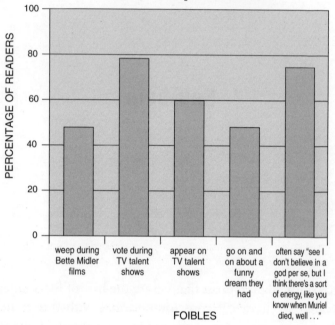

the behaviour patterns of self-help addicts

Another graph.

the Flames. Is someone you love addicted to sex? Then you have to read Mic Hudson's *When Someone You Love Is Addicted to Sex.*

If you are currently battling an addiction to self-help books and find that you can't deal with life without opening a paperback by someone purportedly possessing a PhD, then the next few thousand words should be the first step to conquering your need for the splintered crutch of nonsense. We will have witnessed some of the most peculiar

© Robin Ince

The National Organisation of Statistics and Geometry can be uppity
if you have a graph but no Venn diagram. This is a Venn diagram.

graphs ever drawn, including one for *Inherent Intellectualism
within Sexy Girls and Sexiness Potential.* Discover how to use
telepathy to improve your bedroom technique, and find out
why a glue factory is the place for a first date.

I cannot find the statistics for people who have bought
only one self-help book, but I believe, on no evidence
whatsoever, that it is not many. On the opposite page is
what a graph may look like for personality flaw versus self-
help book buying.

And above is the Venn diagram of this situation.

Usually I would require hard and fast evidence before
uttering simplifications, but as most self-help books I've
become entangled with don't bother, then neither shall I.
There may be a few people who have purchased just one,
perhaps entitled *Embrace the Dragon But Don't Feed The*

Tiger: a Guide to Cutting Away the Dangerous Vines in the Emotional Jungle, and then looked askance as they have thought, 'But this is clearly rubbish, I don't think I even have an inner tiger, I reckon it's just a grumbling appendix.' But from perusing the bookshelves of my more jittery friends, I'm pretty confident that one self-help book is never enough. As each mental kink is cured, it can only make another one more apparent. How else would you know that hiding behind the kink created by your chronic shyness at events organised by jockeys lies a phobia of exuberant hats and dogs with lazy eyes?

The first part of being a self-help priest is to persuade you, the reader, that something is missing. Maybe you didn't even know that something was missing. Perhaps in your happiness you didn't realise you were actually unhappy, but what if your being blindly happy was simply masking your inner everlasting sadness? The Scientology personality test works a little like that. It doesn't matter what your answers are, the result will never be 'Oh, you seem fine, off you pop, no L. Ron Hubbard for you.' There will always be at least one dent in your personality, and to remove that dent takes dianetics. But I'd better not ponder on Scientology again, I can hear their lawyers rasping like vampires at dusk.

To be a really successful self-help guru you must buy some sort of qualification from the internet, pretend you had a backlog of trauma that you cured yourself through positive thinking or a diet consisting of brown things, and possess a shoutiness combined with a bullying streak that may be mistaken for charisma and confidence. The only self-help going on really is the self-helping of the author to all of your money. They don't even need to bottle the snake oil to dupe these metropolitan hicks, though it is worth coming up with a series of spin-off products to maximise revenue. Gillian McKeith, formerly Dr Gillian McKeith, has books, TV shows and a full line of snack bars, pastas and energy powders, and all from gaining a hint of notoriety from sieving wobbly people's poo.

Problems in the time of scullery maids and gaslight

The first self-help book I freed from a table in a jumble sale did not have the whiff of charlatan bamboozler, it had the aroma of a well-meaning group of doctors, vicars and Women's Institute members trying to guide society correctly. The first issue I turned to had me hooked:

'Should a Manager Marry a Factory Hand?' This question highlighted the danger of crossing the class divide. Can happiness ever last when worlds collide? It is one thing for a duke to foist himself upon a maid forced then to bear a bitter bastard offspring, but to exchange rings and vows with someone without an entry in Debrett's is another matter entirely. In your heart, you know the answer to this one.

'No . . . although you may be the least snobbish person in the world, it would grate upon your ears, as an educated man, to listen to badly phrased and ungrammatical speech all the time.' Furthermore, imagine the look on your cultivated friends' faces as this stained guttersnipe mangles sentences like an itinerant hammering scrap.

Real Life Problems and Their Solutions by R. Edynbry covers the quandaries of modern living when living was modern in the 1930s. It appears to be based on contributors' letters, and should you ever be uncertain about the onward-moving nature of thoughts and ideas, whether positive or negative, looking back to Edynbry's ideas for the individuals of 1938 shows just how war and a brief bout of socialism can change a nation.

'Should one marry out of pity?'

Here is a question that is triggered by a scenario that might have come from a long-forgotten touring play or early radio drama. A man loved a girl when they were teenagers, but some cad came bounding in and swept her off her feet. After six months of jealousy pangs, he heard news that the cad had involved his love in a car accident that means she will be infirm for the rest of her life. The bounder has bounded off, and the young, now mainly bed-bound girl has realised, in her infirmity, that her first love was the true one. Should the man marry this weakened woman? Maybe, but only if she bucks her ideas up and heals herself.

The pitying chap is congratulated for his thoughtfulness, but reminded that an invalided wife may not be able to provide happiness and the husband may require 'stern self-discipline'. 'Your best plan here is to make no rash offers of marriage, until this improvement is obvious and has lasted for some time.'

Other concerns afflict the young gentlemen of the day:

'My girl has had a shock. How can I make her forget?'

The shock is initially non-specific. The reader might presume that it may have been a man in a raincoat on Clapham Common, or a seedy man with roving hands in a railway carriage compartment. All the reader gathers is that the girl returned from a walk looking 'very pale and agitated'. Soon all is revealed: a motorist, so frequently a cad as we are increasingly discovering, pulled her into his car, forcibly kissed her and threatened far more. Even after the doctor has given her a tonic, she remains a nervous wreck.

The good author firstly stresses that this sort of motorist is a blackguard, and sadly more prevalent than the reader might hope. The solution is simpler than in modern times, where a lengthy and costly bout of counselling may be the thing. Back then, a jolly holiday and amateur dramatics would take your girl's mind off any unpleasant sights or touching. Once any lingering shock has been forgotten, marriage agreed and family spawned, concerns become less about you, and more about your offspring, of course.

'How can a backward child be cured?'

Worried parents fear that their two-year-old is dull compared with others and has not inherited their personal vivacity. The solution is a simple calm down and don't be pushy, as relevant now as it was then. I spent my early working years in a children's bookshop in a smart part of London. Every day a snooty parent would appear and declare that their three-year-old was remarkable and had the reading age of a Latin professor in their mid-fifties. After going through a few books for ten-year-olds, we'd try books for five-year-olds. They would be rejected too. In the end it would seem they had the reading age of a middle-aged professor, but one who liked books made of cotton that made a rustling or ringing sound when squeezed.

Should you still wish to know how to treat 'a girl who wants to show off' or whether young girls should holiday in seaside camps or if art photographs contaminate, the answers are contained within. I'd be surprised if you manage to find a copy, though; who would give up ownership of such a vital volume to the charity shop and risk living the rest of their life unguided?

Me no how letter write

Letter-writing was an old way of communication before the email and text message were invented. Whereas emails and text messages require little decorum and much abbreviation and ugly slang, especially for the debased young people who loiter on our streets nowadays, the letter required etiquette. Some people still write letters in ink, but the Royal Mail is mainly used for the distribution of catalogues and information about beaten dog charities. Should you wish to write a letter, and it is a challenge, then *The Correct Guide to Letter Writing* will help steer you toward some semblance of shape and meaning. It can be relied on as it is written 'by a member of the aristocracy'. Being a member of the aristocracy, the author is not so crass as to use their name and title. Over five hundred different letters are set out for you to just copy out and add relevant names at the 'Dear . . .' and 'Yours sincerely . . .' sections. The first hundred or more cover basic business letter templates from 'From a Commercial Traveller, suggesting special terms' to 'To a customer, acknowledging receipt of order and offering alternative goods'.

The book starts to heat up with section two, which deals with letters to schools and from students such as 'From a foreign student, asking what qualifications are necessary for entrance to Oxford University', but even this is a preamble to the main event of The Ladies' Letter Writer and The Gentlemen's Letter Writer. It should be obvious at once that 'Accepting an invitation from a Gentleman to Lunch at a Restaurant' is not at all the same as 'Accepting an invitation from a Gentleman to a Dinner and Theatre Party' or 'Accepting an invitation from a Gentleman to his firm's staff dance'. The options for declining are also spelled out. How sad it must be for the man constantly rebuffed in written form to notice that the letters have not the slightest personal touch, but vaguely whiff of rejection from a member of the aristocracy.

Writing to the bereaved is very difficult, as an attempt to avoid cliché or not say the blindingly obvious is almost impossible. *The Correct Guide to Letter Writing* offers a variety of templates, including a short letter to an acquaintance on the death of their husband, and a longer one. There is a 'Letter of thanks from an invalid' and even a 'Letter of condolence to a lady on the death of her little boy'. If you fear that this isn't specific enough, then take note of 'From a lady to her brother-in-law, informing him of the death of her husband' or 'Requesting a friend to break the news of the death of her husband to his wife'. I think they've covered just about everything.

Love, as well as death, is also dealt with. 'I hate writing this because I know it is going to make you very unhappy, as unhappy as it makes me to have to say it. But we should never be happy together.' Read in a Celia Johnson voice with the sound of heart breaking like sticks crackling in a fire, this letter is, of course, for 'Rejecting a proposal'.

'I have been so unhappy lately, thinking you did not love me as you used to, that I hardly knew what I wrote . . . Why do you write so seldom?' This is another lachrymose tale that nowadays would be dealt with curtly and with abbreviated swearwords in a text, but at the time was the only recourse for a woman 'To her Fiancée, excusing herself for her jealousy'.

Meanwhile, the to-the-point 'I was extremely sorry to hear of your disappointment' will pretty much suffice if you're writing 'To a friend who has met with a disappointment'. Please bear in mind though, ladies, this is from the Gentlemen's Letter Writer chapter, so may well not be applicable to women wishing to write to a friend who has also been disappointed of late.

Should you wish to find a pen in your drawer and take

to writing letters asking a suitor to desist or an actress to open a bazaar, *The Correct Guide to Letter Writing* will be a most pleasing volume and possibly a shock to those who had forgotten such dignity and language were still in existence. How charming the past looks from the pages of advice books, as long as you forget about the smell of sewage and whooping cough.

But we have lingered in the era of Ealing films for long enough; it is time to leap from the fifties over the chasm of the sixties and into the almost modern world.

Feel the fear and then punch it in the face with your crystal

Milling around a Methodist chapel, I was, as usual, drawn to the small selection of charity books on sale to help fund roofing tiles and prayer book purchase. And there I found a book of paranoia and redemption nestling between a haunted house pop-up book with a few ghosts missing and a guide to pony trekking.

'If I expose my nakedness as a person to you – do not make me feel shame.' Why am I afraid to tell you who I am? Because people can be spiteful and need to arm themselves with as much as possible to be top dog or at least have a sense of power, so tell them too much and they'll blab it out and make you foolish. Then you'll cry in the toilet and everyone will laugh at your smudged make-up, that's why. Although that is not John Powell's answer in his book of 1968, *Why Am I Afraid to Tell You Who I Am?*

I am wary of any self-help book that begins with a biblical quote, though considering the location of discovery, I shouldn't have been surprised: 'Then the Lord God said, "It is not good for man to be alone . . ." Genesis 2:18.'

This verse works very well out of context; human beings should not be on their own unless their solipsism is perfected. On the other hand, it's at this point in the Bible that God snatches a rib and makes a woman, who then is lured by a snake to eat some fruit and so realises her nakedness before suggesting her husband takes a bite too, thus bringing about the end of paradise for everyone. If the serpent hadn't been hanging off the Tree of Knowledge and man was still alone in the Garden of Eden then we wouldn't need self-help books in the first place. We would be dull but satisfied and lambs would still be hanging with lions.

'My person is not a little hard core inside of me, a little fully formed statue that is real and authentic, permanent and fixed; person rather implies a dynamic process. In other words, if you knew me yesterday, please do not think that is the same person you are meeting today.'

I fear this thought is reminiscent of the Sally Field epic of multiple personality disorder, *Sybil*. Sybil had an unpleasant mom who foisted colonic irrigation upon her, so the only way she could deal with it was to develop thirteen different personalities. Like many true-life TV movies of the week, some people have debunked the story and of late the whole multiple personality disorder scene has been scrutinised. If only Sybil had turned to amateur dramatics then she could have got over the shock and put the thirteen personalities to good use too. I hope this particular book does not encourage people into the confusing and distressing world of deciding that one personality just isn't enough. Putting aside John Powell's rapidly changing psyche, it's pretty clear we will become fearless in telling people who we are by the end of 167 pages. I won't count page 168, as that is just a drawing of three heeled shoes and I have no idea what it means. We are all shoes; our buckles change over time and become laces?

The crux of the book is that we all wear masks, but dare we remove the mask and reveal our mask-less self, or is there any point, as we might be someone entirely different tomorrow. As Powell says: 'Inside each of us, there is a tape recorder which plays a psychodrama which is constantly being enacted.' In other words, every one of us is an afternoon on Radio 4, a chamber-piece psychodrama of children and parents and smashed egos. I'm only up to page 22 and I am more fearful of telling people who I am than I was at page 1. Fortunately, geometry saves the day with a triangle, each corner representing a facet – intellect or will or feelings: 'To tell you my THOUGHTS is to locate myself in a category. To tell you about my FEELINGS is to tell you about ME.'

You will have accepted the challenge and proved that you are no longer scared to tell people who you are if you wake up one day and have no fear of your friends knowing that you read books like *Why Am I Afraid to Tell You Who I Am?*.

I still don't know what the drawing of those shoes means.

Memorial Stone

While attempting to break from relentless touring and bookshop rifling, I had a brief walking holiday in the Peak District in my secondary search for the best Bakewell tart. Dammit, why would I think Bakewell would be without charity shops, and how on earth did I imagine I would be able to resist one if it was there? After filling my belly with jam and pastry, I found a book by 'mother, producer, actress, human rights activist, and an officer of the order of arts and letters' Sharon Stone.

Something to Hold is a predominantly photographic guide

to bereavement. It includes references to the Kabbalah, which seems to be up there with dianetics as the guidebook for the Californian and wealthy. There is not much writing involved for Sharon; I imagine a word count would be hard pushed to hit one thousand, but it is for charity.[1] It is mainly a collection of photographs of angels in cemeteries; sculpted stone angels that is, not visitations caught by a psychic cameraman. Sharon Stone didn't take the photos, which were the work of Mimi Craven,[2] but as she's the big star, hers is the name above the title for such sentiments as:

'You touch me every day.'

This particular sentiment takes up a whole glossy page. Some of the pages have slightly more text:

'Peaceful is as peaceful does.'

But some have less. Opposite a monochrome image of a praying stone angel, just one word appears:

'Why.'

Even a question mark isn't required. This book is designed for those who have lost someone – 'a gift for someone contemplative or grieving' – and its profits go to charity, but in my cold, callous, cynical English heart, I feel there should be just a little more. I suppose the Hollywood showbiz set know how to grieve, and they save demonstrating the depth of their emotions for caterwauling in movies. Some pages are just blank, and that is for the best. Use them as competition space, see if you can fill them with something more meaningful about loss than Oscar-nominated actress Sharon Stone does. On the plus side, there is an addendum informing the reader that the Kabbalah tells us we each

---

1 AmfAR – the foundation for AIDS research.
2 According to the book, 'Mimi Craven is a photographer and human rights activist, as well as an aunt and a friend.' She also appeared in *Vampire Clan* and *Swamp Thing*.

have three angels watching over us. There is a full rundown of angels so you can match up the ones that are meant for you. One of mine is Eiael, who is currently looking down on me with a frown because I've been belittling a charitable effort.

Husband choice via glue factory tour

According to Alfie, the eponymous anti-hero played by Michael Caine in the 1966 movie, the best way to get a married bird was to get her laughing, but you should never do that with a single bird as that would be all you would get. I don't know about this; the only married bird I have ever got with is my wife, and even when I do make her laugh, afterwards she looks at me as if I am an idiot. But then, although advice may not necessarily produce the desired results when acted on, it is very easy to give, and only slightly harder to get published.

Despite all the years that women's magazines have existed, and despite the acres of ink they have spent dispensing their advice, women are still choosing the wrong man. This is very fortunate, as if women weren't constantly choosing the wrong man, an entire arm of the magazine industry would crumble. Without failed romance and bad choices, you wouldn't be able to get your weekly fix of normal people telling their tearful tales of marrying men who were secret slave traders, greedy bigamists or sexual deviants who enjoyed secret intercourse with their wife's favourite pet. On top of that, there are the racks of celebrity magazines that rejoice in tacky weddings of weathergirls, and then follow their descent into despair as it is discovered that their husband is a love-rat drug addict with an addiction to whipping dungeons.

All of this could be avoided if they had just bought one book, Margaret Kent's *How to Marry the Man of Your Choice*.

The cover declares its intent with an image of two champagne flutes clinking in love harmony. Follow Margaret's instructions and it could be your be-ringed finger and nail-varnished hand clasping hope. The book promises to lead you from 'the singles' jungle to a happy marriage'. Margaret Kent is a practising lawyer 'specialising in taxation, international law and divorce law in Florida', and if you can't trust a Florida divorce lawyer for love advice, then surely the world has gone topsy-turvy.

My copy, found in a PDSA shop, is inscribed 'To my darling Katy, happy hunting, love Justine.' Above this inscription is another one: 'I hope it sets you on the right path! K.' Does this mean that K, very possibly Katy, used the book, found her man, and passed it on to another loveless friend?

Margaret prepares the reader for a catfight. 'You see women who are not as attractive, youthful, slim, bright, educated or financially secure as you. But some of these women have men you want.' How come that stupid, fat, old, ugly, impoverished bitch has got a man I want? Don't worry, this book will reveal how they have managed it, and how you can get what they have too. Then you'll beat them on all fronts and laugh in their faces, 'See, scum queen, I am now better than you in all ways.' Despite these initial misgivings, Margaret reveals that she is not on the side of 'bitchy women' who make their men feel honoured to have them, but she will nonetheless teach you how to make men feel pathetically grateful that you are in their arms.

To find your man, you must ask yourself some serious

questions. What can you offer him? It seems that many women have a long list of requirements from their suitor, from rich and witty to young and capable. Problems arise when the woman is asked what she offers back and replies 'Me.' As Margaret points out, '"me" is a poor, unspecific answer.' For those who still think that 'me' is a good enough answer, the book points out that you do not get a cup of coffee for free because it is 'for me'. So you see, maybe if you imagined men as beverages, this would put it all into some sort of perspective.

Now you know how to buy coffee, we can move on to 'A few words about manipulation'. There is nothing wrong with manipulation; remember, sometimes it's for your own good. 'The techniques in this book are benign manipulation, like the incentives to use seatbelts.'

So now you're nearly ready to get your cup of coffee, pop it in the front seat and buckle it in. You must also remember that man-seeking is like gold prospecting: 'You won't expect to find gold nuggets in your front yard.' So don't just hang around by your daffodils; get a sieve, stick it in the boot and drive carefully into town.

Now what are you going to wear?

Chapter Two deals with this. But not before Margaret first reminds you that being clean is important. After all, perhaps you've never found your man because you stink like an old canal during high summer. On sartorial advice, little is left out – from the colour of clothes to fabric, which should be silky. Do not wear things that are 'metallic, corduroy or nubby wool' – so that's your folk-singing robot costume out of the window. It is perhaps surprising that this book was first published in 1988, after the feminist revolution and the works of Andrea Dworkin that

I've already mentioned,[3] particularly when this chapter suggests that you should wear a blouse that reveals your breasts, but not too much, and you should try to have buttons at the front as it allows the man to imagine taking it off. Even better than a blouse, 'T-shirts are great. It doesn't take much male imagination to know that in less than five seconds they are off over your head.' Similarly, pants, shoes, pantyhose, shorts, hair, teeth, perfume, make-up, eyeglasses, fingernails are all carefully scrutinised.[4] On teeth, try to avoid having missing ones and don't have loads of food stuck to them is the general advice (everyone knows you don't order anything with spinach in until you're married, and even then not on the honeymoon). As far as fingernails are concerned, just don't let them get too long: 'Long nails may indicate to many men that the woman is unwilling to do household chores and is unavailable for recreational activities.'

Drifting back to my drunken, dating youth, I don't remember any of this being an issue. Did I ever look at a woman and think, well, that T-shirt should be off in five seconds, but look at those fingernails; there's no way she'll be able to unblock my sink in the morning or shake out my antimacassar. I think I'll give her a miss.

As with *The Secrets of Picking Up Sexy Girls* (see Chapter 1), *How to Marry the Man of Your Choice* tells you where to go to find your companion. Unlike *The Secrets of Picking Up Sexy Girls*, venues include libraries, night school enrichment classes, boating groups and doctor's waiting rooms. It's

---

3 'Men who want to support women in our struggle for freedom and justice should understand that it is not terrifically important to us that they learn to cry; it is important to us that they stop the crimes of violence against us.' (Andrea Dworkin.)

4 My favourite children's joke: Why do women wear perfume and make-up? Because they're ugly and they smell. Do not tell this on a first date or at an Andrea Dworkin memorial event.

important to remember that doctor's waiting rooms stop being a good place to meet up with men 'if you are going to an obstetrician or gynaecologist'. If none of those venues work out, then you might have to choose your job specifically to meet men. It's at this point that I can't help feeling that Margaret Kent is taking the piss or deliberately trying to up the divorce rate to increase her sales.

Pause for a moment and ponder just what professions you would put in a list of man-meeting opportunities? Don't turn the page and look; just think about it for one minute.

Have you been thinking for a minute? You may turn over now.

'Boat repair and service.'

Did you think of that one? If you say you did, then I say you are a bloody liar.

According to Margaret, 'If you enjoy boating, why not meet men with a similar interest? If you can repair and service a boat, you will be sought after as a crew member.' So that's why you've remained alone all this time. You've never learnt how to repair a high-powered speed boat.

If you are a hydrophobe, you can always choose another career on Kent's list, such as men's shoe sales: 'Since every man must buy his own shoes, you can meet large numbers of men by selling them shoes.' This sentence has actually made me scared of buying shoes. I didn't realise the shoe shop was such a predatory place. From now on I'll buy my ethical baseball boots via mail order.

By Chapter Four we've got to the date-planning stage. I won't make you go through the rigmarole of using your imagination to work out what might be the best venue to visit, but I presume you didn't immediately think of 'the oldest building in town'. Perhaps the advantage of meeting at something old is that it will make you seem younger. Frequently the oldest place in town is the church cemetery, and I'd imagine there are more than a few people whose ideal first date might not be spent wandering around a graveyard. Equally there are those, such as Smiths fans, Goths and undertakers, who may enjoy it too much. Having said this, in many ways walking amongst stone plinths dedicated to the dead might be a good way to work out someone's character. If you find yourself hearing your man say, 'I don't know what it is about wandering on sacred ground filled with decaying corpses, but it always seems to make me horny', then at least you have been warned. As Margaret is a Florida native, 'the oldest building in town' may well be something very different to what it would be in England. Antiquities may include a fifties roller rink or a plastic surgeon's office. Other locations for your date might include a visit to 'an ethnic restaurant' or 'a manufacturing plant that offers a tour'. Imagine the joy of those conversations: 'Good Lord, I never realised that was how they made glue. I had no idea that horses would make such a terrible din in a rendering plant.'

Self-help books are, at most, a sticking plaster for an unsightly sore that soon becomes dislodged as the gunk of your wound loosens the adhesive. Publishers would gain nothing should they publish a book that could cure all your mental and social ills. If such a book existed, it would be brutally suppressed, for it would make the self-help publishing industry obsolete, which would have a knock-on effect on daytime television. Before you know it, commissioning editors would be forced to try and make decent TV again, and that's just too much bother when you can have someone with a pretend PhD spouting fortune-cookie philosophy to weeping divorcees.

What have we learned?

- Shoe selling can lead to marriage, or at least a passionate fling over an arch support
- The working class must not marry the middle class for fear of sending the language into the gutter
- Men who don't build things are not worth marrying
- 'Wotcha!' is not the correct opening for a letter dealing with bereavement

Further reading

Don't read any more for heaven's sake. Cut the apron strings before you journey down another road less travelled or feel the fear or hug the inner you or cure heartache via hypnotic regression or release the child within and end up crayoning all over your stairs.

Conclusion

Over the last five years of picking up fleas in junk shops and paper cuts in the PDSA, I have learnt a lot. Just as the hippocampus portion of a taxi driver's brain grows as their directional knowledge expands, so whichever part of my brain that deals with pantomime facts, ghost-spotting techniques, alien civilisation architecture and arthritic horse knowledge has swelled like a tumour. I find myself attempting to flush some of this knowledge out by spraying water up my nose, but it has stuck like a bluebottle on fly paper in a butcher's shop.

Once the smell of yellowed pages has got caught in the fine lines of your fingertips and your clothes have the odour of the last table at the jumble sale, it is too late to think you can return to the polite, well-ordered but characterless world of the chain bookstore. It's hard enough to walk through the supermarket, with its crass and minimal books stacked high, without ramming your shopping trolley into the simpering, buy-me faces of that week's chosen TV-related titles.

The charity shop, and its century-traversing bookshelves, will offer far more. You'll find outdated astronomy books by Fred Hoyle, to whom the Big Bang was the preposterous idea of a few mad scientists; psychology books that talk of the kindly routing-out of the feeble-minded via a little castration; cookery books with lurid colour plates where the chicken legs have strange little chef hats on their bone and the gammon steaks are covered in brown sugar, brandy and thick double cream (how long ago did that TV chef succumb to heart disease?). The charity shop bookshelf can act as a history of the changing thoughts of human beings in the twentieth century, whether these thoughts have centred around how a junior gamekeeper should garrotte a stoat or romantic cowboy fiction where the hero succumbs to venereal disease so that God's morality can be understood in a gun-toting, penis-burning scenario.

Should the laptop book, or whatever new technology the consumer society wants to overtake the traditional page-turners, take over, will we see the demise of the second-hand bookshop, to be replaced by a series of downloadable dots that unfurl into impersonal texts of great and dull works? I don't know (but I do know that being middle-aged is wonderful, as bemoaning modern trends looks so much more authentic once your hair is grey and you squint over your glasses at things that shouldn't be).

Sometimes, though, the charity shop can be its own enemy. There is a snootiness that has overtaken some of those in charge of deciding what goes on the shelf and what goes to making papier mâché mulch. It is getting increasingly difficult to find rabid animal horror novels, bike-chain epics, and self-published poetry; it's as if they would sully the message of helping the poor build a well or ridding the old of their cataracts. There are certain branches of charity shops that would rather fill their shelves with bland, lengthy and shiny-covered books that are sub-Judith Krantz or plain Dan Brown rather than delightfully bad or wrong. The banal and glib book has overtaken the odd or obscure book.

Although I sit here in praise of the world of weird literature, I think I need a break from hysterical zoological romances, mystical world adventures with musclemen and anti-commie paranoia pamphlets. I want to box up all those books and put them in a storage depot that resembles the great big warehouse of artefacts at the end of *Raiders of the Lost Ark*. But even then, escape from my obsession would be impossible. I can box up the books and put them aside in a lock-up, but how do I then ensure that I ignore all the charity shops of every town that I go to on my travels from Victorian theatre to room above pub? And what if the pub, like the one in Lincoln I sat in post-show, is lined with books and the landlord says, 'Take what you want'? Only the strength of my holdall and spine would prevent me from snatching the lot.

I was once warned that there is a line that can be crossed, where the urge becomes too great and the collector goes from bibliophile to bibliosexual. I fear I'm perilously close to this. But how can you not go into that second-hand bookshop or rifle through that table of books at the school fete? You don't want to. You circle a few times, go somewhere else, waste a little money on the tombola and browse the jams, but inevitably you have to just briefly glance at those books, because maybe this table or shelf will be the one, the one with the book you must have, and every table has one book that you need, you really really need that one, and how silly to buy just one book, because that one is a very reasonable price too, and it is all going to charity.

You know your wife is out with friends, so you should be able to get home and hide the books so she'll know nothing of this fresh infestation. You crawl through the undergrowth behind the house so you can sneak in the back gate, just to be on the safe side. But what's this? The kitchen light is on already, so you'll have to secrete the books in that small space under the shed that seems perfectly sized for four New English Library paperbacks. Too late; you are spied and offered a wave before her face drops.

'You know, you're the sort of man who is going to be found dead surrounded by carrier bags full of stuff,' she says.

Sadly, maybe happily, yes, I know.

List of Sources

Abolition of Britain, The by Peter Hitchens (Quartet 2000)

Ants, The by Peter Tremayne (Sphere 1980)

As Seen on TV: Your Favourites by Trudi Purdy (Arrival Press 1993)

Be Your Own Psychic by Sherron Mayes (Mobius 2004)

Book of the Netherland Dwarf, The by Denise Cumpsty (Spur Publications 1978)

Cats, The by Nick Sharman (New English Library 1977)

Correct Guide to Letter Writing, The by A Member of the Aristocracy (Frederick Warne and Co. 1945)

Crabs on the Rampage by Guy N. Smith (New English Library 1981)

Croak by Robin Evans (Littlehampton Book Services Ltd 1981)

Cult of Softness, The by Garth Lean and Sir Arnold Lunn (Blandford Press 1965)

Elvis: His Life and Times in Poetry and Lines by Joan B. West (Exposition Press 1979)

Elvis: The King on Film by Chutley Chops (Creation Books 2000)

Fast Gun by Walt Coburn (Trojan Publications 1970)

Flying Saucers, The by Dr George King

Freddie Starr: Unwrapped (Virgin 2002)

Frontier of Going by John Fairfax (Panther 1969)

Ghost Hunting with Derek Acorah by Derek Acorah (Harper Element 2005)

God is For Real, Man by Carl Burke (Fontana/Collins 1967)

Godless by Ann Coulter (Three Rivers Press 2006)

How to Be a Supernatural Lover by Sherron Mayes (Hodder & Stoughton Ltd 2004)

How to Marry the Man of Your Choice by Margaret Kent (Robson Books 1988)

Immortal Highlander, The by Karen Marie Moning (Delacorte Press 2004)

Keeping it Real by Jodie Marsh (Metro 2006)

Little Goes a Long Way by Syd Little (HarperCollins 1999)

Littlejohn's Britain by Richard Littlejohn (Arrow 2007)

Lord of the Dance by Michael Flatley (Sidgwick and Jackson 2006)

Love Poems by Danielle Steel (Sphere 1988)

Major Major by Terry Major-Ball (Gerald Duckworth and Co. 1998)

Man's Book: Phyllis and *Death of a Tom* omnibus (Odhams 1963). Individually *Phyllis* was published by Andre Deutsch and *Death of a Tom* by Cassell and Co.

My Secret Garden by Nancy Friday (Virago 1975)

Night of the Crabs by Guy N. Smith (New English Library 1976)

Old Testament and Apocrypha in Limerick Verse, The by Christopher Goodwins (John Hunt Publishing 2002)

Out of the Stewpot by Ed Stewart (Blake Publishing 2005)

Pop Goes the Gospel by John Blanchard, Peter Anderson and

Derek Cleave (Evangelical Press 1983)

Psychic Adventures of Derek Acorah, The by Derek Acorah (Element Books 2004)

Roger Moore and the Crimefighters: The Siege by Malcolm Hulke (Alpine 1977)

Sex is Not Compulsory by Liz Hodgkinson (Sphere 1988)

Sex Link by Hy Freedman (New English Library 1978)

Sing Lofty by Don Estelle (Don Estelle Music Publishing 1999)

Slither by John Halkin (Hamlyn 1980)

Something to Hold by Sharon Stone (Assouline 2005)

Starlust by Fred Vermorel and Judy Vermorel (Comet 1985)

Swarm, The by Frank Schätzing (Regan Books 2004)

Tenth Pan Book of Horror Stories edited by Herbert van Thal: 'The Necklace' by Dulcie Gray (Pan 1969)

This Creeping Evil by Sea-Lion (Hutchinson 1950)

What God Does When Women Pray by Evelyn Christenson (Nelson 2005)

What Would Jesus Eat by Don Colbert (Thomas Nelson 2006)

Which One's Cliff by Cliff Richard (Hodder & Stoughton 1990)

Why Am I Afraid to Tell You Who I Am? by John Powell (Argus Communications 1968)

World According to Garry Bushell, The by Garry Bushell (Metro 2008)

Worms by James Montague (Futura 1979)

You Couldn't Make It Up by Richard Littlejohn (Mandarin 1996)

You, Me and Jesus by Cliff Richard (Hodder & Stoughton 1985)

Your Psychic Power and How to Develop It by Carl Rider (Piatkus 1996